In Memoriam

Peter Abbs
(1942–2020)
Writer, educator, poet.

For all those who journey at night

Sleepless

Also by Annabel Abbs

NON-FICTION

Windswept: Why Women Walk

NON-FICTION (AS ANNABEL STREETS)

52 Ways to Walk

The Age-Well Project: Easy Ways to a Longer, Healthier,
Happier Life (with Susan Saunders)

FICTION (AS ANNABEL ABBS)

The Language of Food

The Joyce Girl

Frieda: A Novel of the Real Lady Chatterley

Sleepless

Discovering the Power of the Night Self

ANNABEL ABBS

JOHN MURRAY

First published in Great Britain in 2024 by John Murray (Publishers)

3

A CIP catalogue record for this title is available from the British Library

Hardback ISBN 9781529366471
Trade Paperback ISBN 9781529366488
ebook ISBN 9781529366501

Typeset in Bembo MT by Hewer Text UK Ltd, Edinburgh
Printed and bound in Great Britain by Clays Ltd, Elcograf S.p.A.

John Murray policy is to use papers that are natural, renewable and recyclable products and made from wood grown in sustainable forests. The logging and manufacturing processes are expected to conform to the environmental regulations of the country of origin.

Carmelite House
50 Victoria Embankment
London EC4Y 0DZ

www.johnmurraypress.co.uk

John Murray Press, part of Hodder & Stoughton Limited
An Hachette UK company

Contents

Prologue ix

1. The Night Self 1
2. Disobedient 15
3. Imaginative 25
4. Receptive 35
5. Raging 47
6. Ruminative 59
7. Anonymous 71
8. Curious 81
9. Restless 95
10. Changeable 115
11. Courageous 123
12. Wild 139
13. Enchanted 151
14. Reckless 161
15. Fearful 171
16. Revelatory 187
17. Healing 207

Author's Note 221
Acknowledgements 223
Notes 227

Prologue

Why does one feel so different at night?
Katherine Mansfield, 'At the Bay'

This is a book about a journey I neither planned nor prepared for. A journey I never expected to take. A journey that would once have terrified me. This is a book about a journey into darkness and sleeplessness. Even these two simple words – darkness and sleeplessness – are freighted with all that we have come to fear and loathe. Inevitably, my journey was precipitated, rather than chosen.

And yet, despite my frequent fears, I found a world that was utterly new, one that soothed, intrigued, distracted, enticed and exhilarated. To my surprise, the inhabitants of this strange and unfamiliar place became my companions. They ranged from the tiniest of nocturnal insects, to the stars above, to women who welcomed a darkness thicker and purer than we have ever known. But, of all my companions, none astonished me more than my Night Self.

This book is about the Self we find at night. In recent years it has become evident that we humans are subject to manifold and constant circadian change. Chronobiologists have discovered that our bodies and brains behave differently according to the time of day, and that we all work to a set of biological patterns, often referred to as our circadian rhythms or simply our body clock. This 24-hour clock is bound to light and dark, day and night, and etched so deeply in our biology that we cannot shake it off.

In nocturnal darkness, the contents of our blood, breath, bones, saliva and skeletal muscle change. We produce different hormones, which rise and fall according to the hour. Breast cancer cells divide more quickly. Our muscles weaken. We metabolise alcohol more slowly. Our bones are rebuilt. Our fat cells, kidneys and intestines operate with a peculiar sluggishness. Dead cells are shed from our skin. Our temperature falls. Our appetite fades. Our blood pressure drops. Thanks to a litany of metabolic, cardiovascular and endocrinal alterations, we are physiologically different at night.

Our brains are altered too, most notably as they cycle through a series of sleep stages. But early investigations into the awake-at-night brain suggest that it too swims in an altered sea of biochemicals, making us feel *different*, rendering us (as the writer Virginia Woolf once put it) no longer quite ourselves.[1]

For women (who are twice as likely to experience insomnia as men),[2] these endless shifts are compounded by barely under-stood infradian rhythms and hormone change, adding to the complexity of our nights. Awake in the purring, softly melan-cholic darkness, we are no longer our Day Selves. We are subtly altered, our brains now wired for nocturne.

Women are also powerfully and disproportionately affected by the absence of light.[3] Dwindling illumination penetrates our brain, nudging it into a heightened state, amplifying our inner voice and compounding the alterations that strike after dark. All of which is to say, we are different. We are our Night Selves. I didn't know it at the time, but my Night Self was to become a powerful instrument of consolation and imagination, of healing and hope.

This book is not a paean to insomnia. Rather, it is an attempt to remove some of the anxiety that now accompanies *not* sleeping, to understand why we don't always sleep, and to remind ourselves that women throughout the ages have suffered from periods of sleeplessness, and survived, even thrived. It seems to me that insomnia is neither illness nor affliction, but our body and brain's attempt to express and comprehend loss and absence. This could be the loss of someone we love or the loss of darkness, silence, rest.

For millennia, women have snatched time from the night – to write, paint, learn, reflect – finding a solitude, creativity and productivity rarely available during daylight. For millennia, women have endured sleepless nights caring for the young, the old and the sick. Indeed, new research suggests that females may be in possession of uniquely robust circadian clocks that enable us to do this, without as much detriment to our health as headlines suggest.[4] And yet, our relationship with darkness is fraught with complication. While private darkness has long been female territory, public darkness has invariably been male space. And so, this book is as much an exploration of our fractious relationship with the dark as it is a deeply personal account of what happens when we accept our night wakings, embrace our Night Self and open our hearts to the disappearing dominion of darkness.

I

The Night Self

Truly, poor Night, thou welcome art to me.
Mary Wroth, 'Sonnet 15'

It's Sunday 6 December, and I'm running down a narrow country lane. It's the first time I've run for months – I usually prefer the slower, more contemplative pace of walking. But on this particular day, which is to change the balance of my life for ever, I am running.

The air is thin and glittering, and so cold it pinches the insides of my lungs. I feel the virtuous exhilaration that all morning runners feel and decide that my New Year's resolution will be to run more often. It doesn't occur to me that there might not be any New Year's resolutions. Or that these feelings of virtuosity and exhilaration could be the last I experience for some time.

As I approach our cottage, my phone rings. Which surprises me, because it's only 8.45 a.m. I expect to see my husband's name, Matthew, on the screen. To my surprise it's my father's wife, who I shall call L.

'Hello,' I puff, wondering if she's phoning to discuss our Christmas plans. I've invited her and my father for the traditional meal we always celebrate with them – supper on Christmas Eve. Since my parents divorced, Christmas has been a delicate navigation. For twenty-two years, my siblings and I have juggled growing families, jobs that don't stop for the holidays, elderly parents, acrimoniously divorced family members, multiple locations, diverse dietary requirements, and so on. Which is to say, all the usual complications of a family Christmas. This year, things have been compounded by the Covid-19 pandemic, meaning that only a certain number of family members can be together. And because of the growing death toll and the lack of a vaccine (although early batches will be made available within the next two weeks), a heightened feeling of anxiety pervades this year's festivities. My father is particularly alarmed and has gone to excessive lengths to avoid catching Covid. I'm half expecting him to cancel our supper plans.

All this bubbles into my head as I shout into the wind, 'Hello?'

'Your dad . . .' says L. 'The paramedics are here . . .'

I don't understand what she's saying. Why are the paramedics there?

'He's dead,' she says.

She sounds so calm, so dry-eyed, I assume I've misheard her. Besides, her words make no sense. Firstly, he can't be dead because I spoke to him two days ago – and he was fine. Secondly, if he's dead what are the paramedics doing?

'A heart attack,' she adds.

'I'll drive over,' I say. 'I'll be there as quickly as I can.' I can hear voices in the background, as if L. is conferring with someone. Why aren't they resuscitating him?

'They say you must drive very carefully.' Her voice is still oddly calm and measured. 'The police, I mean,' she adds.

The police? Why is L. with the police?

I hang up, and then I start to scream. I am running and screaming and crying all the way home. Three words play over and over in my head: I'm not ready; I'm not ready; I'm not ready.

This is where it starts. And later, much later, I think how strange it was that something so decisively *ending* was also something that was so clearly *beginning*.

Matthew drives while I call my sister, and then my brother. My sister drops the phone and I hear her screaming and screaming. My brother is very calm. Later I realise that I was too blunt with my sister and too vague with my brother. I know this because, after an hour, my brother calls back and asks how the paramedics are getting on. And I have to tell him that our father has been dead for nearly twelve hours, that there was never any chance of resuscitation.

Then my brother says the very thing that had struck me when L. called, 'He can't be dead because I spoke to him last night,' and I know he's thinking exactly as I am – that this is too soon, too fast. That we need more time. That we have not had time to say goodbye or I love you.

The flat is full of uniformed men writing reports, talking into phones, drinking tea. Their presence – with its intimation of order and certitude – is immediately calming.

L. asks me if I want to see Dad, and I cannot answer so I nod. Because I do and I don't. And I'm working excessively hard to regulate my emotions, to stay calm. Like L., who is calmer than I've ever seen her.

Dad is sitting in his red chair. He looks asleep. Peaceful. We comment on this, and for the next few months we repeat it over and over . . . How peaceful he looked. I touch his hand. It's as cold as glass.

The coldness of him stayed with me for months to come. But it was the silence of him I remembered most of all. A silence that was lost at first, lost in all the people milling around. Until I caught a snatch of it: no hiss of breath escaping his lips; no creak of bone or joint; no grind or gnash of teeth; no twitch of cloth; no words. Without life inside us, we are soundless.

For the first time I saw death close up – and it was silent. And I wondered if this was the reason we so often fear silence. For in its folds and creases, silence carries unavoidable indications of our own mortality.

A week before my father died, I had helped my mother bury her partner of twenty years. Douglas and my mother weren't married, but I'll call him my stepfather because that is how I thought of him. My mother was mourning him. We were all mourning him. His drawn-out death in a nursing home he loathed – where, thanks to Covid, we could not even visit him, let alone hold his hand – had left a vinegary taste in our mouths and a tight feeling in our ribs; like thousands of others, he hadn't been accorded the comfort and dignity in death that he deserved.

This tightness in my chest may have been the reason I was running on the day my father died. Perhaps I hoped to outrun its vice-like grip, to breathe so fully I'd shake off the vestiges of anger and sadness still swilling around.

Instead, the grip tightened.

I stayed at my father's house that night, sleeping in his study on a camp bed with orange sheets and an orange duvet, my head squeezed up against his desk. His books were all around me. His pen was just as he had left it, mid-sentence on his notebook. His cardigan lay slung over the back of his chair. My father had always attached great meaning to particular objects – stones, feathers, shells, small sculptures. These objects were all around me, placed with great care on particular surfaces and shelves where he might see them as he wrote. The room was heavy with his smell, his presence, his hopes.

That first night, I had no expectation of sleep. No desire to sleep. Instead, I chose a few of his books and settled in for a teary night of emotional but wide-awake intimacy. But to my surprise, the night passed in a thick blanket of dreamless sleep. I awoke, shocked and ashamed: instead of crying all night, I'd had one of the best nights of sleep I could remember. How could I sleep so well after the most upsetting experience of my life? What did this say about me? I read later that a response like mine wasn't uncommon, that the brain shuts down when it needs to – an evolutionary mechanism designed to preserve us, to ensure our survival.

It was not to last.

For the next ten days I lived at my father's house and busied myself organising the funeral; seeing to the post-mortem and the death certificate; informing friends and family; writing tens of obituaries; decorating his (cardboard) coffin; shopping and cooking for L.; and all the other chores and errands that accompany a sudden death. L. was a ghost of herself, and I sometimes wondered where exactly she was – later I learned that she was in shock, a state of mind that protects us from extreme pain. I would come to think of 'Shock' as a place, a cross between a hospital and a hotel, to which L. had quietly and involuntarily removed herself.

I took this absence as an excuse to become ever busier and more 'competent'. But when darkness fell, as I lay tucked up between the orange sheets, staring at the outline of my father's books, I could no longer maintain this pretence. Every night, the claw tightened so determinedly around my chest I thought I, too, was having a heart attack. I cried, and gasped, and gulped, and focused on slowing my breath. And then I got up and began another manic day of organisation. Clearly, that first night of uninterrupted sleep had been an aberration. I rummaged through my chest of sleep aids, determined to fight my ever-longer nights. I threw back quantities of Nytol, melatonin and magnesium; doused the pillow in chamomile and lavender oils;

rid myself of blue light, caffeine and alcohol; and hunted for old prescription sleeping pills. To no avail, of course.

And then I made myself even busier. Convinced I had the answer to my family's grief, I found a puppy online, arranged its collection for the day after my father's funeral, and went shopping for puppy toys and food. What better way to heal this sudden loss than by bringing new life into the home? And who better to lavish our homeless love upon than a puppy?

But our puppy was sick from the minute we got her home. She lay around listlessly, occasionally lapping at water. Looking at her limp little body filled me with foreboding. On Christmas Day I drove her to the emergency vet in our nearest town. The vet suspected she had parvovirus. He explained the long process of testing, the escalating costs, the slim chance of survival. The process would take longer than normal, he added, because of the raging pandemic with its endless rules and regulations, and because it was Christmas.

'She's probably come from a puppy farm,' he said with a shrug of his shoulders. 'Likely the whole litter is dying.'

Our puppy stayed in the veterinary hospital for five nights. We weren't allowed to visit her and, because parvovirus is both fatal and highly contagious, she was kept in isolation. We called for news repeatedly. Each time, the vet asked if we'd prefer to have our puppy put down. The costs were mounting by the day, and she still wasn't eating. But until the tests came back, we had no diagnosis.

'Is there any hope? Even a sliver?' I asked through a veil of tears. And every day the vet said, 'Perhaps a sliver . . . there's always hope.'

On the fifth evening, the vet called and said, 'She's taken a turn for the worse. I don't think there's any hope now.' Our puppy was put to sleep in the arms of a veterinary nurse. And we never saw her again.

For weeks I was haunted by the size of her – that she had died so small caused me endless anguish. I had taken her from her mother and allowed her to perish. I had failed to protect her. That an animal we'd lived with for less than three days could give me so much pain astonished me. We had no relationship as such, no shared history. And yet even now I cannot write about her without crying. For she had also carried on her tiny shoulders the weight of hope. And, in some inarticulate way, she had been a crucible, a means of remembering my father and stepfather. And suddenly that seemed too great a weight – and so everything swung back, again, to the smallness of her.

I didn't want to terrify my children with my wild, monstrous grief. And I had grieving people to look after. I was no use to anyone as a flailing sobbing mess. So I spent my days busily tracking down justice for our puppy, and my evenings busily buying up my father's out-of-print books. Stay busy. Stay busy. Stay busy.

Still I could not sleep.

Then one greyish dawn it occurred to me that I was night-grieving, and that this was how it would be. And so I put away my chest of sleep aids and accepted my wide-awake nights. At which point, I noticed that this wasn't my usual insomnia. Slowly my sleepless nights were metamorphosing into something I hadn't expected: they were becoming a vital place of refuge. For while my days were overfilled with organisation and caring for others, my sleepless nights were becoming oases of inner reflection.

And in this dark and comforting place I began to understand the necessity of my wakefulness.

Those long wakeful hours were like nothing I'd ever experienced before. This wasn't my normal insomnia, with its habitual fears and anxieties. This was different. The darkness seemed to shift and soften, and yet it had weight and density – so that I often felt as if I were enclosed in something resembling the inside of a marshmallow or the sweetly pillowy interior of a meringue. At other times it felt like a downy protective skin, a soft pelt in which I could lose myself.

What I recall most clearly is the sense of being *held* by the darkness. It never pressed upon me – it simply held me. It asked no questions, and it made no demands. It gave me space and secrecy, silence and anonymity. And yet it seemed to breathe and pulse beside me, like a sleeping companion, so that I never felt alone. This companion wasn't entirely silent – my nights came with their own soundscape: planes, traffic, inexplicable scrapings, scufflings and rattlings. I came to understand that a whole other world was awake alongside me. And I heard, for the first time, the infinitesimal noises of what I would later call my Night Self – the beating heart, the sump of saliva, the rasp of my heel against the sheet.

Every night, after my eyes snapped open, my father appeared in my mind's eye. Puppy and Douglas followed, reminding me of what I had lost and would never recover. A void opened in the pit of my stomach, and the boulder lurched against my chest. And then the darkness seemed to rush in, as if to say, 'But I'm here. And I'm yours.' A sort of buffer between me and bodily pain. A feeling of relief would wash over me: I didn't need to get up; I didn't need to be 'strong'; there was nothing to organise. I could lie alongside my sadness, dredging up memories that I was terrified of losing, searching for the answers to my questions: Where was my father? Where were Douglas and Puppy? Where do the dead go?

As an agnostic, I was preoccupied by this question. During the day I had little time to ponder it. Besides, during the day the question seemed faintly ludicrous and without any possibility of an answer. At night it seemed entirely reasonable. We've all searched for things in the dark where the *process* of seeking – groping and fumbling for anything from a door handle to our car keys – feels perfectly rational. We rummage patiently, with good grace. In bright light, our search reeks of incompetence. We reproach ourselves for our stupidity. We become harried and frustrated. I sensed that my quest to know the whereabouts of the dead was a night quest, one that should be carried out under the cover of darkness.

As the night passed, the darkness changed from silky, sooty black to something opaque, tinged silver-grey, thinner, sparser, grainier. The dawn light pushed its way into my room, the traffic grew more insistent, the birds trilled. My questions seemed ridiculous. The darkness had gone into hiding and no longer held me. My eyes ached, hollow and empty: I longed for sleep. And yet those black hours gifted me something more profound than sleep. They gave me undiluted time and space, but they also released me from what I later called 'daytime thinking'.

One sleepless night, I heard floorboards creaking in the hall. And it occurred to me that perhaps all my children were awake, their wide-open minds ranging over the questions that were occupying me. My mind spun on – hundreds of thousands of people had recently died of Covid, and surely this meant hundreds of thousands of us were awake, inhabiting the same liminal, anguished, insomniac place. This image – of so many 'siblings of loss', alone but dimly connected, occupying the same half-formed world – took hold of my imagination. I began wondering who my fellow sleepless mourners were, and what they were doing, thinking, feeling.

As it happens, insomnia is frequently prompted by loss. According to a recent study in *Sleep Medicine Reviews*, 'Bereavement is consistently associated with ... problems initiating sleep, problems maintaining sleep and sleeping fewer hours than usual.' Put simply, the bereaved rarely sleep well. The more intense the grief, added the researchers, the more fractured, fragmented and aborted is the sleep.

Biological sex plays a role: several studies found a higher occurrence of sleep disturbances in bereaved females than in bereaved males. Age, too, can compound our sleeplessness – the younger we are, the less troublesome our subsequent sleep will be. The nature of the death also has a bearing, with some studies finding that sudden, unexpected deaths are more likely to disrupt sleep than expected deaths.[1]

Little wonder that I, a middle-aged woman who had recently experienced several unexpected deaths, was now struck by the worst insomnia of my life.

But those of us in mourning don't just sleep less; we sleep *differently*. Researchers using EEG* have measured the sleep waves of bereaved people and found their sleep to be unique, with more REM (dream-laden) sleep and less deep, physiologically restorative sleep. The more intense the respondent's grief, the more their sleep changed.[2] And, of course, the more time they spent *not* sleeping.

By the time my father died, I'd had insomnia off and on for more than twenty years. I fully expected *not* to sleep. I fully expected an exaggerated version of my usual insomnia, in which I groped about for sleep aids, then furiously tossed and turned, before eventually falling back to splintered sleep with an audiobook clamped to my ears. During past bouts of sleeplessness, I often gave up on sleep, rising groggily and grim-eyed in the dawn, cursing the night, the dark, my inability to sleep.

---

* An electroencephalogram, where sensors are attached to the scalp in order to read the brain's electric signals.

But now, with a mind charged by grief, I found my nights were changing. I began looking forward to my nocturnal awakenings – the inky consolatory blackness, the softly mournful silence, the stillness. At night I could escape my resilient, capable persona. I was no longer Annabel, the daughter in charge. I could grieve, without inadvertently affecting anyone with my own sadness. I could just be.

There was something pared back about the darkness that I liked and *needed*. I couldn't see the cobwebs that needed sweeping or the mounting piles of laundry across the floor. I couldn't see anything. And so my gaze turned inwards. Once, this would have meant hours ruminating. At the very least I would have catastrophised about being awake, about the many 'mistakes' my sleep-deprived brain would allegedly make the following day. Or the chances of my blood pressure rising, my brain fogging over, the terrible mood that would hound me.

But because I was in the throes of so much loss, wrestling with the shadow of much bigger, more important questions, these concerns quietly floated away. I no longer cared about the threatened effects of a sleepless night. If I looked exhausted or was a touch grumpy the next day, so what?

Once the Christmas holidays were over, my family returned to London. I decided to stay in our cottage outside the city near L. and my mother. I wasn't ready to face the bright, fraught frazzle of London. The world suddenly seemed louder and noisier than ever. I felt as if layers of insulating flesh had been peeled from the insides of my ears; the urban noise pained me. Aircraft, car alarms, ambulance sirens, the rip and tear of motorbikes – all seemed amplified and unusually shrill. I heard them now as the panicked sound of death.

The night soundscape in the country was gentler. I liked hearing the wind, the sheep coughing and bleating in the neighbouring fields, the groaning and creaking of the willow tree by the front door. I liked the way rain became music at night. It seemed to fall in different notes and keys: the sheets of rain against the glass, the drip-drip-drip on the lead roof, the spongy mizzle spitting into the darkness. And in between swung moments of absolute silence. A silence that at once mirrored my own emptiness while hinting at other possibilities.

And yet there was something I craved beyond silence: darkness. Dense unadulterated darkness. I spent hours taping over blue blinking wi-fi lights and fixing cardboard panels to the windows. Every pinhead of artificial light was an affront. This sudden longing for dark confused me, because in the past I'd always been frightened of it – the threatened oblivion, the oppressive-ness, the terrifying imaginings it spawned. But now darkness seemed freeing and comforting. Its mystery spoke to me of hope and redemption. And I had learned to recognise its many shades and textures; it could be feather-light and as supple as skin, or as black and bulky as a blanket. To my surprise, when the darkness changed, I changed too. A sorcery of sorts.

Sleep continued to elude me, but this was of little consequence. In the absence of light and noise, I felt the stirring of another Self. It was inside those limbic, wakeful night-time hours that I encountered – for the first time – my Night Self.

In the heavy hush I heard her softly elegiac voice. In the stillness of a hazy half-consciousness, I listened and I learned. Initially I noticed my Night Self in the smallest of things, in the subtle shifts in my thinking, feeling, sensing, remembering, being. At night I could not think in my usual ordered, logical way. Nor was I as cheerfully optimistic. I often felt wistful, pensive. I needed to turn ideas, conversations, memories, over and over. Time itself seemed to dilate. Thoughts, feelings, perceptions moved in slow motion. I was more inclined to question, to doubt, to mull. My hold on the world felt less assured. All this seemed to be a good thing – reflective, less frenzied, less striving – as long as I could maintain a modicum of control. And yet control came less easily. I was more likely to bubble into rage, which came and went like lightning. I could slip – at the drop of a hat – into regretful, swallowing sorrow. There was a volatility to my Night Self that sometimes unsettled me. But there was also a way of thinking that I liked: looser, unstructured, gauzy. Thoughts, feelings, sensations, memories seemed borderless, edgeless – like water. And my night brain made no attempt to define, order, shape or judge.

At first I attributed these traits to the madness of grief. But then I remembered past nights, unencumbered by sleep anxiety. And I realised that the reason my Night Self seemed so familiar was because she had been with me all along. I simply hadn't noticed her. In my habitual determination to wrest as much sleep as possible from my nights, and in my zealousness for artificial illumination, I had merely blotted her out.

This time, I decided to welcome her in, to befriend her.

2

Disobedient

'I used to think,' Nora said, 'that people just went to sleep,
or if they did not go to sleep they were themselves, but
now,' she lit a cigarette and her hands trembled, 'now I see
that the night does something to a person's identity . . .'
Djuna Barnes, *Nightwood*

June 1484. Brescia, northern Italy – a fifteen-year-old girl slips
silently from her bed and tiptoes past her sleeping sisters. The
shuttered darkness is as thick and black as treacle, but her feet
guide her over the wooden floorboards. She knows every raised
ridge of grain, every warp and knot. Through the soles of her
feet she recognises the chill marble of the hall, then the warm,
undulating flagstones of the kitchen. Of course, she smells the
kitchen – spit-roast lamb, garlic, rosemary – long before her feet
find it. She hears, with relief, the soft sputter of embers in the
fireplace. No need to grapple with the tinderbox, which can
lose her ten minutes of precious, stolen time. She runs her hands
along a stone shelf, feeling for the candle chest. She must avoid
the expensive beeswax and find the soft, sticky press of a mutton-
fat candle. She takes the candle to the embers and watches the
kitchen spring into wavering amber light. Already the fog of her
single hour of sleep is clearing, and her heart beats a little faster
in readiness for the hours ahead.

She knows that tomorrow is washday, that she must supervise the laundry of the entire household as well as give lessons to her brothers and sisters. She must also complete the week's ledger of expenses, help the cook stone four pounds of raisins, and oversee the gardener as he removes moths from the apple trees, and at 7 p.m. she must accompany her father to a dinner. Her chores are interminable and as dull as ditchwater. But she won't think about that now because this is her secret time, plundered from a life of drudgery.

She takes her candle to the table then lays out paper, quill, inkpot, books. Astrology, philosophy, the Old Testament and the New Testament – she will read until she hears the 3 a.m. cry of the watchman. And then she will write until the first crow of the cockerel. Already her mind is revolving, disobediently. A thought swims just below the surface. She needs to tease it out, to twist and turn it. She knows she cannot transmute it into words until her mind has ranged freely, from north to south, from sun to moon. This is how she bends and tests an idea: will it hold at the centre? Will it burn as clearly as her candle? More importantly, dare she make it public?

Her hand trembles, then clenches. Because these are night thoughts, unconstrained, free to flout the rules of church, home, her own heart ... Laura Cereta pulls her shawl around her shoulders, flaps at a mosquito, then opens a book. Her night is just beginning.

As scientists understand more about our circadian rhythms, a picture is emerging of a night brain that appears more reckless than its diurnal counterpart. Researchers have noted a greater chance of 'disinhibited', 'maladaptive' and 'dysregulated' behaviours when we're awake at night. They've noticed that many of us are more inclined to take risks, to break rules, to behave impulsively, to think and do things we might not think and do during the day.[1] A tentative finger has been pointed at the nightly brew of biochemicals sluicing through the brain, and at the peaking of dopamine during the later hours of darkness. Dopamine gives us drive and motivation, but, when it's combined with lack of sleep (meaning fewer 'supervisory' dopamine receptors), we take on altered hues, our perceptions and feelings are brightened or heightened or skewed. Some researchers think this results in 'sensation seeking, impulsivity, delusional thinking'.[2] But in constrained and circumscribed women, could this altered mix of biochemicals liberate a devil-may-care chutzpah? A brazen emboldening inconceivable during the day?

My own mind – still swimming in grief – felt neither rebelliously delusional nor daredevilish. But as I examined the works and writings of other sleepless women, I sensed a pattern of dangerous thought – as if their 'maladaptive' nocturnal minds had kindled ideas too unconventional to countenance during the day. I wondered if these women, emboldened by a brain-on-darkness, had enjoyed pockets of sleepless solitude unexpectedly free from fears of impropriety, disapproval and judgement.

On nights to come, I too would find a quiet recklessness. I too would find moments of meaning made impossible by daylight. And I too would think thoughts that, in all likelihood, I would have suppressed during waking hours. But first I found Laura Cereta: pioneering fifteenth-century feminist, purveyor of dangerous ideas, sleepless since childhood.

For Cereta, insomniac nights were her only opportunity to nourish the brain, to expand morally, spiritually, philosophically. But Cereta did more than this: she used her nights – 'those profitable occasions when unable to sleep' – to develop radical ideas that were unheard of in medieval Italy.

'This grand volume of epistles . . . bears witness, letter by letter, to whatever muses I have managed to muster in the dead of night,' she wrote in 1486. She was seventeen years old but already feted for the scholarly letters she exchanged with other eminent Renaissance thinkers – all of which were written during her 'sweet night vigils', her 'night watches'.

At first, Cereta's 'sweet night vigils' were her time for contemplating ideas of self and consciousness, for trying to understand who she was. As her nights passed, she became less introspective. Her mind turned to marriage, biology and the Church's oppression of women. Her epistles show her becoming increasingly angry, her mind 'afire' and 'thirsting for revenge'. 'Because of this,' she wrote, 'a sleeping pen is wakened for insomniac writing. Because of this, red-hot anger lays bare a heart and mind long muzzled by silence.'

Three hundred years before Mary Wollstonecraft and four hundred years before the suffragettes, Cereta argued for women to be allowed an education, and for an end to the slavery of married women. She exhorted friends to listen 'not to voices of authority . . . but to the secret voice within'.[3]

Laura Cereta's 'secret voice within' intrigued me. But how to explain its audacity?

It's long been known that the brain region responsible for competently managing our thoughts, making plans, assessing risk and ensuring we behave appropriately, loses its grip as we become tired. The longer we're awake, the more difficult it is for our 'command and control' prefrontal cortex to keep us in check. But new studies suggest that our prefrontal cortex might also be bound to light and dark. In which case, even if we aren't tired, it cannot function with its usual diurnal deftness at night.

This is particularly significant for women – not only are we restrained by cultural expectations, but we have a greater and more active volume and complexity of prefrontal cortex, reflecting (according to the researchers who discovered this) our particularly tyrannical 'impulse control'.[4] Shrugging off the bullying voice of conformity has always been a Sisyphean task for the female sex.

And so Cereta joined a long line of night-spinning women who opened my mind to the daring, disobedient possibilities of a Night Self. From George Sand to Vita Sackville-West, from Simone Weil to Madonna, from Dorothy Parker to Fran Lebowitz, from Mary Wroth to Judith Wright, from Louise Bourgeois to Joan Mitchell – and the list went on. During the day, the idea seemed risible. But awake at night, the idea seemed perfectly plausible. Either way, my lengthening list of night spinners – with Cereta at its top – showed me that my world didn't need to shrink to a pinhead after dark, and that I alone had the capability to liberate myself.

Cereta experienced her first bout of insomnia when she was eight years old and living in a convent. The prioress showed Cereta how to make use of her empty nights, teaching her to draw pictures with an embroidery needle. Suddenly the nights seemed less 'terrifying'. Much later, Cereta recalled how night embroidery had given her 'gentle breezes of hope'.

By the age of ten, Cereta had been summoned home to help raise her five younger siblings. By the age of twelve she was running the household. By the age of fifteen she was married and managing her own home. With her days weighted beneath 'toil and duty',[5] Cereta relied on 'the dead of night' for time to herself. 'I have no leisure time for my own writing and studies unless I use the nights as productively as I can,' she wrote. 'I sleep very little . . . But by staying up all night, I become a thief of time, sequestering a space from the rest of the day.' Her insomnia provided the time and space to think, to come to the dangerous conclusion that 'nature imparts one freedom to all human beings equally – to learn.' These ideas were entirely her own, forged on the twin anvils of insomnia and night.

Is it possible that Cereta's insubordinate thinking had its genesis in a Night Self freed from the grip of a diurnal brain? We can only speculate because, although hundreds of studies have explored the effects of sleep deprivation on our Day Selves, few have examined the sleepless mind at night. And none (at the time of writing) have investigated the sleepless female brain. But, as understanding of our biological rhythms grows, a more nuanced picture is emerging. In 2016 sleep researcher Michael Perlis published a pioneering study in which he noted the sharp rise in suicides among people awake between midnight and 6 a.m.[6] A subsequent study led by sleep researcher Andrew Tubbs found *thoughts* of suicide also peaked during this time.[7] Perlis and Tubbs wondered if this might have something to do with neuronal and physiological change to the nocturnal brain.

Their hypothesis of an altered, awake-at-night brain was extended in a 2022 study presciently titled 'The Mind after Midnight', which identified an amplified tendency for criminal activity, violence, self-harm, substance abuse and unhealthy eating during the night. Even reformed smokers were more likely to lapse after midnight than at any other time. Why, pondered Tubbs and his team, might so many of us behave differently at night? After examining dozens of papers, they identified five possible explanations for the brain's nocturnal shape-shifting.[8]

First up is the theory of synaptic saturation. Simply put, our brain fills up during the day and requires a nightly prune in order to create space for the following day's learning. Just as a muscle fibre in constant contraction tires and loses strength, so does our central nervous system, say proponents of this theory. If we're awake at night, having been up all day, our brain is working at a time when many of its synapses are saturated.

Unable to respond with its diurnal efficiency, the brain gropes around for new pathways.

Secondly, our altered night mind might be explained by our altered hormones.[9] At night the hormones that keep us cheerful (serotonin) and energetically alert (norepinephrine) drop away as our bodies prepare for sleep. Meanwhile we are flooded with drowse-inducing melatonin. Curiously, dopamine, the hormone of motivation and reward (of *wanting*), peaks at night, while testosterone (also associated with impulsivity and risk) rises steadily before peaking at dawn – which is why some researchers speculate that impulsive, risky and sensation-seeking behaviour is more likely to happen at night. Moreover, if we're awake and stressed, angry or anxious, our bodies also produce surges of adrenalin, inevitably colouring our thoughts and emotions.[10]

Thirdly, our moods appear to change in line with our circadian rhythms. Repeated studies show that many of us are more likely to feel upbeat during the day and downbeat between 1 a.m. and 4 a.m. Whether this is chemical, circumstantial, genetic, evolutionary, cultural or social is still unclear. But numerous reports indicate that feelings of wistfulness, doubt, melancholy, regret and guilt are more manifest at night. In the 'Mind after Midnight' paper, Tubbs calls this the theory of positive and negative affect.

A fourth explanation for an altered mind-after-midnight takes its cue from evolution, proposing that our nocturnal brains are wired to prompt behaviours that help us survive. At night we behave and react differently because, millennia back, darkness was supremely dangerous. For example, hunger faded after dark to deter us from foraging for food, while a ready supply of nocturnal aggression on tap meant we could respond instantly to attack.

Fifthly, and as mentioned earlier, the prefrontal cortex (the main driver of inhibition) behaves differently both when we're severely sleep-deprived and when we're awake at night. Not only does it become particularly fatigued at day's close, rendering it less effective, but connections between it and other brain regions appear to weaken and tear at night. Some scientists think that dreams are partly caused by the loosened grip of our sleepy prefrontal cortex. Liberated from its draconian control, our brain runs amok, producing content at once beguiling and inappropriate, vivid and nonsensical, familiar and strange.

Our night brain changes in other ways, too. Certain neurons increase the number of receptors and molecules on their surface, making them more sensitive (to circulating hormones or drugs, for instance). According to Tubbs, these could result in subtle changes, leaving us more acutely at the whim of our emotions, less proficient at balancing risk versus reward, and more inclined to ruminate.

But let's put this another way: awake at night we might feel more deeply, imagine more vividly. We may be more spontaneous in our behaviour, we may be more emotionally open, we may be more inclined to reflect, to question, to doubt. We may feel emboldened. Dangerous, unusual and surprising ideas might come to us.

Unpicking this data is extremely complicated. Are we more likely to think and behave differently at night merely because we are otherwise occupied during the day? Or because we're alone (which also prompts its own cascade of biochemicals)? How much of our altered feelings is the result of our unseeing eyes? According to neurobiologist Andrew Huberman, the minute light drains from the sky and our eyes switch to night vision, new pathways open in our brain.[11] We can no longer see colour, we can barely make out shape or size. Our vision becomes peripheral: we see the edges of things but not the heart of them. Because our brain prioritises vision over all other senses, our indistinct nocturnal vision unsettles us, making us feel instantly vulnerable and unsure.

Our distant ancestors were accustomed to the dark and adopted techniques that made it less intimidating. They slept in huddled groups. They navigated by the stars, planned by the moon, knew the terrain through the bare soles of their feet. They probably had better night vision too – some geneticists think our earliest mammalian ancestors were once nocturnal.[12]

But we live in the twenty-first century, navigating not by the stars but by a Google dot. We wear thickly soled shoes, making our feet impervious to the substance beneath them. Our night vision has weakened through lack of use. Many of us sleep alone. And to compensate for our fear of shadows, we have saturated our lives with artificial light. Little wonder so many of us are terrified of darkness and of night. Little wonder we are deeply disconcerted by our sleeplessness.

All this ran over my wakeful brain as I lay in my swaddle of black, listening to the wayward voice of my Night Self urging me to surrender, surrender, surrender. And it struck me then that my decision to forgo sleeping pills, to desist the call of my usual trove of sleep aids, was my first act of disobedience. My first heretical idea in an age when a ballooning billion-dollar sleep industry has us in its anxious clutches.[13] When eight hours of unbroken shut-eye – perfectly apportioned into *deep* and *dream* sleep – is considered a universal panacea.

Laura Cereta was considered a social deviant by her contemporaries. Not only had she dared to publicly voice her revolutionary ideas, but she had dared to use her insomnia to occupy male space and make it her own. Her letters show the extent to which she was attacked and lampooned – for her dangerous thoughts and for her audacity. When it all became too much, Cereta returned to the calm of embroidery. Her designs were as unconventional as her thoughts, like a shawl on which she stitched dragons and leopards. For three months of wide-awake nights, she combed, carded and spun the wool, she sketched out her image, she embroidered, and wrote proudly of 'the things I have made before the first rays of the dawning day'.

But then Cereta's nights of creative production stopped. No more epistles flowing with radical ideas and written with 'swimming eyes, a drowsy mind, and my pen itself as if in a dream'. No more dragons and leopards. No more 'long vigils of study'.

After the death of her husband and then her father, Cereta's 'secret voice within' became subsumed by grief. She swapped her 'all-night bouts of writing' for wordless mourning. She was too sorrowful to be eloquent, she explained: 'My accustomed thoughts . . . dissolved into tears.'

This is the nature of grief. We cannot sleep, but nor can we turn our thoughts provocatively outwards. We are compelled to mourn, to sob, to search. We have no idea how long our sorrow will endure. As Cereta wrote, 'Time is not something that belongs to us, it depends instead on the nature of the sun's journey.'[14]

Later, I traced the origins of this book to my grieving open-eyed nights. How else had I ended up embarking on a project so contrary, so unwieldy? A project, needless to say, that my practical Day Self would never have agreed to.

3

Imaginative

It must be dark . . . It's not being *in* the light, it's being
there *before it arrives*. It enables me, in some sense.
Toni Morrison, *The Paris Review*, no. 128, Fall 1993

Thinking about Laura Cereta sparks a restlessness in me. For weeks
my nights have been a time of braced and silent immobility. A time
to sink into the full heaving slosh of my sadness. But now I sense
the fingers of my newly recognised Night Self creeping through
my mind, loosening windows, opening doors, pulling things –
images, memories, recollections – from far-flung corners. It
reminds me of an earlier time when I wrote a novel, in secret and
at night. For three years I crept daily to my darkened kitchen and
wrote, stopping only when the children stumbled sleepily downstairs. I hadn't recognised the Night Self's presence then. But I see
her clearly now, and I wonder if that first novel was *her* doing.

I may not have recognised my Night Self but, writing in the
silent tenebrous hours of night, I'd had an inkling of a brain that
operated differently, of a mind that preferred the byways to the
highways. At first I forced myself to think in what I now call my
'day' mode, straitjacketing my sleepy slurring mind with bullet
points, timelines, plot points, underlinings, character lists. My
brain objected to this: the lists were ramshackle, the diagrams

haphazard, the crossing-outs copious. Although the note-taking came easily enough, the written book crawled along. Words didn't flow in the ordered, punctuated way I wanted. Characters seemed thin and sparse. Timelines jumped. My brain ached.

Eventually I changed tack. I lay on the sofa, read for a bit, then turned off the light and let my brain dance free-form. Suddenly my characters fleshed themselves out, as if by osmosis. Scenes sprang to disordered life. The shape of my novel came in tattered fragments. In among the flotsam and jetsam I found the snatches of plot, character, insight, description and dialogue that became my raw material. It seemed to me that darkness had fostered a sort of brain-drifting where improbable and whimsical connections were made – memories, images, colours, shapes, words, anything really.

I began thinking of night and darkness as a portal into empty space and empty time – a void so neutral I could weave myself into it, imaginatively reinvent myself as a string of characters from another world. No questions asked. No judgements made.

Later, I came across a line from the poet Linda Pastan: 'While I'm lying in the dark, the solution to a problem I've been struggling with in a poem actually, and magically, comes to me.'[1] Her words – with their coupling of 'dark' and 'magic' – made complete sense: ordered, rational, logical sense.

Darkness – even during daylight hours – seems to free our imaginations. A decade back, a group of researchers ran a series of experiments in which people were invited to come up with new uses for household implements (among other things). The experiment was repeated under different levels of lighting, and on each occasion ideas proliferated as the room darkened. The ideas also became wilder and more original. The darkness 'improved creative performance', wrote the researchers, noting that the participants had felt freed by the lack of light, and that the darkness itself seemed to have unleashed 'a risky, explorative processing style'.[2]

It wasn't just my thinking in the dark that was different. In the depths of night and by lamplight I read differently too. During the day I read from start to finish in a linear, ordered, efficient way so that I never lost my place. By night, I dipped and fished my way through a book. I skimmed entire pages, then read a single paragraph over and over. Sometimes I read backwards, but still grazing and gorging. This, I decided, was night reading. During the day I didn't have time to lie around on the sofa. Besides, my day brain didn't like skimming (cheating) or needlessly rereading (wasteful). It certainly didn't approve of reading in reverse (ridiculous!). I was beginning to see that my day brain was duller, more limited and more predictable than I'd ever realised.

The writer Greg Johnson once carried out a survey of female writers and noted their 'special capacity' for turning their 'sleepless hours into creative profit'.[3] Johnson was right: women have often demonstrated a remarkable ability to salvage something from their restless nights, particularly when it involves harnessing the imaginative powers of their night brains.

You only have to flick through Mason Currey's *Women at Work: How Great Women Make Time, Find Inspiration, and Get to Work* to see just how many women found space for themselves at night – from Pina Bausch to Josephine Baker, from Madame de Staël to Tamara de Lempicka. But what is it about night that has allowed so many women to profit 'creatively'?

When Edwin Land, the inventor of the Polaroid camera, examined the work of hundreds of scientists in his firm, he discovered that the most important and original inventions were made by those who had 'freed themselves from a way of thinking held by friends and associates'. In a 2022 paper on creativity, Stephan Schwartz of Saybrook University listed 'strategies for inward looking' as an essential component of learning to think with originality. 'It is essential to develop . . . some way of connecting with the factor that lies outside of . . . the intellect,' he wrote.[4]

Neuroscientists are now unpicking some of the mechanisms that might contribute to the looser, more connected thinking that often takes place in the hours when we should be sleeping. Kenneth Heilman thinks inventiveness comes from 'associative and convergent thinking', which happens when different brain circuits meet and meld.[5] He argues that the hormone norepinephrine (the brain's equivalent of adrenaline) stops this happening, by carefully restricting each circuit to its own zone. At night, when norepinephrine falls away, the brain loosens, becomes more fluid, reaches in and out of itself.

A sleepless Virginia Woolf often made 'creative profit' from her nights. After finishing each of her books, Woolf was always plagued by acute insomnia. But as she lay in bed, her mind fizzing restlessly, she began plotting out her next work of fiction. Her most inventive novel, *Orlando* (1928), recounts the bizarre escapades of a time-travelling, border-crossing, gender-bending poet who lives for a mind-boggling 300 years. Which is to say, it bears all the hallmarks of an unleashed night brain.

Described in the *Evening Standard* as 'a play of fancy, a wild fantasia', and in the *Sunday Times* as combining 'images and historic facts, possibilities and impossibilities . . . with scenes from a dream-world', the novel was essentially a nocturnal composition. 'I make it up in bed at night,' Woolf explained in a letter to Vita Sackville-West.

According to Woolf scholar Maggie Humm, 'It was the fantastical nature of *Orlando* which prevented it being banned.' Humm thinks that if *Orlando* had been a less original (day) composition, it would have been deemed a lesbian novel – and censored by the authorities, just as they had banned *The Well of Loneliness* (also published in 1928). Instead, the law enforcers were too baffled to spot *Orlando*'s transgressive undercurrent.

In *Orlando*, Woolf combined two of the Night Self's most obvious traits – original thinking and a reckless disinhibition. But her stroke of genius was to cleverly obscure a dangerous theme of same-sex love with a flummoxing flight of fancy. Although *Orlando* was dreamed up by her Night Self, Woolf needed to do the hard work of ordering, structuring and editing by day. 'I find my head [at night] full of pillow stuffing: hot; inchoate,' she later scribbled in her journal. And yet it was night that continued to spark her creative epiphanies. After protracted struggles with the novel she eventually called *The Years*, Woolf had a dramatic breakthrough 'owing to the sudden rush of 2 wakeful nights', writing ecstatically in her diary (17 August 1934) that she was finally able 'to see the end' of her novel.

As we've seen, the hormone norepinephrine* dips during the small hours. But that isn't the only hormone to fall away at night. Cortisol (the hormone that makes us alert and focused) also drops, typically reaching its nadir around midnight. Studies have repeatedly found that cortisol suppresses connections between remote brain regions, just as norepinephrine does.[6] As Heilman points out, 'creative ideas are produced by looking *inside*' and anything that inhibits this threatens our ability to think imaginatively. He adds that as many distractions as possible should be removed if we want to create an environment conducive to inventive and original thought.

Moreover, the night-peaking dopamine covered earlier also helps us think imaginatively. Dopamine, it turns out, is as much a molecule of creativity as a molecule of motivation. When people with Parkinson's disease were given dopamine replacement therapy, one of the unexpected side effects was a surge of

---

* Also known as noradrenaline.

creativity: many reported a flood of ideas, several began painting and writing poetry. Neuroscientists speculated that dopamine was an essential ingredient in the creativity recipe, peaking in the latter half of the night because that is when we dream.[7]

I thought of all this as food for the Night Self. Liberated from daytime distractions, free of controlling cortisol and inhibiting norepinephrine, awash in dopamine and with her prefrontal cortex on standby, the Night Self readily turns inwards, weaving, mixing, diffusing, transforming. The French mathematician Henri Poincaré once described his own experience of a sleepless night like this: 'ideas rose in crowds; I felt them collide until pairs interlocked, so to speak, making a stable combination'.[8]

A profusion of ideas isn't the only gift bestowed by our liminal brains. For writer Alice Vincent, 4 a.m. darkness gives an unfiltered quality to her thinking: 'In that strange nothing time my thoughts are at their purest, they have a day-break newness and novelty that later thoughts don't – they are untarnished by the detritus of daylight.'[9]

This sense of the 'newness and novelty' bestowed by night was exuberantly captured by the frequently sleepless author Katherine Mansfield. Her journal opens with a single entry from 1910 describing a 'night of agony. When I felt morning was at last come, I lighted a candle, looked at the watch and found it was just a quarter to twelve!'

When Mansfield resumed her journal four years later, little had changed: 'I can't sleep or eat. Too tired' (March 1914) . . . 'I have begun to sleep badly again' (April 1914) . . . 'I hardly slept at all' (January 1915) . . . 'I got up in the dark to . . . watch the dawn coming' (11 January 1915) . . . 'I couldn't rest or sleep' (9 January 1920) . . . '[I] Lay awake until 5.30 too excited to sleep' (11 January 1920) . . . 'I cannot sleep. I lie retracing my steps – going over all the old life before' (12 January 1920) . . . 'At night I could not sleep' (16 January 1920) . . . 'I had a very bad night' (6 January 1922) . . . 'In the night I thought for hours' (9 February 1922).

As it happens, Mansfield loved the dark (unless she was alone). The late evening was her favourite time of day: 'the time of times . . . with that unearthly beauty before one'. It was daylight that revealed the difficulties of writing. At night, writing seemed easier. Night, as she confided to her journal, was both a catalyst for her imagination and a powerful memory prompter:

It often happens to me now that when I lie down to sleep at night, instead of getting drowsy, I feel more wakeful and . . . I begin to *live* over either scenes from real life or imaginary scenes. It's not too much to say they are almost hallucinations: they are marvellously vivid. I lie on my right side and put my left hand up to my forehead as though I were praying. This seems to induce the state. Then, for instance, it is 10.30 p.m. on a big liner in mid ocean . . . Father puts his head in and asks if 'one of you would care for a walk before you turn in. It's glorious up on deck.' That begins it. I am *there*. Details: Father rubbing his gloves, the cold air – the night air, the pattern of everything, the feel of the brass stair-rail and the rubber stairs . . . All these details are far realer, more in detail, *richer* than life.[10]

Awake at night, Mansfield metaphorically time-travelled, dredging up distant memories in glorious technicolour. 'I can do this about everything,' she added, 'there's *no end* to it . . . My God! It's a marvellous thing.' So marvellous was her nocturnal ability to imagine that Mansfield called it her 'consolation prize' for insomnia.

Are these vivid imaginings precipitated by sleeplessness or darkness? Or a baffling combination of the two? No one knows. But when anthropologist Polly Wiessner lived with the Kalahari

Ju/'hoansi Bushmen, she studied their language as they gathered round the fire at night. She was intrigued by their altered methods of communications after dark. 'Stories were told,' she explained. But stories that conveyed emotional truths, not just facts. And stories that made use of a different vocabulary: more evocative, imaginative and compassionate. Less didactic, less instructional, less practical and less aggressive.[11] The group's language became more 'rhythmic, complex and symbolic', explained Wiessner. And as the vocabulary and language changed, so the mood and dynamics of the group were subtly altered. The result, said Wiessner, was greater empathy, more tolerance and equality – and a sense of tranquillity conducive to sleeping.[12]

Something about darkness and night loosens our imaginations, but they also lend an urgency to our ears. We listen more acutely, fostering intimacy and empathy. In Europe, the nights were once a time for sharing ghost stories and fairy tales. As imaginations opened and bloomed, bonds were strengthened. A community of Night Selves – as Wiessner found – is nothing like a group of straining, striving Day Selves.

Writing in my London kitchen, a backdrop of urban darkness, street lamps and the soundscape of a city served another purpose. My first novel was set in a city that never slept and included a plot that unfolded largely after dark. Jazz Age Paris, revelling in the still-new thrill of artificial light, came alive at night: flamboyant fancy dress balls, surrealist salons and artist soirées, Josephine Baker dancing naked on stage, underground gay clubs, *bals musettes*, champagne *clubs de nuits* for the wealthy, *boîtes* for the 'brazen, gay and licentious'.[13] F. Scott Fitzgerald's habit of popping in to see a friend at 2 a.m. was quite normal. Proust wrote all night from his cork-lined bedroom. Colette wrote until the early hours, 'wrapped up in a blanket'.[14] Jean Cocteau sat up sketching and puffing on his opium pipe. No one in Paris slept. At least, not at night. And it seemed to me that the explosion of creativity and reckless rebellion sprang directly from a sleepless nub of darkness.

How could I possibly write about this period during the anodyne hours of day?

I later discovered that other writers working on books with a 'darkish' or night theme often did the same – as if they knew night and its uncertainties could seep into the composition of their words. Stephenie Meyer wrote her *Twilight* series by night. Rita Dove often began work at 1 a.m. because she found the 'mystery and confusion' of night an essential condition for writing poetry.[15] A. L. Kennedy writes her 'dark' characters at night, using a dim golden-hued lamp for illumination, and describing the night-writing process as 'quite trippy and intense . . . you can borrow the atmosphere'.

And let's not forget the sleepless Jean Rhys, who wrote *Wide Sargasso Sea* – a novel utterly steeped in images of light and dark – at night. Indeed, Rhys saw herself as 'a lapdog' by day who turned into 'a wolf' by night. Darkness released her from the expectations of day and this hallucinatory, wolfish freedom pervades much of her work. 'Jean wrote every night,' notes her biographer. 'Once she heard a cuckoo in the morning and realised she had been writing all night and had been doing so for many nights.'[16]

There's one other reason why we're more likely to be inventive wolves than constrained lapdogs at night. Fatigue, it seems, forces our brain to subtly rewire.

According to Andrew Tubbs, 'sleep deprivation can increase connectivity between disparate brain regions; typically the brain balances local connectivity (related regions communicating with each other) with global connectivity (unrelated regions communicating with each other). But as some regions become exhausted, global connectivity increases so that other parts can compensate. It's possible that as the brain processes information in unusual ways, it throws up novel and unusual ideas.'[17]

In other words, our tired brain works like a deft driver traversing a city full of roadworks. As one street is dug up for repairs, so the driver finds a new route through a new area, inevitably discovering unknown parts of the city.

And so, from the dregs of an exhausted mind, answers, images, ideas come to us – as if from another world. Like wolves, they are unpredictable. Like lapdogs, they should be protected, inspected and groomed in the clear, orderly light of day.

I buy a Dickensian candle holder with a loopy handle and a beeswax candle. When I wake – which can be any hour from midnight on – I light the candle, plump my pillows and pull the duvet to my chin. Then I write by hand, avoiding the electric glare of a screen and the bland tap-tap-tap of a keyboard. Night calls for embodied writing – I want to feel the movement of my hand, the solidity of a pen held between thumb and forefinger. I want to hear the scrape of pen on paper, the soft riffle of pages turned. I want the candlelit intimacy of nib and notebook and Night Self. I want to sense the darkness twitching around us, throwing us together like orphans.

From my wavering puddle of light, I begin a sort of night purging, scrawling out the memories I am terrified of losing – my father tossing pocketfuls of coins into the sea, stirring marmalade into yogurt, smiling into his steepled fingers, striding seaward with an ocean wind in his hair. The memories pour onto the page, raw and uncensored. For the first time in weeks, I feel the boulder lift from my chest.

And for the first time in weeks, I feel the gradual shifting of an imagination that has been crushed by grief and sadness. I sense her, rising, loosening, lifting, like tangerine peel that must be eased from the fruit – slowly, carefully, a single spiral of ragged ribbon. My own creative profit.

4

Receptive

> I was literally burning like Saint Theresa; I stopped
> eating and sleeping . . . In a word I was in ecstasy,
> my body had no feeling, it no longer existed. My
> thoughts took strange, impossible turns.
> George Sand, *Histoire de ma Vie*

As the weeks passed, I scrutinised my Night Self. I had noticed her tendency to disobedience and her skill at whisking the mind to an inventive froth. But she had several other traits, one of which took me months to identify. This aspect of my Night Self often floated silently on the horizon, producing nothing but open to everything. I struggled to understand her, for she resisted all attempts at comprehension and definition. I sensed that this Night Self was exceptionally old, ancient, primal, although she was utterly new to me. She was at ease with magic, mystery, the inexplicable, the divine. She saw hope in the places where my sceptical Day Self saw only quackery and woo-woo. I sought words to describe her – thin-skinned, credulous, curious, open-minded? No single word seemed to do her justice. Eventually I opted for 'receptive'.

It was 1.30 a.m. on a frost-bitten February night when I woke with a sudden need for clean cold air in my lungs. I hopped out of bed and opened the window. The sky was overcast, starless, moonless. I stood shivering while my ears picked out the barking of a dog, the soft hoot of an owl, traffic receding into silence. Suddenly I heard a sound that was so misplaced I froze. But there was no mistake: birdsong, a plume of notes soaring and scissoring through the black air. Dawn wasn't for another six hours. So why was a bird singing with such dazzling vim in the depths of night?

Since my father died, birds had appeared constantly and inexplicably. By day I knew this was simple coincidence. But on this night, with my ears full of nocturnal birdsong, I pondered our avian visitations, and found within them a rich thread of hope and possibility. It seemed to me that birds were coming to our rescue, carrying us into another dimension – a dimension that bridged two worlds, the one in which I lived and breathed and another that I could not articulate, except to know it contained something of my father, and of those we had lost.

The bird encounters had begun a week after my father died, when my daughter Bryony, exultant and astonished, reported having seen seven barn owls on her night drive home. From there, the bird sightings became both more dramatic and more unlikely.

On the morning of my father's funeral I opened the cottage gate and a buzzard swooped down from a branch, almost grazing my head with its sharp-tipped wing before rising and disappearing into the horizon. It was the first time I'd felt the breath of birdwing on my face.

The strangest sighting happened three hours later, as we drove to the crematorium. 'An eagle!' shouted one of the children, pointing out of the window. I swivelled round from the passenger seat, but I didn't have my glasses on and saw only a blur of brown fields and bare hedgerows.

'It's huge!' they shouted. 'It's a golden eagle! Just sitting there!'

I'd seen a golden eagle only once – high in the Pindus Mountains of Greece. There was absolutely no chance of seeing a golden eagle sitting in a Sussex field. On our sombre drive home from the funeral, the children pointed and yelled again: the eagle was still in the same field. 'It's plastic,' I said sharply.

But as I listened to the trill of nocturnal birdsong, I remembered the eagle, the owls, the buzzard (more were to follow), and my Night Self whispered to me, 'not coincidence or chance – they have come as consolation'. I thought about this long into the night, my mind as open and welcoming as a smile.

When morning came, I dismissed all this irrational bird business, but then my hands reached, unbidden, for my laptop. I tapped the words 'golden eagle' and 'Sussex' into the search engine. Up popped birding chat sites suggesting that a golden eagle appeared sporadically in East Sussex. Apparently, a decade earlier a golden eagle had escaped from a falconry centre not far from the crematorium. In the intervening years it had, on rare occasions, been spotted.

In the months that followed my father's death, birds came to us again and again. A duck hatched eight chicks beside our front door, then disappeared with her brood from under our very nose – leaving neither feather nor bone. Robins perched on spade handles, blue tits flew through windows, cuckoos called, doves visited, snipe drummed, swallows plunged, thrushes burst from drainpipes, hundreds of starlings appeared in the trees behind our cottage. And unseen birds broke into song at midnight. Had they always been there, unnoticed? My no-nonsense Day Self nodded. My Night Self wasn't so sure.

Birds have long been twinned with events of agonising significance. When the writer Rosamond Lehmann lost her daughter – 'the one flawless joy of my life' – the tragedy was presaged by a bird. Lehmann, holidaying on the Isle of Wight, had no idea her daughter was unwell. But at the exact minute her daughter died, a blackbird flew into Lehmann's French windows, dying instantly.[1]

Lehmann's mystical experience continued, bringing with it the '*blinding* certainty' that her daughter was still present, still with her. The blackbird that died flying into her French windows, she realised, *was* her daughter. 'She didn't *send* the bird with a message,' wrote Lehmann, 'she was *there*.' Lehmann's revelation was met with embarrassment, evasion and scoffing scepticism. None were more derogatory than her Bloomsbury friends, who promptly cut her from their circle.

Lehmann's account was one of many that crossed my desk: again and again, birds were harbingers of death and recovery. During the day this all seemed faintly ridiculous and very much like coincidence. But at night I sensed that it was dimly connected to our surfeit of grief. Why shouldn't the souls of the dead appear as birds? Why shouldn't birds sense our anguish and come to us as gifts? Why not? asked my Night Self.

By now I thought of my sleeplessness not as insomnia but as my own 'sweet night vigil', a time for contemplation, reflection and magical thinking. I liked the way images floated involuntarily before my inner eye. They came, I guessed, from some part of my imagination normally waylaid by the exterior world – or by the iron junta of my day brain. Sometimes my mind swam between a wordless sadness, a restful abstract emptiness, and these sharply delineated images that appeared without preamble or explanation. I thought of these meanderings as a form of agnostic 'prayer'. There was no God or asking involved, but I was experiencing darkness in a way that felt so serene it was almost holy or sacred. I could find no other words for it.

This is nothing new. For millennia the night has been a place of prayer. Darkness was embraced by early mystics, several of whom barely slept. Saint Christina, Saint Colette, Saint Catherine de' Ricci and Catherine of Genoa were among the religious women who – allegedly – forwent sleep in order to pray or care for the sick. The Carmelite nun Saint Teresa of Ávila slept on a straw pallet for four and a quarter hours a night. Catherine of Siena slept for thirty minutes every other day, which she called 'paying the debt of sleep to the body'.[2]

Until recently Christian nuns routinely rose for matins (sometimes known as the night vigil), a lengthy service of prayers, readings and song that took place between midnight and 3 a.m. The nuns then returned to bed before rising three or four hours later. In fact matins was deemed of such spiritual significance that it became the lengthiest of all eight canonical services.[3] A few orders continue to pray at three-hourly intervals, like the Poor Clare Colettines, following the centuries-old canonical hours, and the practice of Judith in the Old Testament: 'At midnight I rise to praise you.'

The 'hour of God' wasn't reserved for monks and nuns. For hundreds of years, sleep and darkness were intimately bound up with the spirit and the soul. Night was a time for faith, prayer and thoughts of God, as our ancestors protected themselves from the vulnerability bestowed by sleep and darkness. According to historian Sasha Handley, our medieval forebears prayed and read from devotional texts by moonlight, looking for emotional and spiritual consolation to 'ease the passage into restful slumber'.[4] For our ancestors, night was divine.

Years back, I'd come across the work of historian A. Roger Ekirch and his discovery of biphasic sleep (sleeping in two segments separated by an awake period of between one and three hours). After trawling hundreds of letters and diaries, Ekirch identified the sleepless middle of the night as a historically popular time for prayer, meditation, spiritual contemplation and dream analysis. As far as Ekirch was concerned, segmented sleep was neither insomnia nor 'an inexplicable disorder' but an entirely natural mode of sleeping, rooted in the habits of our distant ancestors.[5]

All of which is to say that for hundreds – possibly thousands – of years, we encountered night in a way that was open-minded and other-worldly, with darkness providing a bridge to a spiritual or transcendent dimension. For many Indigenous people (some of whom continue to sleep in two phases), the night remains a time and place for worship, for nourishing the soul, for remembering the dead.

Perhaps it was inevitable that my sleepless nights morphed into mysterious occasions of vigil. Perhaps it was inevitable that I stopped thinking of myself as a 'bad' sleeper and began thinking of myself as a 'good' watcher. After all, we are neither wholly logical nor rational. Ambiguity, paradox and contradiction are our natural habitat. Why fight them?

My Day Self was still a little sceptical: Do the night-rising nuns really know something we don't?

A few years ago, a team of researchers persuaded a handful of Californian monks and nuns to be tracked and monitored as they slept. The researchers wanted to understand whether the nightly awakenings of the monks and nuns had any physiological effects. For the duration of their monastical lives, these monks and nuns had been setting their alarm clocks for matins at midnight, enforcing a biphasic sleep pattern that had existed in convents and monasteries for over a thousand years. The researchers then compared the sleep of the monks and nuns with that of a control group who slept all night. Subtle but significant differences were spotted immediately. Firstly, the bodies of the monks and nuns quickly adjusted to their nightly waking, with their temperature rising in anticipation of their nocturnal rousing.[6]

Secondly, the monks and nuns slept for a shorter length of time in total – almost an hour less of sleep each night. Was this because their bodies remained in a state of deep rest as they prayed and chanted during matins? We don't know, but they also reported 'more frequent hypnagogic hallucinations' than a control group of 'normal' sleepers. As if the space between their two sleeps acted as a portal to a state of mind that was wide open, without judgement, more receiver than producer.

Rather like my receptive Night Self.

At the beginning of spring I meet Allison, an osteopath and shamanic practitioner who facilitates darkness retreats in her spare time. Here, participants live for either five or ten days 'in total blackout', alongside trained guides. Her retreats – billed as 'a pilgrimage to the midnight sun . . . an encounter with our own luminosity' – are always fully booked with a waiting list, but I want to ask her about relearning the lessons of darkness.

'The dark is a great leveller,' she says. 'When you can't see other people you get to know them in a different way, less judgementally. You listen more acutely because you can't see their gestures, face or body language – so *what* we say becomes more important.' Allison explains that, in darkness, different senses are heightened in different ways and at different times. 'Smelling and listening take on greater significance. People move differently – we all become more embodied. Most people come away having made a new connection with their bodies.'

'It's particularly liberating for women,' she adds. 'They stop seeing themselves through the eyes of others. And many want to reclaim darkness – men don't usually have this need. Some women come because they're terrified of the dark and they think a darkness retreat will help.'

Allison suspects that it was once quite normal for women to remove themselves to the darkest of places – caves – either for protection or to give birth, and that our fear of the dark is more modern than we think. 'Many of us feel powerfully drawn to the dark,' she says. 'We can re-emerge changed or reinvented in some way. The idea of losing ourselves in womb-like darkness so that we can renew ourselves is very, very old. And perhaps the disorientation of darkness is part of its appeal.'

In the 1990s, researchers at the University of Pennsylvania scanned the brains of a group of nuns and monks as they prayed. They found that a small region near the front of the brain – known as the posterior superior parietal lobe – quietened down. This particular lobe plays a vital part in navigation, prompting the researchers to ponder whether the experience of spiritual communion required the blotting out of spatial perception. Rather like being in the dark.

Perhaps we can only find what we're searching for when our feeble, straining eyes and our logical linear brain accept defeat, when we surrender to the habitual unease of darkness. It seems to me that some of the greatest gifts of night reside in the unseen, the unfathomable, the unknown.

Allison thinks one of these 'unknowns' comes directly from the pineal gland (the main source of sleep-inducing melatonin), precipitated by the dark itself. Having been involved in darkness retreats for twenty years, she's noticed that most participants have an epiphany, a startling realisation about themselves or their lives. 'Darkness means we turn inwards, and this deep inner dive is a really important part of a dark retreat. It's why people come. But the extended darkness also ushers in a sort of altered state of perception – and it's here that we encounter the spirit of darkness.'

She pauses, her eyes fixed on mine. 'Some people think the change of perception is triggered by DMT, released from the pineal gland. But no one really knows.'

★

For months I read and reread chaotic, conflicting papers on DMT, short for N,N-dimethyltryptamine. DMT – which sometimes goes by the name of 'the spirit molecule' – is a psychedelic compound made in the body using enzymes from the pineal gland, the retina and the brain.* In fact, all mammals and plants make DMT. Rick Strassman, a clinical psychiatrist who investigated the effects of synthetic DMT, described it as 'universally present in nature'. And yet its biological function remains a mystery.

Users of lab-made DMT say it possesses unparalleled, highly visual, ego-dissolving effects. Researchers think it might play a part in the hallucinatory phenomenon of near-death experiences, mystical visions, out-of-body experiences, pyschosis and dreams. Some describe it as a neurochemical catalyst of creativity. In 2018 a group of London researchers investigated DMT by injecting it into thirteen volunteers, then measuring their brainwaves. To the researchers' surprise, altered spikes were spotted in the volunteers' theta waves, mirroring the brain changes that occur when we dream. Researcher Christopher Timmermann described the experience as 'dreaming with your eyes open'.[7]

Researchers speculate that endogenous DMT – a very simple molecule that increases with stress – plays an overlooked (and still barely understood) role throughout the body and brain, but particularly in dreams. In which case, is DMT yet another circadian ingredient in the altered Night Self?

It's too early to come to any conclusions, but a researcher I spoke to thinks DMT probably follows a circadian pattern, playing a part in both dreams and hypnagogic states. 'It's our

---

* DMT is also made synthetically in laboratories or from plants, most famously in ayahuasca, which has been ritually drunk in South America for centuries.

own in-body psychedelic, constantly shaping how we see the world, affecting our perception of time and space,' he explained.[8]

I often pondered the way in which time seemed to move more slowly when I was awake at night, drifting rather than ticking by. I thought of this as *dark time*. I noticed that my hold on space felt different too, although not in the way I had anticipated. Allison's conviction that a chemical might be responsible for the *receptive* nature of my brain-on-darkness made sense, whether or not it was my own 'in-body psychedelic'. I frequently found myself in obscure landscapes as I drifted, semi-oblivious, along the borderland between wake and sleep. These frontiers were as strange as dreams and yet I was awake. One night I came face to face with a Siamese cat in a turquoise collar. She disappeared, only to be replaced by a black cat who slid away into the shadows. Another night a very clear image of a Greek church with a huge bronze bell flashed before my eyes. Unlike dreams, these images had no improbable narrative. They came merely as pictures, bereft of meaning or explanation.

Once I would have dismissed and forgotten them. But now I thought about them. Where had they come from? And why?

Seeing things as we slip in and out of sleep is not uncommon. So-called hypnopompic hallucinations are those that appear as we emerge from sleep, and hypnagogic hallucinations are those that appear as we fall into sleep. And in 86 per cent of cases, these 'sleep-related perceptions' are in fact visual, marked by moving shapes and colours, animals and people.

But here's the thing: women are more likely to experience these semi-hallucinations, as are the sleepless and those with fragmented sleep.[9] My sleep-related perceptions became a source of solace, mysteriously hinting at the existence of parallel universes, and alternate realities where I might – possibly – find my father.

I didn't find him, of course. But in the process, I stopped thinking of night as a *time*. Instead, it became a *place*, with geographies and topographies of its own. And eventually it morphed yet again and became a *companion* – a friend in whose company I wanted to be. My Night Self resisted all attempts to find a mechanism – loosened prefrontal cortices, fewer dopamine receptors, surging DMT – but by day I still longed for an explanation. Surely science could explain the mysteries of darkness, of dreams, of death, of the strange breathing I sometimes heard at night?

In truth, science could explain very little. Even the researchers I spoke to were unsure and would commit only to speculation. But the message from my Night Self was as clear as the midnight sun: mystery meant possibility and possibility meant hope. My father hadn't gone, he was merely elsewhere. And the 'hour of God' was my passage to the elusive land of elsewhere.

5

Raging

The beast in me, which wakes me up at night, it is hate.
Louise Bourgeois, 1964[1]

Six months after my father died, I still couldn't sleep. My days
were as crammed as ever, and so my night awakenings remained
a time of rest and respite. I was well acquainted with my (indoors)
Night Self by now – her receptive meandering mind, her
moments of disobedience, her florid imagination – and assumed
there was little left to discover. But as winter turned to spring
and then summer, and the nights grew shorter and lighter, I
realised I was wrong.

For the first time, I felt my grief flare into overwhelming
anger.

I was angry with the doctor who hadn't noticed my father's
weakening heart. I raged at the woman who told me to 'get over
it'. I was furious with my dad for mistaking the signs of a heart
attack for heartburn. I was mad at anyone who bought a puppy.
I was incensed by politicians, faulty wi-fi, lengthy queues. I
fumed when the neighbour's dog yapped at 10 p.m., when the
children slammed the front door at 2 a.m., when the planes
roared overhead at 4 a.m., when Matthew breathed too noisily,
when I couldn't get back to sleep. I raged at injustice and mortality. Even my *anger* enraged me.

At first I assumed these spikes of night fury signified my smooth progression through Elisabeth Kübler-Ross's Five Stages of Grief: denial, anger, bargaining, depression and acceptance. I congratulated myself on successfully suppressing my anger during the day but wondered why it revealed itself so candidly and irrepressibly after dark. And then I discovered the raging sleepless nights of sculptor Louise Bourgeois. If anyone knew how to make 'creative profit' from their twinned rage and insomnia, it was her.

In 1998 the *Daily Telegraph* reviewed a London exhibition of some new works by Bourgeois. 'It's the continued intensity of Bourgeois's rage that I find so repellent,' wrote the reviewer, before accusing Bourgeois of 'savouring her hatred like some vintage wine she can roll around on her tongue'.

He was right to spot her rage. But why was he so disgusted by it?

'I use anger . . . it is really the anger that makes me work,' said Bourgeois, who spent much of her life transmuting her fizzing fury into sculptures, installations and prose. A few years before her death, aged ninety-eight, she was still exploring blood-red fantasies of wringing the neck of her childhood governess. Age had not mellowed her.

Bourgeois also spent much of her life wide awake. Awake and angry. She once told an interviewer that her life had 'been regulated by insomnia', which began when she was twenty-five, four years after the death of her mother, and never left her.[2]

In 1994 she used her sleepless nights to make a series of 220 drawings – many with accompanying text – that she called her 'insomnia drawings'. A year later, these were exhibited at the Basel Art Fair, whereupon they were snapped up by a Swiss family of art collectors. As I stared into her restive drawings, I wondered at the source of this angry Night Self. I'd seen signs of her in Cereta's 'red-hot anger'. I'd felt her flare during my own nights. Where had she come from?

It seems that anger too has a circadian rhythm. At least three separate studies of Twitter content show that anger is at its most vocal 'in the evening through to early morning'. The acme of circadian anger is – apparently – 2 a.m.[3] Nor is this unique to Twitter users. Studies of mice also indicate a circadian pattern to anger and aggression mirroring that of humans: mice are more likely to attack each other an hour after lights are turned off.[4] Why the connection between darkness and anger? Is it because we're tired? Is it because our controlling prefrontal cortex loosens its vice-like grip in preparation for sleep? Or is it an evolutionary surge designed to protect us from predators? No one knows. Nor is it gendered: studies suggest that anger is just as prevalent and intense among women as among men.[5] We're just better at keeping it under wraps, apparently.

Either way, my night rage suddenly made sense. Under a shroud of darkness I could lie, inflamed and burning and utterly private. No need for shame, or apology.

But studies also show that keeping anger under wraps doesn't mean relinquishing it. Women, it seems, are often more proficient at making use of their anger come the cold light of day. Less dumb impulsive aggression. More 'selective deployment' and 'alternative routes'. Which might explain why it's not Bourgeois's insomnia drawings that glitter with unspeakable fury, but the Cell installations she worked on during those exhausted days. She called these her Red Rooms and, in my opinion, they are the most violently raging works she ever made.

Bourgeois once said that her insomnia drawings came 'from a deep need to achieve peace, rest and sleep'. Some were drawn from her unconscious memories. Others were 'problems to be solved', or a means of obliterating bad memories. In other words, producing these pictures was a method of self-calming. 'For me the state of being asleep is paradise,' she said. 'It is a paradise I can never reach . . . My drawings are a kind of rocking or stroking, and an attempt at finding a kind of peace.'

Bourgeois kept stacks of drawing paper, scrap paper and manuscript paper by her bed so that she could doodle when she was awakened by 'mental and physical spasms'. Music paper was a favourite: 'there's a sort of peaceful impression . . . it is very peaceful to look at the lines of the staff paper. It gives a rhythm,' she explained. In the same way as she used whatever paper came to hand, she also used any available pen or pencil: ballpoint pens, red felt tips, pink ink, stubs of charcoal, blue biros. Her drawings – of clocks, time, connected shapes, the houses she'd inhabited, rivers and ripples, spirals, vortices, mazes, shoes – make references to stars and constellations, silence and waiting, day and night.

The Louise Bourgeois narrative is well known: born a girl instead of the boy her father longed for, she became her mother's principal carer while still a teenager. Her mother had contracted a chronic lung condition during the Spanish flu epidemic and young Bourgeois accompanied her on trips for her health, made her meals, and kept track of her appointments and medication. Bourgeois missed great chunks of her education in the process.

As her mother weakened, Bourgeois's father began an affair with the live-in governess, who was only a few years older than Bourgeois. The affair lasted ten years, and Monsieur Bourgeois felt no need for discretion. A man of singular cruelty, he sashayed around publicly with his mistress, children in tow, even as his wife wasted away. To Bourgeois's perpetual bafflement, her mother turned a blind eye.

Bourgeois spent much of her childhood in the company of an all-female weaving team, employed by her mother in the family's tapestry repair business. By drawing the outlines needed to restore antique tapestries, Bourgeois nurtured her fledgling artistic talents while absorbing many of the ideas that were to preoccupy her for the rest of her life: the female body, motherhood, power.

When her mother died, Bourgeois was devastated. She began studying for a degree in maths at the Sorbonne, craving the clarity and certainty of numbers, which she described as dependable, constant, safe: numbers 'never betrayed you'. But numbers weren't enough. A year later Bourgeois enrolled at art school.

The malice and cruelty of Bourgeois's father had a lasting impact on her. Throughout her life, he was consistently uninterested in her or her work. He taunted her, making fun of her deeply felt emotions – including the grief she experienced at her mother's death. He made her complicit in his adultery while simultaneously propelling her into the position of 'favourite child', a precarious position that came with an additional layer of expectation. And yet the shy, self-doubting and confused Bourgeois always played second fiddle to the live-in mistress. From this swill of pain, confusion, humiliation, betrayal and rage, Bourgeois made art, thereby 'taking possession of that which possessed her'.[6] But she also stopped sleeping.

Bourgeois's rage crystallised when her father unexpectedly died, forcing her to face years of unrequited filial love and denying her any opportunity to confront him. With his untimely death he tricked her out of a day of judgement: she would never have the chance to tell him what she thought. Instead, she sank into depression, withdrew from the art world and embarked on an intensive programme of therapy that was to last for thirty-five years.

From this point, Bourgeois began to keep notes and journals in 'a wild jumble of English and French' that were 'shocking' in their violence. 'The spiralling cycle of her reproaches and self-reproaches, her entreaties and self-entreaties, her agonizing suspicions and envies, her revenge fantasies, her hate and self-hate are hard for the reader to bear,' wrote curator Ulf Küster, reeling from the fury contained in Bourgeois's diaries. Here, Bourgeois wrote of prowling the house at night, of her fear that she would do violence to her husband and sons. 'I break everything I touch because I am violent,' she wrote. 'I destroy my friendships, my love, my children.'[7]

In her old age Bourgeois asked for the pages of these diaries to be read aloud to her so that her memories might endure. 'What is important to me is the recall,' she said. So great was her need to remember that she refused the medication that might have helped her sleep, terrified it would whittle away her memory and sedate her out of her rage. Instead she surrendered to her sleeplessness, letting it fully inform her work.

And so there is only one way to look at Bourgeois's insomnia drawings: in the thin-skinned, unsteady hours of a sleepless night. By all means turn the lights on – Bourgeois always did. And the radio too – Bourgeois often tuned in to talk shows to relieve her loneliness. If she felt hungry or thirsty she made herself a cup of black tea or ate an individually foil-wrapped slice of Kraft cheese. And then – as New York slept around her – she began sketching, doodling, scribbling, remembering.

Bourgeois's insomnia drawings weren't made for the public eye. Looking at them makes me feel as if I'm peering directly into Bourgeois's undiluted head, seeing *her* nights and darkness, *her* Night Self, rather than my own. One critic described the insomnia drawings as akin to 'the compulsive sketching of mental patients'.[8] Others have called them intimate, innocent and endearing – and this is what I love about them. There's no pretence at craft or technique. I look at her insomnia drawings and think that I too can night-doodle, I too can take a ballpoint pen and make a few spirals, I too can jot down the unhoned phrases swimming in my limbic brain.

One evening, when Bourgeois was a child, the family ate dinner at the bottom of their garden, in blackness so dense they couldn't see each other. Monsieur Bourgeois decided to teach Louise 'not to be afraid' and asked her to fetch something from the house.

Louise – aware that her sex was a continuous source of disappointment – 'braced' herself for the challenge and 'started through the blackness; the sky could not even be seen because the trees met over the lane'. She was 'beset by anxiety. I couldn't tell right from left or orient myself. I could have cried out with terror at being lost.' But she didn't. Instead, she found a gap in the canopy and studied the sky, 'determining where the moon would come out, where the sun would appear in the morning. I saw myself in relation to the stars. I began weeping, and knew that I was all right.'

Bourgeois never forgot her fear of the dark, always turning on dozens of lights at night. The notes on her insomnia drawings – diary jottings, memories, musings, lists – suggest repeated attempts to drown out, and overcome, her fear of darkness. 'During the night I am afraid to be alone,' she wrote. 'Artists are afraid all night long,' she added.

Bourgeois maintained that her violent anger germinated solely from her fear: '[anger] is my way of defending myself,' she said. But I keep thinking about all those blazing lights at night, wondering if they exacerbated her bad mood. She wouldn't have known what we know – that bright light shuts off the body's production of sleep-inducing melatonin. To boot, sleep researchers now think that bright artificial night light tips us 'towards negative mood'[9] and heightened emotions,[10] even if we're well slept.

I knew instinctively that my eyes preferred indigo obscurity at night. Even opening the fridge – with its violent white lights – irritated me. Despite this, it takes two days of wading through studies offering statistically significant proof before I feel compelled to bulk-order beeswax candles and turn my iPhone to 'red mode'. From now on, it's candles or red bulbs if I need my night vigil illuminating.

How else to keep my Night Self from tipping into torrid rage?

One night I place a stack of paper and pens beside my bed. Perhaps I too can sketch and scribble my way out of rage and into serenity. When I wake at 2.25 a.m. I reach for a pen and paper, intending to doodle myself back to sleep with a Bourgeois-style spiral.

Because of my recent light-mood reading material, I doodle in the dark. The pen scrapes soothingly against the paper, until it slips off and disappears into downy nothing. When I turn on the lamp, I see that my white duvet cover is scratched through with black marks from my pen.

I light one of my new candles and return to my mindless spiralling and, as I do so, my mind circles back to the past. As a child I drew constantly – but it was colouring that I found most soporific. Like spiralling, colouring required very little thought. The pen moved and the eye followed. And bingo – just like that, I am returned to my past with its childhood certainties and comforts. To slip back into a longed-for past is deeply calming, reminding us of where we came from, what made us – little snatches of assurance in the disquiet of darkness.

Bourgeois never had this. And when she tried to recreate a new family to anchor herself, she became furious all over again. Furious at being called a housewife, at not being taken seriously as an artist. Furious at the demands placed on her by small children and domesticity. Furious at the art world's neglect of her.

'I'm not afraid of violence,' said Bourgeois, who found release and relief in 'aggressiveness', which she called 'self-expression'. Merely admitting to her rage took courage at a time when women weren't supposed to show anger. Even today, studies report that angry men are seen as strong, decisive and powerful while angry women are seen as irrational, shrill and unfeminine.[11]

By the end of her life, rage and insomnia had become two of the certainties of her past and of her present – a pair of faithful and hugely productive companions, combined into a single, very angry Night Self. And yet her insomnia drawings are oddly peaceful. As if the constant circling of her hand had rubbed away the sharp edges of her fury, softened it, removed its sting.

There is no consciousness to compete with our Night Self. No one to challenge, soothe, support, question, interpret. Instead, she becomes a prima donna, ranging freely – and sometimes furiously – through our wide-awake minds.

Studies suggest that sleep deprivation may be partly to blame. Sleep-deprived men typically become more aggressive, while women become moodier and more anxious. Both sexes are, apparently, more susceptible to feelings of hostility and anger.[12] Scientists think that, when we're excessively tired, the part of our brain that suppresses activity in the amygdala (the brain's emotional and fear headquarters) becomes impaired, leaving our emotions in freefall – and so we vent and rage. Meanwhile, the brain region responsible for 'control' (the prefrontal cortex) is in partial, circadian hibernation, further exaggerating our night rage. In other words, our emotions don't change. Instead, our ability to *control* our emotions changes.

When Japanese researchers used MRI to investigate, they

found that blood flow between the 'emotional HQ' amygdala and the 'controlling' prefrontal cortex slows downs when we're sleep-deprived, making this (possibly) a simple case of insufficient delivery of oxygen and nutrients.

Either way, the emotions we carefully button up by day can gallop roughshod and unrestrained as we lie awake at night, superseding and erasing our fatigue and exhaustion. Our Night Self in furious freefall.

And yet Bourgeois turned her sleep deprivation into 'creative profit'. Because with the grumpy anger of sleep deprivation comes a refusal to care. In Bourgeois's time (and arguably today), this was deemed a bad thing: women were supposed to be kind and caring. But for Bourgeois, sleep deprivation merely added to her chutzpah – she didn't give a damn about the opinions of others.

Instead of following the dictates of the art world, she experimented – with fabric, metal, wool, wood, anything she wanted. How can we not love her willingness to experiment, to recycle, to go utterly against the grain? It seems to me that she reshaped and reused her things – Pucci blouses and Chanel dresses, her mother's skirts, her husband's shirts – just as she remoulded her fear, rage, remorse and insomnia – in an endless cycle of inventiveness.

A few months later, I went to a Bourgeois exhibition at Tate Liverpool. I looked for rage but found none. Instead, I saw tenderness in her prints of hands, patience in her stitching and embroidery, determination in her sculpture, sadness in her spiders. A line of hers kept coming to me that I'd thought exaggerated and overwrought when I first read it, but which now made perfect sense. It was a line written sixty-six years after her mother died: 'I miss her every day.'

The weight of loss doesn't go, it merely changes. And I was

beginning to see that although grief has a clear, definite beginning, there is no clear and absolute ending. To expect or hope for one was mistaken. I knew now that I would always miss my father. And that was OK.

When we stepped out of the gallery we found ourselves in the midst of an exhibition of light sculptures and installations, flaring into dazzling life across Liverpool's old port. Hundreds of lights that looked like lilies floated on the water. Towers of light – lilac, lemon, tangerine – flashed from clustered bulbs in every shape and size. From dark industrial corners shot kingfisher volts of radiance. Lights in every hue, blinking, winking, flashing, brightening, dimming. Crowds emerged from the darkness to point and exclaim, to *ooh* and *aah*. We joined the shadowy, happy throng. And I had a feeling that I would always remember this evening – tumbling out of the metaphorical darkness of Bourgeois into the neon glow of Liverpool, as light and bright as fireflies.

Did Bourgeois's night drawing help? Did she eventually sleep? It appears so. 'I still try to conquer the insomnia, and to a large extent I have done it,' she explained in 1995. 'I draw . . . until I feel peaceful and I fall asleep . . . It is conquerable,' she added with arresting optimism.

And so it is Bourgeois who shows me how to reinvent the fury and shapelessness of grief. Just as she transformed everything in her life, from old clothes to childhood emotions, from unwanted plates to raging memories. Bourgeois is the sleepless master of metamorphosis, her personal Night Self an incubator of rage but also an unending source of creative fuel.

Night after night, I draw. There's something about it I like – the movement, the slowness, my Night Self's refusal to rate or rank. The pencil seems to suck up my rage. And all my thoughts are concentrated, distilled into drawings, which are very, very small. And the size feels right too. Like curling up, as tight as a seed, beneath the germinating warmth of a winter duvet. Curtains closed, light shut out. Every inch of me crystallised into something small and containable. For my eyes only.

And so, just as we shed dead skin most profusely at midnight, my Night Self sheds her rage and fury most effectively at 3 a.m., pencil to paper. In the morning, I rise calm and purged. And, yes, tired. But hopeful that the next night I will fall into deep and exhausted sleep. The dangers come when sleep deprivation rolls on and on, day after weary day. As I was about to learn.

6

Ruminative

I can stay awake all night, if need be –
Cold as an eel, without eyelids.
Like a dead lake the dark envelops me . . .
Sylvia Plath, 'Zoo-Keeper's Wife'

Every now and then my night watch spirals out of control. A run of nights in which I barely sleep leaves me snappish and sluggish, eyes aching, brain straining. I survive on coffee, snatched naps and the words of the French philosopher Simone Weil, who relished her sleep-deprived exhaustion. 'Sometimes I'm crushed by fatigue,' she wrote. 'But I find in it a kind of purification.'

I didn't feel 'purified' by my insomnia, but I liked Weil's defiance. There was another line of hers that I liked too: 'Right at the very bottom of my exhaustion I encounter joys that nothing else can give me.' Weil wrote these contrarian words at the pinnacle of her sleeplessness when, according to her biographer, she 'kept an exhausting schedule, seldom sleeping more than three hours a night . . . occasionally resting by putting her head down on her desk'.[1]

I never discovered Weil's exhausted 'joys'. Instead, I observed my Night Self's growing propensity for rumination. Eventually I taught myself to break the bouts of broodiness before they spilled into doubt and doom, regret and remorse. The onset of rumination, I learned, was the very moment for leashing my Night Self, for strenuously reining her in. Because a surfeit of darkness, sleeplessness and despair can tip us over the edge of sanity.

No life illustrates this better than that of Sylvia Plath, whose apocryphal story is a reminder of what can happen when we overdose on a synthesis of exhaustion, darkness, medication and emotional devastation.

And yet during her wide-awake nights, Plath brought forth poems unlike any she'd ever written. She described the process as akin to 'writing in a train tunnel, or God's intestine', and the poems she produced as 'the best poems of my life'. Critics, poets and readers agreed. Robert Lowell called them 'a triumph'; Anne Stevenson called them 'astonishing'. The collection (titled *Ariel*) sold 15,000 copies in ten months.

Plath's husband (the poet Ted Hughes) believed Plath's final poems represented her 'real self'. But did they? To me, the poems in *Ariel* wear all the disordered brilliance of a Night Self teetering on a tightrope. Eerie, damaged, dazzling things, forged in an excess of nocturne.

In a letter written in the summer of 1962, Hughes confessed that he had changed 'in April or so, & since then this marriage, house, Sylvia etc have seemed just like the dead end of everything'.[2]

It was only seven months since Hughes and 29-year-old Plath had moved into their dream home, a large thatched house amid the greenery of Devon. And it was a mere three months since Plath had given birth to their second child, Nicholas. The birth hadn't been easy: Nicholas was born at midnight, after fifteen hours of 'very strong' cramps and pain. Plath then endured a ten-day wait for her milk to come in: 'the baby starving and crying all night, culminating in two nights of 103 degrees milk fever'.[3] Plath started the last year of her short life with a string of broken nights, familiar to most mothers.

In fact, the previous two years hadn't been much easier. Plath's first 'colicky' daughter, Frieda, was breastfed for ten months. Plath then had a miscarriage at four months, swiftly followed by an appendectomy and a ten-day hospital stay where her fellow patient snored incessantly. Plath described the subsequent winter as 'full of flu, miasmas, near bankruptcy, nights full of teething yowls from our changeling'.

By spring of 1961 Plath's health was on the mend, but by then she was pregnant again. She soldiered on – typing up her husband's work, writing her own poetry, working on her first novel *The Bell Jar*, giving readings, attempting to be the perfect wife and mother, and moving from London to Devon, where she had neither friends nor family.

In the spring of 1962, as Plath was nursing Nicholas – her 'hands full, with cooking & two little babies' – Hughes returned from London with a young woman he'd met at a poetry reading. She was elegantly dressed, her hair groomed and styled, her well-slept complexion soft and dewy. Plath tried to compete ('I managed a girdle and stockings and heels'). But a newly nursing mother – breasts like overblown balloons and desperate for sleep – carries no whiff of excitement, no promise of escape, no hint of the exotic. Quite the reverse.

The marriage began to break down. Visiting friends noticed the 'palpable tension' between Plath and Hughes. Plath scrawled in her journal of her need to 'purge myself of sour milk, ruinous nappies, bits of lint and the loving slovenliness of motherhood.' Meanwhile, a poem she started at dawn, on 12 April, hinted at her old depression: 'I am terrified by this dark thing / That sleeps in me'.

It barely needs saying that motherhood magnifies the difficulties and complexities of sleepless nights. In 2018, researchers linked poor post-partum sleep (isn't most post-partum sleep 'poor'?) to 'greater symptoms of depression and anxiety' in new mothers.[4]

I often found a rare and quiet intimacy nursing my babies in the darkness and silence. Even so, there were dozens of wrung-out days when I felt my Self derange and dissolve. Neither Night Self nor Day Self. Instead I became a hollow empty creature I barely knew.

By the summer Hughes had started a far more serious affair with the wife of a friend, Assia Wevill – a renowned beauty free of the demanding milky taint of small children. He told his sister that he was 'aghast' at how he had 'confined and stunted [his] existence'. He was referring to the family trappings he'd acquired: children, house, garden, wife. All of it holding him captive, curtailing his imagination so that he could barely write. While Plath held everything together – bee-keeping, daffodil-selling, cooking, entertaining the neighbours, breastfeeding, even her writing career, which was racing ahead at this point – Hughes privately simmered with resentment. To his brother he wrote, 'It's a good thing every ten years or so to smash your life to bits.'[5] Which is exactly what he did next.

The story from here on is well known. After nights of 'no sleep & horrid talk', Hughes left for London – and his new lover. Plath was devastated. 'I care to a frenzy,' she wrote in a letter. 'I cannot sleep. I cannot eat . . . I keep having to run off to cry and be dry-sick . . . I can't imagine a life without Ted . . . My marriage is the center of my being . . . I feel ugly and a fool . . . I am just sick.' Plath's milk dried up, she sobbed all night and she told friends she couldn't live without him.

Her grief was compounded by ongoingill health: she 'had a recurrence of my old flu fever & chills & weakness . . . I almost died from influenza.' Little wonder Plath couldn't sleep. And little wonder she began throwing sleeping pills down her throat by the handful.

Plath had a long history of sleeplessness. Her journals express a deep ambivalence towards the act of sleep and she was frequently so hungry for life that, on many occasions, she happily sacrificed her slumber. In August 1951, she (a 'passionate, fragmentary' eighteen-year-old) wrote, 'I am very tired. I wonder why I don't go to bed and go to sleep. But then it would be tomorrow, so I decide that no matter how tired, no matter how incoherent I am, I can skip one hour more of sleep and live.' Later in the month she declared: 'I want to stay awake for the next three days and nights, drawing the threads of my summer cocoon neatly about me . . .' And a month later, she asked, 'Why, instead of going to bed . . . do I sit up later . . . and lash my brains into cold calculating thought?'

Further on in her journal, she moaned, 'Tomorrow I will curse the dawn,' before optimistically adding, 'but there will be other, earlier nights and the dawns will no longer be hell laid out in alarms, raw bells and sirens.' A little later in the same month, she stayed up late: 'In spite of vowing to go to bed early, because it is more important to capture moments like this, keen shifts in mood, sudden veering of direction – than to lose it in slumber.'

Four years later, Plath was still complaining to her journal that 'such a fraction of this life we live: so much is sleep . . . sleep is like the grave'. And yet Plath's attitude had begun to change, as if she'd recognised an intractable need for sleep in spite of her preference for *life*.

In January 1953, she wailed: 'All I need is sleep . . .' Later, she described 'hellish sleepless nights' and 'miserable tense knotted sleepless nights'. She wrote of the ache that arises 'from little sleep and taut strung nerves' and the difficulties of teaching 'on 3 days & nights of no-sleep'. Her nights were often disrupted by terrible nightmares – of drinking poison, of losing her mother, of chasing Ted through psychiatric hospitals, of giving birth to dead babies, of swimming in a river of corpses, of a sword-wielding man hacking off the legs of costumed bystanders, 'of deformity and death', of her dead father shooting a deer, of tearing a 'youth' apart with her 'teeth and hands'. 'My feverish dreams', she called them, her 'troubled' night-hauntings, her 'worm-eaten nights'.

And on it goes. Excruciating in its drift.[6]

Plath didn't know what we (now) know: that endless threadbare nights increase our risk of depression, weakening our emotional resilience, making it more and more difficult for us to counter the ups and downs of everyday life. The more exhausted we become, the more challenging we find it merely to live. Night Self and Day Self destroyed in a single, sustained swoop of sleeplessness.

And yet Plath knew she needed sleep. At the age of nineteen, she wrote herself a list of ten 'Back to School Commandments'. Eighth on her list was 'Get a lot of sleep: afternoon naps if necessary.'

In the aftermath of Hughes's betrayal, Plath's insomnia returned. 'The degraded and agonising life I have been living has . . . just about ruined my sleep,' she wrote in August 1962. But this time she made use of it to write poetry – a practice instigated by Hughes a year earlier when he'd suggested she write when she couldn't sleep. On that occasion she'd written one of the most evocative night poems ever composed – 'The Moon and the Yew Tree'. This time, it was Plath's home help, Winifred, who suggested that Plath get up and write instead of ruminating.

She began a routine of rising at 4 a.m. (when her sleeping pills wore off), then 'madly writing' poems until 8 a.m. Plath knew these poems were 'the best ever', and 'all marvellous, free, full songs'. She loved writing 'in the blue dawns, all to myself, secret and quiet . . . this quiet center at the middle of the storm'.

Around this time she decided to return to London. She needed company, support and the literary network that would enable her to work and so provide for her children. Alone, she found a new home, packed up the Devon house, and relocated herself with baby and toddler to a chilly undecorated apartment without electricity, a gas stove or a telephone. 'We moved in by candlelight,' she wrote to a friend. Unfazed, she set to work painting the floorboards, organising furnishings, sending out her work, catching up with friends, galleries, films.

By December, Plath was in trouble. She told friends that she'd become addicted to sleeping pills and needed her doctor's help to wean herself from them. But then the babies caught colds and the weather changed. A subsequent letter suggests that instead of getting her off the sleeping pills, Plath's doctor prescribed more: 'tonics to make me eat, pills to sleep etc.'.

By January she was taking an antidepressant – with side effects that included both insomnia and drowsiness – alongside her usual sleeping pills, as well as over-the-counter medications for her 'flu'.

Within days of Plath's arrival in London, snow started to fall in thick drifts – it was to be the bleakest winter in 150 years. In some places, the snow reached depths of twenty feet. Pipes and ponds iced up. People slipped and died on the treacherous pavements. The north wind blew, day after day, night after night. The sea froze.

January 1963 was one of the darkest on record. Thirty-seven power stations went on strike over pay and overtime. A third of the British power supply became erratic and unpredictable, with the country frequently plunged into darkness. The London

Underground often lurched into smothering darkness; babies were born by candlelight; church services were held amid the dim flicker of a few candles; theatres and cinemas frequently snapped, mid-show, into blackness.[7]

In the endless dark Plath wrote poems by candlelight, 'with cold fingers'. To her psychiatrist friend in America she described her new poems as 'very good but, I feel written on the edge of madness'.

As Plath created extraordinary poems in semi-darkness, humiliation continued to rain down on her: *Difficulties of a Bridegroom*, Hughes's radio play that was full of barely veiled allusions to their failed marriage, aired on radio; and Hughes and his two mistresses were paraded, discussed and gossiped about in the literary circles Plath had once occupied. *The Bell Jar* was rejected by American publishers. Plath and her children became sick again – fevers, infections, flu. Her daughter woke regularly in the night, 'tearful and obsessed with [Hughes] . . . it is like a kind of mirror, utterly innocent, to my own sense of loss'.[8]

Between 28 January and 5 February Plath wrote eleven poems – not poems of rage and fury like those she'd composed on autumn nights, but poems of despair and resignation. She described them as 'dawn poems, [written] in blood'.[9] The final lines of the last poem she wrote ('Edge') denote the Night Self at its bleakest – isolated, minuscule, abandoned – watched over by an indifferent moon 'staring from her hood of bone' as 'her blacks crackle and drag'.

The long weeks of exhaustion, loneliness and sickness were beginning to show. Plath stopped writing. Friends expressed alarm at how she looked – bony and underweight with darkened rings around her eyes. On the final weekend of her life, she stayed with new friends Gerry and Jillian Becker. Accounts of this period show how fragmented Plath's dwindling sleep had become: at 10 p.m. Plath took her sleeping pills (and possibly the opioid she was taking for her respiratory illness), then 'rambled' about the past, about Hughes, about her disappointment at the reception of *The Bell Jar*, finally falling asleep at midnight. Four hours later, Nicholas woke and needed feeding and 'Sylvia was wide awake again. She could not sleep and wanted to take what she called her "pep" pill because it took "hours" to work.' Two hours after feeding and settling Nicholas, Plath fell back to sleep for a bit, before waking and embarking on another 'grim' and gruelling day, ashamed, disappointed, jilted. And exhausted, her brain and body cracking beneath the emotional and physical strain and the debilitating fatigue that accompanies chronic sleeplessness.[10]

The pattern of her sleeplessness changed on her final night, when she knocked on the door of her neighbour, Trevor Thomas, at 11.45 p.m. asking for airmail stamps. Trevor lay awake, listening to Plath pacing the floor, until 5 a.m., when he eventually fell asleep. It was Plath's closing night of sleeplessness. And Trevor Thomas was the last person to see her alive.

A fortnight later, the literary editor of the *Observer* declared Plath 'the most gifted woman poet of our time', and described the 'loss to literature' as 'inestimable'.

Some researchers speculate that 'circadian factors may contribute to suicidality'.[11] The traits of the 'Mind after Midnight' (introduced in Chapter 2) – less rational, less logically analytical, less able to plan or assess risk – are most marked between the hours of midnight and 6 a.m. Of course, these traits have a flip side (the originality and audacity that radiate from *Ariel*), perhaps explaining Plath's predilection for 'that still blue, almost eternal hour . . . before the glassy music of the milkman, settling his bottles'.

But in acutely depressed people, these traits become amplified.[12] Sleep researcher and co-author of 'The Mind after Midnight', Michael Perlis, calls this 'hypofrontality', a condition resulting from sluggish blood flow and poor glucose uptake in the brain regions responsible for judgement and impulse control. The greater the fatigue, the more the depressed brain struggles. 'It's a perfect storm,' Perlis tells me. 'Our ability to think reasonably is compromised and we're more likely to have, and act on, negative impulses.'

Studies suggest that sleep-starved young women with major depressive disorder experience a heightened and exaggerated form of hypofrontality.[13] Their brains can't function with their usual clarity and foresight because fuel and nutrients (blood and glucose) are effectively blocked. To boot, they are less likely to sleep because their bodies produce less melatonin. These women are, quite literally, *not themselves*.

There are many Plath biographers, and all have their own carefully sleuthed explanation for her suicide. Some think she was bipolar at a time when bipolar disorder was undiagnosed. Some blame the toxic cocktail of medication she was taking. Others think she reacted unfavourably to the antidepressant medication she had recently started taking. One or two speculate that Plath's earlier electric shock treatment had left her with undiagnosed PTSD. Her latest biographer, Heather Clark, points the finger at undiagnosed postnatal depression. Plath's doctor blamed her paternal genes, saying she'd 'inherited a chemical imbalance that causes . . . depression'. Hughes believed she had 'tapped too deeply into her creative powers, releasing emotions that she was not equipped to handle'. Meanwhile, Plath's mother believed she was 'overwhelmed . . . by the bitter cold and darkness of the winter'.

Most recently, Juliet Nicolson has suggested that Plath suffered a 'sort of heart attack of the brain, a catastrophic failure of the wiring of the mind', precipitated when Plath turned her intense mental energy inwards rather than exorcising it in the creative 'outward' act of producing poetry.[14]

We'll never know what went through Plath's mind on that final fateful night. But, as I said, our Night Selves are fragile, unpredictable – and darkness is not always a place of solace and solitude. Here, we exist as finely balanced blades. Beware the excess of rumination and despair that can lead us – teetering, skittering, stumbling – to 'an edge of madness' . . .

One night I wake just before 4 a.m. The darkness is thick and empty, a sack of black. The cottage wheezes and creaks. I feel my ears open and sharpen – alert, vigilant, wary. I put in my headphones and listen to a recording of Plath reading from her 4 a.m. poems. As her words pour into my head, unfiltered by space or light, I hear the whimsical gifts of nocturne: mystery, vulnerability, fury, creativity, uncertainty, volatility, jeopardy, wonder. These poems – bald and wild, and rich in their allusions to celestial darkness – are like snatched dreams caught in a rush of words. *Earwig biscuits . . . Nazi lampshades . . . flogged trolleys . . . the word of a snail on the plate of a leaf . . .* There is so much of night here – the rawness, the obscurity, the wistfulness, the casual disregard for convention. As I listen I have an odd sense of my Night Self listening to Plath's Night Self. As if I'm catching intimations, rhythms, sounds, images I wouldn't notice during the day.

When the recording ends I grope through the darkness, down the stairs, to my desk. Then I light a candle and do something I have never done. I write the first draft of a poem. I'm stepping on toes, of course. My father was the poet, never me. But he has gone. And I am here. And poetry feels more naturally the language of darkness than my usual prose. And so I write, until a line of licked-clean dawn rises on the horizon, gold-beaten and shining like water dazzle.

I have learned – from Cereta, Bourgeois and Plath – that writing can blot out a brooding Night Self. So, when I hear the slide of my inner voice towards recrimination and regret, I shuffle to my desk and write peculiar poems by the gulping light of a candle.

But one night I sense a stirring inside me, as if the shift from bed to desk, from upstairs to downstairs, has awakened something. The walls and ceiling of my cottage are not as comforting as they once were, and I have a sudden yearning for escape. My Night Self seems to be tugging at me, urging me outwards, as if she knows I've exhausted all the possibilities of indoor darkness. As if she knows of something more potent than writing to quash her ruminative tendencies.

And yet she tugs and nudges with a wariness that confuses me. I want to roam beyond my bedroom, beyond my home – but I feel hesitant and unsure. What is it that binds me so deliberately to the bricks and mortar of home?

7

Anonymous

In the vast caverns of space, where Sirius lights the traveller, a
genius and a weary invalid are equals – both frail as star dust.
Mary Webb, 'The Spring of Joy'

Leaving my bedroom for several hours every sleepless night
marked a tentative shift in my understanding of darkness and its
possibilities. No longer bed-bound, I was conscious of a profound
vulnerability. Beneath the duvet I felt safe. But stepping out of the
bedroom into bible-black darkness, groping my way along the
hall and down the stairs, I felt exposed, unskinned, wary. I suppose
this is inevitable. We're neither dressed nor made up. We cannot
see. Our brains are addled by sleep – or lack of it. We carry genetic
memories – of predatory animals, poisonous insects, night raiders,
falling, fire – that compound our feelings of vulnerability.

In his book, *At Day's Close: A History of Nighttime*, A. Roger
Ekirch paints a horrifying picture of female vulnerability. Prior
to the Industrial Revolution, public places at night were male
haunts where women were frequently in danger of their lives.
Ekirch explains that women – particularly young women – were
routinely 'beaten and kicked', thanks to the 'gratuitous and
unprovoked violence' of raging drunken men. In his lengthy
and shocking narrative of nocturnal crime and brutality, Ekirch
explains that darkness 'made legions of the weak more powerful',

while enabling the wealthy and religious (men) to behave – unseen – like vandals and thugs.

As if this wasn't enough, fear of spells and sorcery – often believed to work after dark – made any out-at-night woman instantly susceptible to accusations of witchcraft. And if she wasn't a witch, she was surely a prostitute. Arrested, accosted, assaulted, accused . . . after nightfall women were deemed safe only when indoors or when accompanied by men. Little wonder I felt vulnerable tip-toeing around in the dark.

And yet feelings of vulnerability are fundamental to empathy and compassion. That *raw, unskinned* feeling lets us slip outside of ourselves and into the skins of others. Turned inwards, our insomniac dark-induced vulnerability can be agonising. Turned outwards, it becomes quite a different thing – it becomes a torch into human experience. We feel what it is to be sightless, alone, frail, lost, *other*.

And then there's the anonymity of darkness, the sense that we are invisible, that we are protected even as we feel curiously exposed. A bit like being alone on a stage after the curtain has come down. There's a freedom to this, as if darkness gives us a right to roam imaginatively. Dangerous thoughts enter on doves' feet. We consider them, try them on, take them off – liberated from the gaze and scrutiny of others.

Again, Ekirch's history of night shows a long, sad tradition of women making use of darkness to avoid shame, retribution and judgement. Unwed mothers regularly abandoned babies under cover of night (so that they could secretly check their babies had been safely 'found' before escaping unrecognised); women crept out to steal firewood in order to keep the family fire going, to pilfer fruit and vegetables to feed their children, to beg in the concealment of darkness. Night has always been a time and place for hiding, for obscurity. For anonymity.

★

Few women appreciated the anonymity of darkness better than the English writer Mary Webb. Webb, who was diagnosed with the autoimmune condition Graves' disease at the age of twenty, understood the democratising power of anonymous night, where 'a genius and a weary invalid are equals – both frail as stardust'. For the invalid, insomniac Webb, this insight was both liberating and empowering. From here, she developed a series of bold ideas on darkness and earth as a necessary place of struggle, conflict and grief: 'Only through the bravery of the root, its determination to suffer rather than die, does the flower dance in the light,' she noted. Darkness – like the soil – was a place of creative and emotional germination.

One of Webb's favourite metaphors was the water lily: 'every one of those wide spreading leaves, those pure blossoms, has its long, swaying root going down into darkness.' Roots, bulbs, tubers – to Webb these were symbols of the human spirit. As earth was vital for rooting plants, so darkness was essential for grounding and centring her own spirit. 'The more delicate and beautiful the flower and fruit the closer must be the union with earth,' she wrote. For Webb, 'the quietude and secrecy' of 'boundless dark', 'the clear, cold scent of wet starlight', were places of discovery and recovery. As her marriage fell apart, as literary success eluded her, as her diseased body withered away, Webb found a version of what we now call 'radical acceptance' – pain as a path to joy, darkness as a place of hope.[1]

I think about Mary Webb as I creep round the house at 3 a.m. Graves' disease had disfigured her, causing her eyes to bulge, her goitred throat to swell, her hands to shake. She considered herself repulsive, hideous, ugly. She wrapped herself in high-necked blouses and scarves. She wore large-brimmed hats to conceal her protruding eyes. She became deeply self-conscious, always seeking out places where she could be alone. The anonymity of darkness was her salvation – here she could remain unseen and unseeable.

I love the way darkness renders us invisible. During the day, I catch reflections of myself, in windows and mirrors, in saucepan lids and knife blades. It's distracting, reminding me of my appearance, of all the things I should do – get dressed, brush hair, stand up straight, trim my fringe, mend my glasses. Infinitely worse for Webb – every reflection was a reminder of her approaching death. Because Webb found darkness so freeing, it ceased to hold any fear for her. She began spending time in forests at night, watching owls, hedgehogs, moths. She learned to recognise trees and plants by their night scent. Even stream water smelled different in the dark, she noted. Night fragrances became a 'healing perfume' and she urged her readers to embrace 'the fascination of shadows' and 'the dark, still dawns'.

The tragedy of Webb's life keeps me prowling too. Her hatred of her appearance reached an apotheosis when her adored husband began a blatant, brazen affair with a student two decades younger than Webb. Once again, she retreated into the sanctuary of darkness while her husband left her, uncared for. Webb – who often wrote her novels during the night – would eventually become a bestselling author, recognised by Simone de Beauvoir, Rebecca West (who called her a genius) and the British prime minister, Stanley Baldwin. Her books were reprinted, sold in great volumes at home and abroad, made into films and TV dramas. But by this time Webb was in her coffin, dead at forty-six, buried deep in the black earth of Shropshire.

The artist Joan Mitchell also needed anonymity, not because of a disfigured appearance but because it helped in the dissolution of her ego. At first, she found a sense of anonymity in her peripatetic life, moving from place to place, first in America and then in France. But in 1959, as her reputation grew, she bought her own Parisian apartment. Mitchell began painting later and later into the night, as if searching for the anonymity she'd lost. And as her hours shifted, her paintings changed. Even Mitchell was baffled by the change in style, wondering why her paintings appeared more 'violent'. Later, critics noted their 'greater sense of impulsiveness and velocity'. Some art historians saw Mitchell's new night paintings as an expression of rage.[2]

Recently, the art historian Sarah Roberts pointed out that 'these paintings also express tremendous risk-taking ... as Mitchell experimented aggressively'. Mitchell turned and flipped her canvases, painting from all angles, tackling each image from multiple orientations. She threw, flicked and whisked paint through the air to 'create bewilderingly complex threads, shreds and droplets'. She risked 'the total collapse of the painting into a chaotic unsightly sludge'. The dramatic change of style bemused critics. Roberts speculates that Mitchell felt liberated because she now had 'a place where she could throw paint and not worry about cleaning it up'.

Me? I think Mitchell merely unleashed her Night Self: inventive, imaginative, bold, angry, vulnerable. From the anonymity of night, she took risks, making herself yet more vulnerable. But she didn't care. Later, much later, Mitchell described these first 'night canvases' as the 'boldest' pictures she ever painted.

Mitchell liked night painting so much she carried on, feeding from both the anonymity and the sense of vulnerability bestowed by the press of darkness at her studio windows. She painted half-drunk, by fluorescent light ('ten [at night] to four I paint'), saying 'No one can paint – write – feel whatever without being vulnerable.'[3] In order to work, Mitchell needed to shed her ego, to become supremely *receptive*. In 1957 she told a journalist from *ARTnews*, 'The moment that I am self-conscious, I cease painting.'

To help 'make myself available to myself' Mitchell spent her evenings preparing – listening to music (jazz and Bach), reading poetry and drinking. Thus, she began the gradual process of turning inwards to her Night Self exactly as the outer light drained from the sky.

Mitchell never painted from life: she painted from memory. 'I carry my landscapes with me,' she once said. Turning inwards – as we must in order to unearth our memories – is a private practice. If the memories are to remain entirely our own, ungilded by others, we must engage with them in complete solitude. For Mitchell, night provided the necessary privacy. In fact, she was so protective of her privacy that she kept her studio locked at all times, refusing to let anyone in and then sleeping with the key beneath her pillow. 'The solitude that I find in my studio is one of plenitude. I am enough for myself. I live fully there,' she wrote.

As she worked, the sickly light seeping from her studio became a sign: like the bright beam of a lighthouse . . . *Danger: Night Self at Work.*

I liked the anonymity – the hiddenness – of darkness. In my most grief-stricken times, it had allowed me to forget my appearance, and to shed my expectations of myself, as it had for Webb. I was intrigued by the vulnerability conferred by night. I thought of it as a trauma memory genetically bequeathed by generations of women, but Mitchell showed me its possibilities. Indeed, it seemed to me that the vulnerability and anonymity experienced by my Night Self were a means of liberation, allowing me to live more fully, both by night and by day.

And yet there was something else that struck at night. Like anonymity and vulnerability, it wasn't obviously spurred by rerouted circadian chemicals in my brain or by clock-driven hormones in my body. It seemed to come from the darkness itself, riding alongside anonymity and vulnerability. Its name was fear.

As a small child I was afraid of both night and darkness, convinced that strange creatures lived under my bed and crept out when I was asleep. The only way to avoid them was by keeping a light on.

I was quite normal. Studies show that after the age of four, 75 per cent of all children experience night fears. As children become teenagers, this rises to 79 per cent. From the age of eight, fear becomes gendered, with a sudden and startling esca-lation in the number of females intimidated by darkness.[4]

I wondered if grieving had exaggerated my fearfulness. I'd read of numerous instances where sudden loss precipitated an extreme fear of the dark. After the writer M. F. K. Fisher lost her husband, the dark was transformed from romantic to some-thing unfamiliar and terrifying: 'Now I am afraid of the quiet and the dark and my mind . . . makes insufferable such earlier [night] pleasures.'[5] Joan Didion 'started leaving lights on through the night', explaining that she became 'immobilised' in anguished darkness.[6] Following Jackson Pollock's death, Lee Krasner couldn't sleep alone in the house – in spite of her pet dogs. Friends or the child of a neighbour stayed over every night. When the Danish coffee farmer and writer Karen Blixen was bankrupted (a bereavement of sorts), she too became terrified of nights alone and frequently dragooned the young son of a serv-ant to stay over.

Of course, fear isn't restricted to the bereaved. The writer Katherine Mansfield was so frightened at night that she dragged large pieces of furniture across the door of her London flat. 'She wasn't scared of intruders,' explained her flatmate, Ida Baker, 'She was scared of night, of what might be lurking in the dark-ness.' Even Sylvia Plath, an inveterate stargazer with a penchant for night-walking, disliked sleeping alone at her Devon home.

And then there's the singer Joni Mitchell, a self-styled 'night watchman', unable to sleep until the sun comes up.

None of this is unusual – a survey of 2,000 British adults found that 40 per cent were too frightened to walk around their house in the dark, with a shocking one in ten too terrified to use the bathroom at night.[7] And in the course of writing this book, many women spoke to me of their ungovernable fears when home alone at night.

As for my own fear, it lived inside my Night Self like a vital organ – a kidney or lung – sometimes awake, sometimes dozing, but always there. I knew one thing for certain – it was ancient, primal, scratched so deeply into me it *was* me.

Where does all this fear come from?

In 1973, the psychologist Jenő Ranschburg identified three reasons for our fear of darkness. Firstly, he pointed out that darkness makes us feel disconnected and isolated, even if we're in company. Merely being in the dark separates us from the environment we know, rendering it suddenly unknown. This, he argued, caused separation anxiety – particularly in children. Secondly, Ranschburg cited the human imagination, which when activated by darkness allows us to project fantastical imaginings onto our surroundings in a way that often frightens us. The third factor, he claimed, was the lack of safety that automatically accompanies darkness and prompts innate fears of falling, of walking into something, of predation.

Fortunately, our understanding of the brain has progressed in the last fifty years. Fear of night and darkness are both more and less complicated than we ever imagined. And our neurobiology lies at the very centre of the throat-tightening terror that strikes so many of us when the lights go out.

In 2021, Dr Elise McGlashan investigated the effect of darkness on the amygdala, the brain region typically described as our fear centre. Instead of looking at the eye cells that enable us to see, McGlashan decided to investigate a set of cells that have nothing to do with our vision: a group of light-capturing cells (called photosensitive retinal ganglion cells) that help set our internal body clock, making us alert during the day and sleepy at night.

McGlashan found that, as soon as light was turned on, the amygdala went into partial hibernation. Just as entering the code into a security alarm deactivates it, so light switches off our fear centre. And with our fear centre turned off, we inevitably feel calmer and happier.

So it's not darkness that frightens and unsettles us. Nor is it our fumbling night vision. It's the absence of light. A subtle but important difference.

'We're afraid of the dark because we haven't evolved to be active at night,' McGlashan explained.[8] 'Crucially, the presence of light means we can control our emotions more effectively – including our fear.' Meanwhile, other researchers think that fear may be circadian, hypothesising that we are inherently more fearful at night, regardless of illumination.[9] All this is to say that we are *wired* to feel anxious and wary both at night and in darkness. And without light, it's harder for our brain to rein in these feelings. We must talk ourselves down, repeatedly, from the precipice of fear – which takes huge reserves of emotional and physical energy. Much easier to stay home, flood the place with light, stick with a crowd.

But if we fail to make peace with our fears, the many qualities of night are lost, squeezed out of existence by our own unconstrained terror. And if night has its own truths, if a part of ourselves exists in its complex internal landscape, we have no choice but to befriend our fear.

How else do we fully liberate our Night Self?

8

Curious

)

> We have a hunger of the mind which asks for knowledge of
> all around us, and the more we gain, the more is our desire.
> Maria Mitchell, diary entry for the Denver Eclipse

Grief is like an eclipse: we are thrust involuntarily into a land-scape that is at once familiar and terrifyingly unfamiliar. We long for the sun to be returned. We yearn for certainty. We see the terrible brevity of all human life.

Even seven months on, I exist in a seam of fear. I'm afraid of losing others I love. I'm terrified that memories of my father won't hold. I fear that my new cracks are irreparable. I dread my own death. Studies show that the grieving brain is marked by an overactive amygdala,[1] so I know that – in this respect – I'm not alone.

Besides, there are two things that no longer frighten me as they once did: indoor darkness and insomnia, the midwives of my Night Self. But to continue hacking out my fears, I need more. I need to yoke the curiosity of my Night Self to the wisdom of a night spinner.

The legendary humanitarian and activist Peace Pilgrim once received a letter asking for advice on conquering 'fear of the dark when alone outside'. Peace Pilgrim – who slept outdoors and walked the roads at night for months and years at a time – replied: 'May I suggest watching it get dark . . . and looking for the first star.'

Caught between curiosity and compulsive fear, I take her advice and begin watching twilight turn to night. And yes, the first glistering star distracts me from my own fearful imagination. When I next wake in darkness, I put aside my candles, pencils and paper, and go to the doorstep. Until now, I've been a stranger to the night sky. In London, where I live most of the time, 'darkness' (such as it is – a lurid blend of harsh streetlight and ambient skyglow) is a time for hurrying home, eyes only for lurking shadows, fists gripped around keys. In the country, darkness means dangerous country roads where cars race in a blur of blinding headlights. Or perilous paths where unsuspecting feet trip and twist in rabbit holes or hidden coils of barbed wire. Nights are for anxiously looking down, not curiously gazing upwards.

But from my open door, I see another night that is neither small nor dangerous. Quite the reverse: suddenly it's daytime that seems restrictive and confining. I realise that, during the day, my world stretches only to the horizon, to the clouds, possibly to an aeroplane trail. But from a darkened doorstep, my world becomes a galaxy, a universe. I have stepped out of a perpetual light-bound hibernation and into the flickering starlight of infinity.

And as I stare at this universe of stars, I feel a sort of rapture descend. A reverent calm gifted from another world – a world I vaguely recognise but that is no longer mine. A world that is older and more elemental, biblical, where time passes more slowly. Where – for reasons I don't understand – I am utterly calmed.

After a few weeks of gazing into cosmic entropy from my doorstep, I feel the itch of curiosity. I want more. Because doesn't one discovery always leave us hungry for another? Isn't this – rightly or wrongly – the nature of our restlessly enquiring human spirit? Or the wiring of our dopamine-dependent brains?

Whatever the reason, I crave knowledge. I want to put names to constellations and planets and phases of the moon. I want to know if they once called to others, as they do to me. I want to know why I feel so different when I gaze upwards. Suddenly I have a million questions.

Three weeks later L. and I arrive at Herstmonceux Observatory, once the beating heart of European astronomy. The observatory and its six telescopes were built in the 1950s to replace London's Royal Greenwich Observatory, which – after 400 years – was forced into closure thanks to the capital's smog and light pollution. The cleanly scoured night skies of East Sussex promised superior observing. But within three decades the night skies of Sussex were so polluted that Herstmonceux's latest telescope was dismantled and sent to a new observatory built on the peak of an extinct volcano on the Spanish island of La Palma.

Today Herstmonceux Observatory is run as a science centre. We have come for the first in a series of naked-eye astronomy classes. Our naked eyes are unlikely to see anything tonight – the sky is a black cloud and the rain falls in drenching sheets. We shelter inside the observatory as Dr Sandra Voss serves up facts and numbers that are so cosmically colossal they are meaningless. Everything is in billions and trillions. Everything is extravagantly, unbelievably enormous. The sun is the equivalent of 4 trillion atomic bombs (of Hiroshima size) exploding simultaneously. The galaxy contains over 100 billion stars – more than all the people who have ever lived. The figure of 100 billion is conservative, she adds. It could be 400 billion.

Starlight, Dr Voss explains, sometimes comes from stars that have long since died. When we look at their thin bright beam, we are viewing time in reverse. At this, I frown into the darkness of the observatory. Is the star that winks at me each night no longer alive? My astronomically uneducated brain struggles and strains. Amid all these titanic numbers and infinitely unfolding galaxies, I feel completely adrift. I need names and words to anchor me, to stop me floating into outer space.

When Dr Voss puts up a map and instructs us to turn to our planispheres (pleasingly full of diagrams and dotted lines), I breathe a sigh of relief. But as the class continues in its damp fug, my mind drifts off. Will the Milky Way still induce a sense of wonder and tranquillity if I'm peering for constellations and joining dots? What happens when we know more and more and more? When everything is named, labelled and connected with a dotted line?

And all at once my curiosity is piqued by something else altogether: I want to know about the first women who looked upwards, beyond darkness and into unending outer space. Who were they? What sparked the audacity to look so far beyond themselves – to meet God's gaze, eye to eye? How does a woman unused to freedom navigate a space so unwieldy, so vast? And where does she subsequently locate herself?

Because I know from my own minuscule experience that, when we repeatedly lift our eyes to the moon and planets, our world is subtly altered. *We* are subtly altered.

The history of female astronomers is long, rich and little known. It's the story of women who looked upwards into the glitter of a night sky and saw infinite planes of possibility. But it's also the story of women compelled by curiosity. Women who became so familiar with the motions of moon and stars, they could forecast the arrival of storms, the changing direction of wind, the return of ships or migrating birds.

It begins with Enheduanna, who lived around 2300 BCE, in southern Mesopotamia (now part of Iraq), where she was also high priestess of the moon god, working for her father, King Sargon of Akkad. This position carried huge political power and required observing and recording the phases of the moon. During her wide-awake nights Enheduanna also wrote thousands of lines of poetry and deciphered her dreams, which were deemed messages from the gods.

Later came Aglaonice, who calculated how to predict lunar eclipses in ancient Greece. On the other side of the world, an unnamed Maya woman appears in astronomical carvings, dressed in a long skirt and feathered serpent headdress.[2] In Egypt, Hypatia of Alexandria taught astronomy, wrote astronomy books and built astrolabes, until she was murdered by a mob of men in 415 CE. After which comes a lengthy silence.

And yet women continued to watch the night sky. We see evidence of it in their poems and letters. And, from the seventeenth century on, we see evidence of it in actual astronomical work, beginning with Maria Cunitz, Europe's first female astronomer. In 1650 Cunitz quietly self-published her book of planetary tables – but in such small quantities and with such an inconsequential printing house that it was readily over-looked by her male counterparts.[3]

Cunitz was followed by a succession of women who usually worked in partnership with fathers, husbands, brothers or uncles. For weeks I pore over their biographies. Slowly I acquire favourites – like Maria Mitchell, who grew up in the isolated maritime community of Nantucket in the early 1800s, where a knowledge of the stars meant life or death for the sailors who navigated by them.

Mitchell's career started as she observed and recorded alongside her father, a teacher and freelance astronomer. But gradually she began doing more and more solo observing. From the age of eighteen, she watched every cloudless night for fifteen years, wrapped in a thick wool coat and taking notes by the light of a whale-oil lamp. She confessed to her journal that she had become attached to 'certain midnight apparitions. The aurora is always a pleasant companion, a meteor [is] like a messenger from departed spirits and even the blossoming of trees in the moonlight becomes a sight looked for with pleasure.' Mitchell recognised in her nightly stargazing a 'subdued quiet and grateful sensuousness – a calm to the troubled spirit and a hope to the desponding'.[4]

One evening in 1847, Mitchell excused herself from a dinner party and went up to the rooftop. Here she 'swept' the skies and spotted the comet that was to catapult her to international fame, changing her life for ever and making her America's first professional female astronomer and an international celebrity.

When I'm not thinking about Mitchell and her pull-out bed in the rattling observatory dome assigned as her combined accommodation and classroom (in stark contrast to the male professors, who were given apartments with bedrooms!),[5] I like to ponder Cecilia Payne. Born in 1900, and known for discovering what stars are made of (helium and hydrogen), Payne was also entranced by the night sky from childhood. One day she stared into the heavens from her pram and saw a meteorite blast through the sky. Little Cecilia's eye was then guided to the Big Dipper, followed by Orion's Belt. Aged nine, she observed the Daylight Comet. Aged ten, she watched Halley's Comet. These early memories of the night sky, of darkness, never left Cecilia, who described them in her memoir as seeming 'more vivid and more significant than those of later years, when wonder has been blunted by repetition'.[6]

Vera Rubin, the first astronomer to identify dark matter, also dated her passion for the night sky to her childhood. One frosty December night in 1939, eleven-year-old Vera looked out of her bedroom window and noticed the stars. At exactly the same moment, a meteor flashed from the east, swiftly followed by a second blazing trail. Over the next few months the stars 'became utterly compelling for her, calling her'.[7] She would get out of bed and peer at them, astonished to find their positions changing over the course of a night. 'By about age 12, I would prefer to stay up and watch the stars than go to sleep,' she recalled.[8] 'I started learning. I started going to the library and reading. But it was initially just watching the stars from my bedroom . . . There was just nothing as interesting in my life as watching the stars every night.'

I'm not sure what I'm searching for as I read and reread the memoirs and biographies of female astronomers. A theme? A pattern? Something that will illuminate my own night-sky revelation? Instead I learn of unquenchable curiosity. But I also learn how physically demanding the practice of observing was; I feel the long chill nights in remote and isolated places, the aching straining eyes, the bone-tired limbs. And the utter blackness of the observatory. It's a completely new way of experiencing darkness and no one described it better than Vera Rubin:

> The night is cold, the work is tedious, and the long hours pass slowly . . . morning brings the end of observing for the night, and brings the sun . . . with the sun my circadian rhythm is reset and I am wide awake, too wide awake to sleep and too curious to leave the night's plates undeveloped, so I walk down to the dark room. Even though the dark reminds me of my tired body, I know that it is futile to attempt to sleep while wondering what is captured on the photographic plates.[9]

At the Lowell Observatory in Arizona, where the night temperatures fell below freezing, Rubin wrote of working 'in a cold, dark dome with freezing fingers inside heavy gloves' in darkness so dense she couldn't see her own hands. She insisted on blocking every light source – even the luminous clock dial. Icy, pitch black, wide awake, alone – these are the apocalyptic nights most of us dread. And yet for Rubin, they were 'among the happiest nights of my life'.

Rubin's life revolved around her allocated telescope time: 'She found real contentment in the quiet calm of the observatory dome, under an expanse of dark starry sky. Free from . . . cares . . . free to explore whatever questions about the universe grabbed her interest.'[10] As it happened, so many questions grabbed Rubin's interest that between 1965 and 1966 she stayed awake for thirty-three nights, observing and trying to find answers to her questions.

Asking questions, I realise, is another trait of my Night Self. Whether this is due to the voided time and space accorded by my night watch or to my altered night brain isn't clear. But I'm beginning to see that turning questions *out* – to the stars, to my astronomical ancestors, to the cosmos – swiftly leads me away from the ruminative questions that otherwise rush to fill an insomniac vacuum. And so night after night I stand at my window, urging my Night Self to look up and out. Up and out. Up and out.

The night sky may have been open to women (if only through a window) but the doors of institutions and observatories were not. When Maria Mitchell lobbied for access to the Vatican Observatory (becoming the first woman to do so),* she was eventually allowed to visit. But at dusk she was told to leave. What use is a telescope in daylight?

In 1955, Margaret Burbidge was told she couldn't win a fellowship at an observatory because there was only one toilet.

---

* Both Mary Somerville and Caroline Herschel were denied earlier access to the famed Vatican Observatory despite reputations as gifted astronomers.

And when they weren't muttering about toilets, male bosses were muttering about the observatory assistants who might take offence at being given instructions by a woman.

Curiosity was simply not a trait deemed appropriate in women. Despite their astronomical talents and discoveries, it was the smallest of things – a single toilet, a disgruntled male assistant – that frequently kept women out, especially *after dark*. At least, that was the reason given by the illustrious men who controlled these hallowed places.

While Maria Mitchell was teaching astronomy to young women at Vassar College, Emily Dickinson was writing poetry. Hundreds of her 1,800 poems refer to astronomy, stars, darkness and the night sky. Constellations, meteors, eclipses, planets, moons in various phases and 'stintless stars' – all flash, dazzlingly, through her work. According to Professor Renée Bergland, 'Emily Dickinson's best poems are astronomical.'[11]

For (often sleepless) Dickinson, the night sky was more than an aesthetically pleasing view. It provided a means of navigating her own life and inner world. It offered a map of symbols and metaphors by which she could reflect and orient herself – literally and figuratively. As she put it, 'For what are Stars but Asterisks / To point a human Life?'

For women who weren't free to roam (which was most of them), the night sky was a source of longed-for liberation, a space in which they could rove vicariously, curiously and imaginatively, from the benign convenience of a balcony or a window. For women like Dickinson – who never left her house after the age of twenty-eight, presumed agoraphobic by contemporary scholars – the night sky offered both a place of safety and a place in which to journey.

In 1862, just as Mitchell was writing to the newly opened Vassar to audaciously enquire whether there might be a position for an astronomy professor, Dickinson was writing to her mentor confessing that 'I had a terror . . . I am afraid'.[12] For decades, scholars have speculated about her 'terror' and her reclusiveness – post-traumatic stress disorder, panic attacks, grief, sexual assault, lupus, epilepsy, an eye ailment that threatened blindness. We'll never know what caused Dickinson's fear.

At least one biographer thinks it was rooted in a tsunami of suffering: when she was fourteen, four of her friends and family died, including her cousin of the same age, Sophia. Emily crept into the room where Sophia's corpse lay. Here, she stood in the gloom, transfixed by her cousin's pallid, lifeless face. Emily had to be pulled away, but her preoccupation with loss and death remained.

Either way, Dickinson's poetry suggests that the celestial darkness became a place of healing and escape. 'Night', she tells us, 'is the morning's canvas', a place for attending to our 'Immortality'. A place where we can, paradoxically, see more clearly: 'I see thee better — in the Dark — / I do not need a Light'.

In her poem 'We grow accustomed to the Dark', Dickinson writes about the transformational nature of darkness. It is at night, she seems to say, that we encounter our most authentic Self and that 'Life steps almost straight'.

For weeks, this line – 'Life steps almost straight' – sticks in my head. It seems to capture my months of night-grieving, in which I've slowly stopped wobbling and started finding my fatherless feet, and a path out of metaphorical darkness. In which stars have come to me, like jewelled climbing ropes, pulling me out of myself.

As well as helping her 'step almost straight', Dickinson saw 'sweet darkness' as a place for 'the Bravest . . . [to] learn to see'. She referred to nights as 'Evenings of the Brain', where she could 'Peruse how infinite I am'. Darkness fostered the intense introspection and insights that became the hallmark of

Dickinson's work. Night provided the anonymity she needed to plumb her emotional depths. But the stars sparked a curiosity, touching her darkness with a sort of alchemy: for Emily Dickinson, stargazing was self-gazing.

Dickinson never submitted her poems for publication. When she died, aged fifty-five, she'd barely left her room for over a quarter of a century, speaking to visitors from behind a curtain or from the top of the stairs. After she died, her sister, Lavinia, found hundreds of Dickinson's poems, written on sheets of stationery, carefully tied with twine, and boxed in collections of 'packets'.

In among these packets was Poem 932, in which Dickinson articulated her relationship with the 'trusty' stars: her 'best Acquaintances . . . With Whom I spoke no Word'.[13]

As they had for Payne, Mitchell and Rubin, the stars became Dickinson's friends – a source of unending curiosity but also the most steadfast of companions.

My doubting Day Self persists in questioning the therapeutic powers of a night sky – until I meet an Australian astro-photographer called Antoinette Koutsomihalis, whose ethereal, moon-rinsed pictures regularly win awards and appear in exhibitions. Antoinette is adamant that the night sky healed her from unendurable pain and mental illness. 'My father died suddenly when he was fifty-nine,' she tells me. 'A few months later my mother died. I had to pick up the pieces of the family business, which was on the verge of collapse. But then I got breast cancer.'

Antoinette explains that this excess of pain and sadness took a huge toll on her mental health. 'I couldn't leave the house, didn't see anyone; my friends fell away. It was a terrible time.' But at some point she roused herself and looked out of a window at the night sky. 'It saved me,' she says simply. 'I started going outside and just looking at the moon and the stars from my yard. It seemed to reconnect me to happier, more carefree days.' At first this was enough, but then curiosity struck. 'I wanted to know more,' she adds. 'The night sky had inspired me and given me confidence, so I went on an astronomy course and taught myself astro-photography from the internet. I started leaving the house again – to take photographs, to join astronomy groups. I'm frequently out all night now, often alone, usually in a remote place.'

But how did the night sky mend her? I persist.

'I'd seen so much of my life slip away. Nothing seemed dependable any more – not even myself. But the moon and stars are a source of certainty. They're a constant in our lives, making us feel less in flux, making us feel centred, grounded . . . To look up at billions of stars created over millions of years changes how you see yourself and your problems. It's a spiritual experience, it changes you.'

I wonder if it's this that emboldened Antoinette to roam the bush alone at night. But when I ask her, she laughs: 'The first time I went out deep into the bush I met people returning – they told me it wasn't safe and that I should turn back, so I did. But then I got angry and made myself walk back into the bush. I was halfway to the place I wanted to spend the night – about two kilometres in – when my nerve failed and I turned homeward – again! Then my fury got the better of my fear. Why shouldn't I sit out in the remote bush and photograph the Milky Way? So I turned round – a third time. But on this occasion I didn't falter. I spent the whole night, alone, out in the bush. It was amazing. I'm not afraid of dark emotions any more so why should I fear the dark?'

One night, several weeks later, as I'm looking at the moon and the stars, I'm struck by something that makes *me* feel a little more *certain*: this is the very sky my grandparents and great-grandparents gazed at. When I spot Orion and his belt of stars, or Cassiopeia, I'm seeing exactly as my distant ancestors did. I like this sense of being tethered to my own history. In the midst of unrelenting change, I find it vaguely comforting.

By now, I've downloaded several stargazing apps to my phone and bought a pair of huge unwieldy astral binoculars. Stars that once seemed plain white become an alchemical swirl of blue, emerald green, geranium pink, dancing madly like perpetual fireworks. I stare until my arms shake from the wobbling weight of my binoculars. I watch a fingernail moon climb out of the sky. Jupiter winks at me and I wink back. I feel my body lighten as the day's cares are sucked into the night sky. Sounds come to me through the darkness: a cow bellowing, a sheep coughing, something shrieking and pipping – an owl? – the distant roar of a motorbike . . . I feel my celestial curiosity abate and my strange inner stillness slide towards a satisfied sleepiness.

All at once I think of Antoinette, alone in the Australian bush; of Maria Mitchell on the roof of her house night after night; and of Emily Dickinson leaning, hour after hour, from an open window in a room she rarely left. Suddenly I long to spend the night beneath the obstinate indestructible stars, to have nothing between them and my skin but cool black air. It seems to me that when tragedy or sickness strike our world shrinks. For a while we have no choice but to inhabit this circumscribed space. But to fully heal we must allow our world to enlarge again – slowly, steadily. When we encounter the night sky we start this process, even if it is only from a window. I make a promise to myself: that when I am ready I too will spend the entire night sleeping out.

9

Restless

)

> I had a splendid sense of the stillness of the night . . . becoming
> a part of the night and the earth and the surroundings . . .
> Katharine Trevelyan, *Unharboured Heaths*

Eight months after my father's death, my sleep is as threadbare as ever. The planes in and out of Heathrow Airport seem to skim the roof of my London house and their incessant whine – which begins at 4.10 a.m. – lodges stubbornly inside my head, so that I often lie awake tense with expectation, waiting for the first flight. One evening, desperate for silence, I pack up my work and drive to the cottage. I arrive, eyes aching from hours on a clogged motorway, and go upstairs to lie in the quiet darkness of my bedroom. But as I tug at the blind, something catches my eye. The sky seems different. Is it the colour? The height? I look again – the sky is a cloudless swimming indigo. An infinite midnight blue. I look for the moon but there's no sign of her. Perplexed by her absence, I push open the window and peer into the blue stillness. The sky burns with thousands of slow-swinging stars, blazing and beckoning like far-flung guides.

I turn back into my room and begin lowering the blind. The next day is full of deadlines – chapters to be edited, articles to be submitted, emails needing a response. I need sleep. But my hand halts on the blind. I can't seem to close it. Instead my hand pulls on the cord, until the blind is fully open again. The stars flash faintly from the far corners of the universe. And in that moment my room, the entire cottage, feels stiflingly small, cramped, airless.

In a moment of boldness I drag a mattress from the children's bedroom, heaving and shoving it along the narrow corridors. I push it through my window, manoeuvring it onto a sliver of flat roof that lies just below my room. As I tug and shunt, I hear the nag of my Day Self: it's cold out there; it might rain; the roof won't carry your weight; insects will crawl over your face; you won't get a wink of sleep; get into your proper bed, you damn fool!

Something urges me on. My reckless, disobedient Night Self? My father calling from the firmaments? I make myself a bed – pillow, duvet, sheets – and crawl in, hoping it won't rain, that the flimsy roof will hold. Then I lie on my back, gazing upwards. And in the suspended cadence of those gazing moments a subtle but life-altering change takes place within me.

From now on, whenever it's forecast to be dry, I sleep out on my rooftop mattress. Being indoors seems dull and predictable after these nights of near-divine rapture in which I'm wholly absorbed in a world without boundaries, edges or limits.

And yet there's nothing out-of-body about my experience, which is deeply and strongly physical. Even as my eye is guided into the vast unfolding compass above, my body feels rooted in its own clammy mulch, in the sudden chill of a westerly breeze with its scent of sap and nettles. By dawn, I'm cloaked in a filigree of dew – over my hair, along the hem of my pillow, seeping into the sheets.

These nights are always the same. Without clock, screen, book or ceiling I stare into the sky, gazing and wandering. And my mind seems to dissolve, and the protective carapace of my thinking brain falls away – so that I empty out and upwards, neither awake nor asleep.

This celestial wandering typically lasts around fifteen minutes, and then – regardless of how late or early it is – I sink into a drugged and delicious drowsiness. A few hours later, I surface and stare at the night sky again. Once more, I feel a sense of intense and unexpected elation. As if I've woken to a gift dropped from another world, a forgotten, unearthly world that exists outside our own perception and time. Eventually I drift back to sleep. And if the dew is too heavy or the air too chill, I climb through the window back to my bed. Either way, I wake with a mild sense of euphoria, as if the night has imparted something of rare value – even if I'm not quite sure what it is.

I don't tell anyone about my rooftop nights. I'm too embarrassed to admit that I regularly drag my mattress outside. Or that the experience is swiftly becoming one of the most profound of my life.

And yet I desperately want to share it, to find someone else who has been moved by the same unearthly state. This strange swill of embarrassment and transcendence confuses me: if the experience is so powerful, why am I embarrassed, almost ashamed?

I wonder if it's because I'm a woman. Sleeping out for pleasure isn't something we're supposed to do. It's presumed reckless and risky. Not quite normal. Instead we think sorrowfully of Sylvia Plath, who longed to sleep out but felt unable to, famously writing, 'Being born a woman is my awful tragedy . . . I want to be able to sleep in an open field . . . to walk freely at night.'

In the past, only men slept out for pleasure – or tramp-camped, as it was called back then. And so the accounts passed down to us are those of the great male adventurers, like Robert Louis Stevenson with his immortal lines: 'Night is a dead monotonous period under a roof; but in the open world it passes lightly, with its stars and dews and perfumes . . .'

For Stevenson (who slept rough in the French hills with a pistol beneath his pillow), 2 a.m. was the magic hour, when he felt truly liberated from the 'bastille of civilization', unsure whether his elation was due to the stars above or 'the thrill of Mother earth below [his] resting body'.[1]

Following Stevenson, the ranks of men glorying in (and writing about) the thrill of 'vagabonding' swelled.[2] From Hilaire Belloc sleeping under hay in an orchard, to Laurie Lee playing his violin under the Spanish stars, to Stephen Graham writing of 'the long and gentle sleep on the soft grey sand . . . the lying outstretched on the spring turf . . .'[3] For Graham, sleeping out (often on a bed of ferns and birch twigs) was a transcendent experience that reshaped his soul. Patrick Leigh Fermor, on the banks of the Danube, wrote ecstatically: 'I understood, with sudden elation, that my first and longed-for night in the open had arrived.'[4] Meanwhile the painter Augustus John wrote of sleeping beside a Dartmoor river and a peat fire, 'you can hear the stream always and always'.[5]

In their art, these men turned themselves into wild-sleeping legends, transformed by the night skies. The absence of women merely indicated the truth of Plath's plaintive words – being born a woman meant nocturnal confinement.

I test this out on my mother one day, asking if she's ever slept out in her eighty-four years of life. She looks surprised, then says, 'No, never.' Her tone is bemused, as if my question is faintly ridiculous. And perhaps it is. I'd tried to sleep on a bench once – in a Serbian railway station when my boyfriend and I had missed the last train. We'd been shoo'd out by police officers, like a pair of stray cats. But the accounts of Stevenson et al. suggested there was another way – and now I too had experienced it.

★

The truth is, women have been sleeping outside for a long time – sometimes of necessity but often but for simple, sometimes profound pleasure. The painter Gwen John often abandoned her Parisian apartment to sleep out in parks, public gardens, woods and meadows. The entomologist Evelyn Cheesman slept in a hammock while travelling the world. Peace Pilgrim slept out regularly as she criss-crossed America on her crusade for peace, claiming that she preferred to sleep out – ideally without a sleeping bag – writing, 'the stars are my blanket'.[6] Simone de Beauvoir slept on benches and in haystacks while hiking the French mountains. The photographer Margaret Bourke-White relished sleeping out, writing, 'If I *sleep* under the open sky it becomes part of the writing experience, part of my insulation from the world.' She even built herself a special bed on wheels so that she could regularly change her sleeping spot.[7]

The experience of sleeping out often acquired an overwhelming significance. After climbing California's Mount Tamalpais in 1985, the poet and painter Etel Adnan slept out 'under trees', resulting in an epiphany that she later wrote about: 'The night freed us from our obsession with reason. It told us that we were a bundle of electric wires plugged into everything that came along. It was enough to be alive . . .'[8]

Adnan's catalysing sleepless moment reflected an earlier experience of writer Katharine Trevelyan as she crossed Canada alone in 1930: 'I felt homeless in that delightful way which comes out on the other side of loneliness and makes me feel as if I possess the whole world of night and space.' Trevelyan was often gripped by fear as she walked and camped her way across the bleak barren forests and plains of Canada, but her night experiences repeatedly fortified her: 'I didn't seem quite to belong to my body. I felt suspended between the earth I lay on and the three-cornered piece of sky which I could see through

the trees.' She never forgot the 'aloneness in which was no loneliness'. For the rest of her life the night sky was deeply meaning-
ful: 'Often I rose at 2 in the morning . . . and stood looking at
the Milky Way . . . In the night hours God's face appeared to me
slowly in the long moments of watching the sky,' she wrote in
her memoir.[9]

Thirty years after Robert Louis Stevenson published his travel
memoir, the writer Clara Vyvyan – riveted by his description of
overwhelming 'serene possession' while sleeping out – decided
to try it for herself. Time under the spinning stars promised
romance, adventure, mystery.

Clara, who was a child at the time, took a blanket and a box
of matches and 'crept down after midnight, trembling with
excitement'. It was cold and uncomfortable but after a while she
'began to forget my body. I became merely "something that
listens" and all senses other than the sense of hearing were dulled.'
In this state of semi-sensory deprivation she found herself
'listening intently for it was a strange new silence such that I had
never heard before'.

Clara struggled to find words to describe her night out, but
noticed that she slipped into an altered state: 'I was no more
aware of my living parents, sleeping not a hundred yards away in
the house, than if they had been stones. I was listening for the
first time to the silence of the stars. Never before had I been
alone with them.'

As an adult, Clara slept out with impunity. She bedded down
on Irish hills, wrapped in newspaper, her rucksack doubling as a
pillow. She slept beside Welsh mountain streams and in the high
passes of the Lake District, tightly wrapped (again) in newspaper.
She slept in an open boat, curled between the thwarts. She
dossed down on a Dutch heath, and in the Cornish hills. She
curled up in a haystack beside a lighthouse. She was an

enthusiastic and persistent rough sleeper, later describing her open-air nights as 'among the great adventures of [my] life that lead one out from the narrow way of habit towards horizons indisputably distant'. She kept this 'new sense of intimacy with the stars' for the rest of her life, always maintaining that her outdoor nights allowed her 'to recapture [a] long lost intimacy with dark night and dawn', enveloping her in 'an almost religious sense of contentment'.[10]

In a way, it was the *lack* of sleep that enabled Clara to find a 'new . . . intimacy with the stars'. After all, if she'd been soundly asleep, her experience would have been quite different. But, as I was discovering, outdoor sleep is nothing like indoor sleep – just as the beguiling jewelled brilliance of the Milky Way bears little resemblance to the curtained comfort of a bedroom. Different beasts altogether.

Eventually I confess my wild nights to someone I suspect might understand. After hearing the writer Inga Simpson talk about her love for trees – 'actual, real love' – I admit to feeling something similar for darkness and starlight. She nods, and tells me that she spent the summer hiking in the centre of Australia without a tent.

'Sleeping out was life-changing,' she says. 'The simplicity of it; at last, nothing between me and the natural world. And the stars. The whole night sky visible. Who knew there were so many celestial bodies, and so bright . . . The constellations arcing across the sky while I lay so still. That's how it felt, but of course, it was me – Earth – moving.'

Inga's experience changed her: 'It reminded me that I'm only here for a moment, that I'm just a speck on this planet.'

There's something curiously and perversely liberating about feeling so speckishly small, so self-*less*. The novelist and poet Emily Brontë experienced a similar shrinking-of-self while out on the Yorkshire Moors under a bright moon, describing it as 'When I am not, and none beside . . . / But only spirit wandering wide.' Katharine Trevelyan expressed it as 'a liberation . . . that . . .! sets the heart suddenly free from a thousand shackles'. For Inga, the sense of smallness induced by the night sky was akin to a 'stripping away of everything unimportant'. If she woke up in the darkness she watched the stars: 'I would drift off again, rather than getting started on all my little worries.'

When the English writer Edith Durham travelled through the Balkans in 1909, she too noticed how sleeping out stripped away all tendency to rumination. Durham often slept on 'a heap of hay', recalling that 'Over all was the intense blue depth of the cloudless night sky, ablaze with a myriad of stars. I wondered why people ever slept in houses . . . to lie awake under the stars is not the misery of sleeplessness in a room – rather it is pure joy.'[11]

What is it about staring into unending space that makes us feel so serene? So disinclined to ruminate? Neuroscientists now think that panoramic vision – the vision we use to look into the distance – is inherently relaxing. Experiments show that when our eyes can see for miles and miles our stress levels fall. As we sweep the night sky, the brain's threat detection system – the amygdala – is calmed and quietened. No one is quite sure how or why this happens, but researchers think that wide panoramic vision relieves our brain of the close-looking and narrow scrutiny that takes up so much of our time. Evolutionary biologists speculate that, as hunter-gatherers, our vision and brain developed so that we could navigate and spot water, animals or predators calmly, switching to tight focal vision (which is inherently more demanding) only when absolutely necessary. Either way, when we can see all the way to the planets and beyond, the sensation of restfulness is immediate and irrefutable, a balm for our busy, buzzing brains.

For Inga the joy was so revelatory that when she returned home she pushed her bed right up against her window: 'Now the stars are the last thing I see before I fall asleep'. When she wakes in the night she looks directly out to the sky and can tell the time by the position of the Southern Cross.

But it's not just the position of Inga's bed that changed following her nights of sleeping out. Her writing changed too. 'It's changed who I am, so my writing is changing too. It's inevitable, isn't it? *We* change and so what we create, make, write will change too.'

Which is exactly what happened to Daphne du Maurier after she slept out.

In the summer of 1957, Daphne du Maurier was riding high. Her latest book, *The Scapegoat*, had been lapped up by the critics she most respected, and a film adaptation was under way. Even better, her favourite actor (the legendary Alec Guinness) had been cast in the lead role and the script was being penned by the rising star Gore Vidal.

But on Monday 1 July, a few weeks after her fiftieth birthday and two weeks before her twenty-fifth wedding anniversary party, Daphne received a phone call. Her husband, Tommy, had collapsed in London and was in hospital. She rushed to his bedside, horrified to find him sobbing and 'emaciated and exhausted, his body all skin and bone, looking suddenly ten years older'.[12] More shock was to follow: when Daphne returned to the pair's London flat, the phone rang, the caller introducing herself as Tommy's lover. The woman accused a speechless Daphne of causing her husband's breakdown, forcing him to live a double life, making him turn to alcohol of necessity.

Devastated, Daphne took a double dose of sleeping pills, but to no avail. She didn't sleep that night, her mind whirring frenetically. Instead she wrote a long letter to Tommy. The next morning she put the letter into his hand, then fled back to her country house, Menabilly, in Devon. Here, she told friends that only swimming and visiting her increasingly frail mother could soothe her broken nerves. As for writing (her customary means of catharsis), there was no chance: 'I have no writing plans at the moment – can't . . .' she wrote to a friend.[13]

To add to the disruption, Tommy arrived at Menabilly – a place he'd previously inhabited only at weekends – to recuperate. Here, he sat in front of the television surreptitiously drinking. His doctor made it clear that Tommy could no longer be alone. Suddenly, Daphne was cast in the role of caregiver, grimly watching the deterioration of both her husband and her mother while her own much-needed independence and solitude vanished. Friends – frightened by Daphne's incoherent, whispered phone calls – thought she was on the verge of a breakdown.

But something prompted Daphne to regain control of herself. Something gave her the impetus to write again.

During this emotionally turbulent summer Daphne decided to make a bed in her garden. For months she'd suffered from dreams of near-drowning while swimming at high tide. Every morning she awoke with her stomach in painful knots. Her bedroom had ceased to be a place of calm.

Little is known about Daphne's nights of wild sleeping. Was she escaping a house now made oppressive by the presence of her adulterous, invalid husband? Or had she felt the tantalising, healing lure of the stars? Around the same time she described feeling 'a sort of longing . . . for what is beyond'. And shortly afterwards, she began writing again – short stories that were later published in a collection tellingly called *The Breaking Point*. But these stories were different. They were imbued with ideas of the supernatural, each containing a mystical thread and hinting at a new fascination Daphne had for the unconscious and the unfathomable. As it happens, we know that one of her nights sleeping out left her both thrilled and distressed. She awoke in the middle of the black, dewy night 'with a conviction that someone was there, not a real person, but not a ghost. She sensed all around her another time and another world.'[14]

This episode – which she considered psychic, prompted by sleeping beneath the night sky – inspired her short story, 'The Pool', in which a sleepless girl ventures into the garden at night and makes a bed beneath the stars, an experience that becomes a strange, numinous 'introduction to life, like being confirmed'. Daphne once confessed that each of her books represented a part of her: in 'The Pool' she gives us a glimpse of her Night Self: 'Dusk was everywhere, the sky a deepening black . . . the deepening sky lost the veil that covered it, the haze disintegrated, and the stars broke through. Where there had been nothing was life, dusty and bright, and the waiting earth gave off a scent of knowledge.'

Daphne may have been impelled to sleep out by jealousy, guilt, sadness, confusion (and who knows what else) but her subsequent writing, with its 'dreamlike fancy and pitiless introspection',[15] was forged in the revelations of her strange outdoor nights. Beneath the twisted trees of Menabilly and a thick scattering of silver stars, Daphne found her voice again. Her personal 'breaking point' had been averted, in the nick of time.

So how does darkness alter the way we write?

In 2018 two Hungarian researchers decided to investigate this very topic. They recruited seventy-eight participants, then ranked their level of night fear before asking them to write two stories – one in full light and one in semi-darkness. Participants who claimed to have no fear of darkness or night wrote similar stories, regardless of whether they were seated in a brightly lit room or a darkened room. Not so the other participants. Those who confessed to being fearful of the dark produced much longer stories, but only when they wrote in semi-darkness. More interestingly, their stories contained very different language.

The researchers then analysed the changes using a computer programme table to distinguish 'primary and secondary content and language'. Primary thinking is described as irrational, free-associative, creative, unconcerned with purpose or problem-solving, dominated by concrete images and characterised by defocused attention. Fairy tales, myths and folk stories typically show high levels of primary content. Secondary thinking is described as rational, restrained, oriented towards reality and problem-solving, with a narrowly focused attention. Academic papers and research studies typically show high levels of secondary content.

In this experiment, the stories produced in near-darkness by participants fearful of night used significantly more primary vocabulary and significantly less secondary vocabulary. It was as if their tendency to fear had unlocked yet another layer of their imagination. The researchers put it like this: 'We speculate that in individuals who fear the dark, semidarkness might intensely activate unconscious processes that they are unable to control.'[16] In 'primary' language, this might translate as 'for people scared of darkness, gloom can spark wild, inventive fantasies.' You get the idea.

The researchers weren't surprised. Indeed, their findings reflected an earlier study that found people showed greater control and more rational thought processes while in bright light, or, as they put it: 'brightness triggers more controlled and reflective forms of self-regulation'.[17]

All this is to say that a wariness of the dark combined with low light alters how we think and write – our thoughts are less 'self-regulated', and we switch more readily into fantasy, reaching with greater ease into the crevices of our imagination. And so it's perhaps no wonder that Daphne's night-time-inspired stories changed, becoming – in the words of her biographer Tatiana de Rosnay – 'disturbing and troubling . . . [exploring] the meandering of madness and the unconscious mind . . . dreamlike'.[18]

When it comes to sleeping out, no one captures its strange sense of profundity better than the Scottish writer and self-proclaimed 'night prowler' Nan Shepherd. For Shepherd, sleeping out was a means 'of my own discovering', of fully knowing herself. But it also helped her understand the landscape she loved.

'No one knows the mountain completely who has not slept on it,' she wrote in her paean to the Scottish Cairngorms, *The Living Mountain*. 'These moments of quiescent perceptiveness before sleep are among the most rewarding of the day.'[19] But it wasn't only the moments of slipping into 'deep and tranquil sleep' that enchanted Shepherd.

The process of waking up outside also came with its own intoxicating flavour. These were the rare occasions when she awoke 'with an empty mind', something she credited to her starry hours of deep and blissful sleep. Waking with a voided mind allowed her to see the world anew: 'For one startled moment I have looked at a familiar place as though I had never seen it before.'

Shepherd believed the act of waking up outdoors was 'an art' that required the eyes to open and the brain to 'come fully awake' while the body remained immobile. Other mornings, 'the ear awakens first'. Either way, the body had to remain motionless. Shepherd often woke to discover birds hopping up her leg, owls watching her from tent poles and red deer feeding beside her.

I liked Shepherd's idea of the ear awakening before the eye.

On full-moon nights I wore an eye mask and I'd noticed that when I was unable to see, my ear was inevitably roused first. We respond more quickly to sound than to sight, particularly in the dark. At night, sound waves bend towards the cooling earth, amplifying our hearing – which is already exaggerated by the darkness. So that from my rooftop bed I was often awoken by the papery scrapings of two palm trees caught by the wind, or the flapping of plastic sheeting come loose, or the distant drumming of a snipe, or the warning bark of a fox. With my eye mask on, I woke not to light but to strange, unfamiliar sounds.

Like me, and all my outdoor-sleeping night spinners, Shepherd slept differently beneath a diaspora of stars. Outdoor sleep is flimsier, frailer. I thought of it as a sort of light-fingered sleep in which I swam in and out of consciousness, soothed, distracted, comforted, dazzled, bewildered and delighted. The poet Mary Oliver described a similar slumber in her poem 'Sleeping in the Forest', writing: 'I slept as never before . . . nothing between me and the white fire of the stars.' Nothing except her thoughts which 'floated light as moths'. She aptly compared the experience to rising and falling 'as if in water'.

Although these nights didn't meet the requirements of today's sleep experts, they felt supremely satisfying. During the days that followed, I felt neither tired nor grumpy. In an unexpected way, the experience nourished me – as if I had imbibed a restorative cocktail of vitamins. It was a salutary reminder that what we need isn't always what we are prescribed. And that there are many ways to sleep.

Can sleeping beneath a sequinned sky of stars really alter how we behave or the way we think? Quite possibly. Psychologists investigating the effect of architectural space found curious correlations between the space we inhabit and how we feel and think, even the moral decisions we make. Space – it appears – can be subtly transformative.

As one recent study put it, 'environmental spaciousness influences emotion ... and elicits more positive emotions', which, in turn, discreetly shifts how we think. One of the study's more intriguing discoveries was that additional space made people more tolerant and less inclined to make harsh moral judgements, while cramped spaces had the opposite effect, causing people to feel both isolated and more judgemental.[20] Being in a generously sized space (and what can be more generous than the galaxy?) makes us more generously spirited, more empathetic and compassionate.

This isn't all. Back in 2007 two researchers published a paper exploring the effect of ceiling height on how we think. Their investigations suggested that high ceilings promoted more abstract and imaginative thought, while low ceilings were better suited to 'concrete and detail-oriented thinking'. They called this the Cathedral Effect. Their experiments also revealed that looking upwards nudged the mind into thinking more loosely and freely ('creatively'), while looking down was rather like being beneath a low-slung ceiling – participants began to think in a more meticulously detailed way.[21]

The funny thing is that the Cathedral Effect becomes manifest only if we're aware of the space around us. In this study, when participants failed to notice the ceiling height their modes of thinking didn't change. And so the *perception* of space mattered more than its actuality.

The philosopher Gaston Bachelard speculated that when we leave the spatial confines of our 'usual sensibilities', we are challenged by new space – we are 'psychically innovated'. We feel the intimacy of immensity, and we recognise that 'immensity is within ourselves'. Bachelard doesn't refer to dark space – only 'vast' space, which he calls 'the friend of being'.[22] But no space that I inhabit is more 'psychically innovating' than my little roof-top, with its view of infinitesimally tiny stars safely suspended in the cosmic immensity of unending blackness.

I return to London at a loss. My bedroom ceiling seems lower than ever. The planes rumble more threateningly, the sirens of ambulances and police cars sound louder than before, the street lights are brighter than a million full moons. I think of Georgia O'Keeffe arriving in New York and dragging her bed beneath a skylight so she can see the stars. But London no longer has stars. Instead I barricade my windows with enormous pieces of card-board to keep out the LED lights that shine around the clock from the old people's home opposite my house.

After long days in the library I finally come across a reference to sleeping out in London, although *lying out* might be a more accurate description. In the opening chapter of her memoir, *A Land*, the archaeologist Jacquetta Hawkes described nights lying out in her north London garden. 'When I have been working late on summer nights I like to go out and lie on the patch of grass in our back garden,' she wrote. From this 'patch' her eye journeyed through the 'fine silhouettes of the leaves immedi-ately overhead', to 'the black lines of neighbouring chimney-pots' and beyond, to where her mind could 'stray among the stars . . . the two little globes of my eyes, unlit in the darkness, looking up at their shining globes'. As I read these words a sharp lump jumps into my throat. If Hawkes was here now, she wouldn't recognise *my* London night sky. A sky that existed for millennia has been lost in less than a century.

But Hawkes's description of meandering nightly from her 'patch of grass' opens my eyes to something I've never experienced on my sliver of cottage roof – the sense of a sleep-ing earth pulsing beneath the body. All my experiences have been upwards – towards the firmament. Hawkes (as might be expected from an archaeologist) moved both up and down, through the 'hard ground', silently travelling beyond the 'top soil' and 'London clay' to the fire and rock within. Her mind's eye also moved horizontally – not to fields and trees but to the seething mass of the city, 'the railways, roads and canals . . . the people seated in those lighted carriages'. For a moment I contemplate lying out in my tiny London garden. But my garden has no grass – only stone. And my daughter has just watched a rat the size of a guinea pig nonchalantly amble from one side to the other. I decide that Hawkes's London is not mine. But I also wonder if sleeping on a skinny metal roof might be missing half the experience of tramp-camping – the earth half. The connection-with-the-land half. The ancestral half.

After immersing myself in the sleeping-out adventures of so many women, my rooftop mattress feels . . . less radical. Slightly fraudulent, if I'm honest. So one evening when I'm back out in the country I roll out a blanket and sleeping bags on the dark, dewy grass at the edge of a field beside the cottage. My son, Hugo, joins me, and for the first half-hour we lie and split the fluffy feathery seed heads of cock's-foot, creeping bent and Yorkshire fog that have grown tall and pillowy over the summer.

Gradually, the evening light drains from the sky. The pinks and blonds of the long grasses are slowly obliterated. The greens of the trees and hedgerows crawl into shadow. The blue above us turns an indigo grey, the clouds little more than smudges of smoke. Our faces become muted blurs of breath. We lie in a soft soup of indeterminate shapes and lines. Moths appear, dancing clumsily above our heads. The moon sidles from behind a cloud, and then disappears again. And with the absence of colour comes a sudden stillness. As if the light has taken the breeze with it.

And then we see them barrelling towards us – a line of badgers, the white stripes of their faces glowing in the gloom. They scurry into a hedge, as if they've sensed us, perhaps caught our scent on the air. We lie motionless, wondering if they'll return. As blackness drops, the land around becomes nothing but sound, and we hear the badgers – digging, scratching, rustling. They are no more than three feet from us and digging wildly, scraping at the compacted earth, while the hedge rustles violently above them.

'They're digging for slugs,' whispers Hugo.

We close our eyes, and let our ears fill with these strange, disembodied sounds. When we open our eyes, there's silence again. The badgers have gone. We gaze at the sky, a vast prickle of stars, pale spikes of light reminding us of our paltry smallness. Except that something tells me we're not as ant-ishly small as the night sky suggests. We are large and ungainly enough to have frightened off three badgers with our pervasive smell of human, of deodorant and soap and coffee and spaghetti Bolognese. I feel like an interloper. The land, that during daylight feels so obviously ours, no longer belongs to us. We have relinquished it . . . or been released from it. Or perhaps it never was ours.

Sleeping out, I decide, isn't really sleeping at all. Sure, there are periods of prolonged sleep. And the sleep is always wondrous, mysterious, quite unlike indoor sleep. But often I'm awake, too absorbed in the nocturnal world to want to shut my eyes. And this, I think, is the final wonder of a night in the open air: to feel the rejuvenation of deep sleep despite being awake.

Jacquetta Hawkes had made a similar point about her patch of grass. 'In bed I can sleep,' she wrote in *A Land*, but 'here I can rest awake.' Researchers now call this waking rest. And mounting evidence suggests it might almost be as powerful as sleep. In dozens of studies, short periods of rest immediately after acquiring new information – spatial routes, vocabulary, names – yielded greater recall. People who rested for ten minutes were better able to remember what they'd recently learned than their non-resting peers. Not only could the waking resters remember with more clarity and proficiency after ten minutes, but they could also remember with more clarity and proficiency a full seven days later.[23]

Other studies have compared waking rest with actual sleep and found the two to be indistinguishable when it comes to memory consolidation and recall. These extraordinary findings offer hope to the sleepless. As the researchers of a 2021 study explained, the 'neurobiology specific to sleep might not be necessary to induce the consolidation of memory'.[24]

We merely need to rest regularly. Preferably in darkness. Ideally beneath a night sky.

10

Changeable

)

I painted . . . because I couldn't sleep nights. I got tired
of fighting insomnia and tried to paint instead.
Lee Krasner, interview, 1978

I first saw painter Lee Krasner's Night Journeys in an exhibition
at the Barbican in London. Her canvases hung, enigmatically
and enticingly, in their own partitioned section. Entering it was
like walking into a thundercloud on a cerulean summer's day:
unsettling, eerie, thrilling. I sat with the paintings for an hour,
staring at their loops and lines, their curves and coils and corners.
I recognised the spin of her night mind, the restless energy that
strikes at 3 a.m. and must be sloughed off like old skin. It was all
there – in these enormous colourless paintings that looked like
night winds, or currents of energy, or the inner workings of the
nocturnal mind. Their titles piqued me – *Night Watch, Uncaged,
Vigil, White Rage, Moontide, Assault on the Solar Plexus, Fecundity,
Primeval Resurgence*. I wanted to know more.

A quick Google search told me these were grieving paintings
created after her husband, Jackson Pollock, died.[1] But this
confused me. Pollock had died several years before her Night
Journeys were painted. Besides, Krasner's Earth Green paintings
(made in the immediate aftermath of Pollock's death, but during
daylight) were so utterly different. Looking at Krasner's Night

Journeys now, by the shadowy light of a candle from the depths of night, I find another explanation: these paintings were made by her Night Self.

The story of Pollock's drunken death has been told many times. In the summer of 1956, he'd started an affair with a young gallery assistant. Krasner asked him to break off the affair and, when Pollock refused, she left for a holiday in Europe. Meanwhile, Pollock continued his affair, his drinking, his not-painting. One night, inebriated, he drove his lover (and her friend) to a piano recital. The friend took fright and tried to jump from the car. Pollock accelerated and swerved onto the highway. The car hit a hump in the pavement, lurched to the right, before whipping across the shoulder, hitting a stand of trees and flipping right over. The lover survived. Her friend was crushed to death. Pollock flew fifty feet into the air, struck his head against a tree – and died instantly.

Krasner took over Pollock's studio barn and continued painting. But three years later, she was struck by severe insomnia. For two years, perhaps three, she couldn't sleep. Being the most practical and stoical of women, she decided to get up and burn off this sudden excess of nocturnal energy. First she tried walking her dogs at night, thinking it might return her to sleep. It didn't. So she decided to paint.

In contrast to Joan Mitchell's experience, the midnight hours were not Krasner's natural habitat. Krasner preferred to paint by daylight. But her days were spent attending to the increasingly valuable estate of Jackson Pollock (declared the world's greatest living painter by *Time* magazine a few years before he died). And although this gave her a platform and status (as well as cash), it also exaggerated her 'wife' position in Pollock's ever-expanding shadow.

Gallerists keen to cash in on the Pollock connection, and critics in thrall to Pollock, maintained the story that Krasner was blindly influenced by her genius husband. Even six years after his death, most refused to see Krasner as an artist in her own right. Nowhere is this clearer than in the story of her Night Journey paintings.

When Krasner showed her gallerist a few barely finished pictures, he cancelled her upcoming show on the spot. The huge colourless canvases were unsaleable, he said. Bravely, Krasner pushed on, painting more and larger, in the tightest imaginable palette – umber and cream. As night blots out colour, so Krasner blotted out the bright hues she normally used, believing that colour needed daylight to preserve its truth. Much later she recalled her dogged decision to use only two colours, noting that it had been utterly against the grain. Everyone else was involved in vibrant 'colour field painting', but Krasner was 'once more . . . going against the stream'.

Her monochrome Night Journeys were both out of fashion and shocking. Critics called them 'unruly', 'dark' and 'nightmarish'.[2] And yet Krasner believed that curtailing her palette had freed her from thinking about colour, liberating her to focus on 'the primacy of feeling, of struggle and exploration'. As far as Krasner was concerned, working during the austerity of night with a drastically pared-back palette helped her 'to extend the outer limits . . . to expand'. Other painters, she added, were merely going 'from A to B'. She, however, was 'dealing with the whole alphabet'. A night journey that ranged from A to Z.

Meanwhile, critics claimed that Pollock was casting his wily influence from beyond the grave, that Krasner's Night Journeys 'were much dictated by the spirit of late Pollock work'.[3] They said her insomnia was provoked by the recurrent trauma of Pollock's death and that, in her paintings, she continued to 'wrestle' with him. The critic David Anfam spoke for many when he said that Pollock's 'presence is the structuring absence that underlies [Krasner's] Night Journeys'.

Many saw them as 'mourning paintings'. Poor Krasner: still haunted; still grieving; unable to free herself from Pollock's artistic shadow. Others commented on the anger – the 'unparalleled violence' – in her paintings. They asked if it was fury directed at her dead husband, at his infidelities.

And yet Krasner's explanation was simple: 'I painted . . . because I couldn't sleep nights. I got tired of fighting insomnia and tried to paint instead.'

In one interview, when asked about her 'mourning paintings', Krasner retorted testily that 'A lot happens aside from grief for Jackson . . .' No one asked about the recent death of her mother, or the vexation caused by managing Pollock's estate, or the fury and humiliation of having her promised show cancelled. It wasn't until 1978 that Krasner described her Night Journey forerunner, *The Gate*, as 'a struggle', 'very much connected with my mother's death', a painting that Krasner 'was not prepared to explain'.[4]

And yet, even as she mourned her mother, is it possible her Night Journeys were the result of something else altogether?

Krasner's Night Journeys are vast. Even more so considering her size: she was just five foot four. A single canvas could take up the entire wall of a gallery and required a sort of embodied painting – climbing, reaching, stretching, twisting, bending. These emotionally charged and loaded paintings weren't the result of a gentle floppy insomnia. Krasner's brain was wide awake, her eyes relentlessly open, her arms circling, dipping, turning, her legs supporting the full force of it all. Even her brushstrokes are characterised by an unprecedented (and never again repeated) ferocity, which Krasner acknowledged: 'I used to thrust with the brush rather than work the way I'm doing now, or the way I worked prior to these pictures. These are physical paintings. The gesture is a thrust – I don't usually do that.'[5] In a later interview, Krasner explained that she refused to use a ladder, preferring the painting to 'be within my physical scope, including jumping up . . . to hit the top of the canvas . . . I want to be in contact with my body and the work.'[6]

Can you picture her? Darkness pushing at the window of her studio. Thick nocturnal silence broken only by the slop and slap of paint. She's barefoot and in her dressing gown – a long silky robe tied loosely at the waist. She's thrusting her brush deep into the weft of a canvas that looms over her, surrounds her. She's crouching, stretching, bending. And now she's jumping, flinging sprays of paint at the upper edge of a canvas that throbs and pulses with a restless charge of its own.

Unsurprisingly, these paintings were described as 'energies', as possessing 'an extraordinary vigour'.[7] Later, when I peered at their whirling furies, I was suddenly reminded of Charlotte Brontë circling the dinner table all night after her sister, Emily, died. Walking round and round the table was an insomniac activity the two sisters had shared in a desperate attempt to exhaust themselves into sleep. Without Emily, and mired in grief, Charlotte took it to new extremes.

The sleepless often feel compelled to move, believing it might exhaust them into slumber. But we also move because all journeys, at some point, necessitate movement. Krasner leapt and jumped and thrust in order to *move on*. Without partner or parent, and in the perpetual shadow of Pollock, she needed to psychologically relocate herself. She had already relocated geographically (all but one of her Night Journeys were painted in New York City rather than in the home she'd shared with Pollock on Long Island), but I suspect her frenzied vigour was part of a nocturnal reinvention.

There's just one other thing, always overlooked, never mentioned, prosaic in its simplicity. And I wonder if it lies at the monochrome heart of Krasner's Night Journeys.

We know that female hormones – oestrogens and progestogens – affect women's sleep, and that women are more likely to experience disrupted sleep and periods of sleeplessness during times of hormonal change: puberty, pregnancy and the menopause. At these points certain hormones can surge or dwindle, creating physiological havoc that spills into our moods, energy levels, emotions and ability to sleep.

During the menopause transition, our reproductive hormones slip away: estradiol, testosterone and progesterone plummet, plunging the female body into hormonal chaos. Sleep frequently deteriorates, with reported sleep problems rising from around 35 per cent of premenopausal women to 61 per cent of postmenopausal women. In the US, postmenopausal women report the highest rates of insomnia in the entire population. They have more trouble falling and staying asleep, greater difficulty sleeping, and lengthier and more frequent night awakenings. No one is quite sure why postmenopausal women struggle so with sleep, but as one researcher put it, 'This clear correlation between hormonal status and sleep strongly suggests that ovarian hormones regulate women's sleep and may contribute to observed sex differences in sleep.'[8]

The average age of menopause is fifty-one. When Krasner began painting at night she was . . . fifty-one. Is it possible that Krasner's Night Journeys are expressions of her newly altered self at night? Perhaps these paintings should be seen as artistic renditions of the emotional turmoil and sleeplessness bequeathed by midlife change? Another form of 'creative profit', if we choose to see it like that.

As Krasner once said, 'I think my painting is so biographical if anyone can take the trouble to read it'.[9] But why take the trouble when there's a story of 'wrestling with Pollock's ghost' on tap?

After three years, Krasner's insomnia eventually disappeared. She never again painted in monochrome, or on such huge canvases, or at night. That part of her life was complete, folded carefully away, ready for the next chapter. But her Night Journeys show me that sorrow, shock, loss, hormonal tumult – however they find us – can be rehomed. That life restricted to three shades of the mutest colours is still life, replete with promise and possibility.

'I believe in continuity,' Krasner once said. 'That the past is part of the present which becomes part of the future.' And I think of my father, no longer alive but cemented into my past. And I know that, together, we will travel into the sweet disorder of the future.

I like thinking about Krasner's Night Self – leaping, daubing and thrusting in a maelstrom of sepia paint, while New York slept around her. When the world sleeps, space opens up for those who need it. Krasner took that space and made something of brio and bravura from it. But it's her *leaping* and *daubing* that make my restive muscles twitch. It appears that my Night Self is growing tired of lying, sitting, slouching, slumping, curling. She wants to move.

One night the urge to move becomes so strong I pace around the house, Brontë-style, until 5 a.m. The sky is still black, bunched like a bat. The air is clean and sharp. I drive until the sky is the colour of metal. Then I park and walk over the hills, my ears full of the frantic flapping of pheasant wings. I climb over a stile and find myself – astonishingly – inside a Lee Krasner Night Journey. The field ahead of me is vast, rolling and undulating. The rich brown earth – colour of bitter chocolate with an undertow of fox – has been ploughed and tilled, bringing to the surface a scattering of flints in creamy white and buff, some twisted and jagged, some as smooth and elliptical as hens' eggs. I'd once read a description of Krasner's Night Journeys as the 'browns and buffs of make-up, hair dye, bleach, and pantyhose – tools a woman uses to conceal her natural state . . .'

The phrase comes back to me, and I think how wrong it is. For here, in this bare, broken field with its flayed flints and its clods of sticky umber soil, I have an inkling of what Krasner was doing in her monochrome paintings, with their oily scrapings.

This turned field, sepia and shorn of light, feels like an omen. Just as darkness is the harbinger of a new day, so a fallow field is the harbinger of green shoots. But before a field recovers, it must lie fallow. A year of fallowing is good, my neighbouring farmer tells me. 'It's not productive economically but sometimes I let my fields go two, even three years.'

Grieving too is a time of fallowing – and darkness is its handmaiden. During my sleepless nights, abetted by my Night Self, I've been rewiring my brain, gathering strength and energy, collecting the little bits of me that scattered with the shock of so much death and loss. These bits need finding, turning, repositioning. Deep below the surface of grief, aren't we all putting back these bits?

Krasner's Night Journeys show me how to be patient, how to lie fallow in the darkness. The story of her insomnia gives me hope (perhaps I too will sleep again). But from Krasner I also learn that it's time to experience night in a more muscular, less cerebral way. It's time to move.

11

Courageous

In the darkness one may touch fires from the Earth itself.
Nan Shepherd, *The Living Mountain*

Every now and then, if I don't catch her in time, my Night Self slips back into her rueful, ruminative ways. I've learned to yank off her blinkers, pull on her reins, turn her westward. Out of the highways and into the byways. But my time with Krasner makes me wonder whether immobility plays a part in our tendency to insomniac rumination, alongside our altered biochemicals. The supine body and brain are quite unlike their upright, moving counterparts. Merely being upright prompts our body to produce norepinephrine (making us more alert and energetic).[1] But when we're upright *and* moving, hundreds of chemicals shift within us, affecting everything – from our temperature to our mood. We know that a brisk 12-minute walk, for example, changes 502 metabolites in our blood.[2] Put simply, we are physiologically altered when we move.

According to science writer Caroline Williams, 'Brain, body and mind are part of the same beautiful system and the whole thing works better when it's on the move.'[3] Williams – who has studied the effects of movement on our mood and mind – tells me that when we're mentally 'stuck', either unable to sleep or lodged in an interminable loop of gloom, physical movement can break the cycle. 'Psychological studies suggest that this might be a result of how we perceive time,' she explains.

> Most of us think of the past as being behind us, literally at our backs. And we see the future ahead of us – in front of our chests. When we physically move forwards, we are tipped into a psychological sense of progress. Which explains why going for a walk, or even pacing, helps us feel we're moving on.[4]

I've spent enough time with my Night Self to know that she has no interest in working up a sweat, so I'm relieved when Williams tells me that strolling is more nocturnally appropriate than a power hike. 'A gentle pace sends our mind wandering,' she says. 'It temporarily turns down activity in the prefrontal cortex, the brain-part that keeps us thinking in straight, logical, analytical lines.' As we stroll, our thoughts begin to scatter, to wander, shifting us into a sense of 'being' rather than thinking, which is – adds Williams – more conducive to sleep.

Night-walking is more than a solution to insomnia: it's a way of reconnecting with the dark. Most of us go out at night without ever experiencing total darkness. When we're in pitch black, we become indistinct. We lose our edges, our rims and hems and borders. The lines of us blur. We seep into the space around us. No longer separate, no longer other.

Outside, in darkness, we encounter our Night Self anew.

Five years ago, I walked over the Texas High Plains in the footsteps of Georgia O'Keeffe, an enthusiastic night-walker. O'Keeffe's letters were full of effusive accounts of her walks: 'I loved the starlight – the dark – the wind,' she wrote in a letter to her (then) lover, Alfred Stieglitz. To her friend, Paul Strand, she said, 'I want to be out under the stars – where there is lots of room.' She spoke repeatedly of 'the big quiet moonlight', 'the wonderful big starlight', the night wind that whipped at her face and hair. Later, in New Mexico, she described feeling 'the stars touch the center of me . . . out there on the hills at night'. Darkness intrigued O'Keeffe, as much as it frightened her. Sometimes she felt it pursuing her, 'an enormous – intangible – awful thing'. After walking with her sister one night she wrote to Stieglitz, 'I was afraid – didn't say so – but I was – I was terribly afraid – but it was worth it.'[5]

Jet-lagged, I'd tramped across the same plains, my ears full of howling coyotes. It was January, ice-cold, the sky a vast lid of stars. I'd felt excited rather than frightened. But that's the thing about the plains – you can see for miles and miles, even in the dark. As O'Keeffe told anyone who reprimanded her, there was 'nothing to be afraid of – because there was nothing out there'. Nothing – and no one.[6]

O'Keeffe found inspiration in the velvet blackness of night, later making several paintings of it. The more I thought about O'Keeffe out on the Texas High Plains at midnight, the more curious I became: what if women once felt less uneasy night-walking than we do? What if our fear is an entirely modern phenomenon?

The South Downs are a rolling ridge of English hills, running along the coast from Eastbourne to Winchester. In 2016 they became a Dark Sky Reserve – an area in which artificial lighting is closely monitored and, largely, banned. This is where I plan to night-hike. But I don't have the nerve – yet – to do it alone.

By chance I catch the tail end of the BBC news and discover Caroline Whiteman, a night-walking guide, being interviewed on the South Downs. A fortnight later, I meet Caroline and a group of night-walkers at a Martello tower beside the sea. We've been told not to wear clothing that rustles, chafes or squeaks. Now, we are told not to use torches, headlamps or phones. Not to talk. If we need to communicate, we must howl like a wolf.

No other sound is permitted. Caroline says we are to walk in single file and to follow her pace – exactly – which will be slow. I like her authority and clarity. In the borderless and boundaryless night, this despotic leadership has an appeal that would irritate me during daylight.

'It's for our safety,' she says, as if she can read my mind.

And I suppose it is. But we are all feeling tentative, unsure. More so, as our route has been blocked by police for the local town's annual fireworks party. Caroline must navigate us through a route she hasn't previously walked, beside cliffs that tilt precipitously to the sea, and in winds that keep disappearing, then reappearing to gulp greedily at our hair, our clothes, our limbs. We do not know each other, we are not familiar with the landscape, we are at the mercy of the elements – and we cannot see. For once I want a little tyranny.

We quickly fall into line, watching our feet – which we have been urged to 'trust'. As I become more familiar with the land beneath my boots, I raise my head and look around. The moon is rising, a yellow pearl in an inky cowl of mist. She ducks and dives, vanishing behind hills and clouds, then re-emerging, bald and bright. Her shape and position change constantly, so that when we round a cliff she is somewhere else. Or so drenched in cloud that she is more like a ragged spatter of gold, and I mistake her for a distant light or an unruly star.

We walk on, silent but for the rush and roar of the sea, the whip of wind in our hair and hoods, the soft scrape of twenty-eight booted feet. I can just make out the sea's pale foaming fringe, the spiked mounds of hedgerows and shrubs, the outlines of the hills ahead. Every now and then the clouds drift apart and I see the steadfast gleam of Venus and Jupiter. Once or twice I hear the startled cry of a bird, or glimpse a far-off pair of headlamps winding through the darkness.

Way out on the oil-black sea, the red lights of wind turbines pulse eerily. The town we've left shrinks to nothing. Suddenly we're on top of the Downs – and there is only emptiness, darkness and wind. This place, which by green-blond day is busy with dog walkers, is utterly alien by night.

My senses have been thrown into disarray. With sight knocked from its pedestal, my sense of sound and smell are amplified: the briny sea wind, the earth scuffed up by our boots, the faint odour of smoke. The sounds and smells come and go with the wind, as does the light of the moon. It strikes me that the wind – merely a nuisance by day – is master by night, helping and hindering our movement.

We walk, on and on, until Caroline stops and lights a candle. This is our sign to stop too, to sit silently in this sheltered dip of land. The wind has dropped but the sea rages in my ears. I lie down and feel, with a jolt of shock, the aloneness of this place. I can feel it more acutely because the presence of other people has removed my fear. And without the endless distraction of fear, we are open to the subtleties of a landscape, and to the quieter emotions that live in the undercurrent of anxiety.

I try to comprehend the aloneness of this place. The darkness here feels elemental, primal. Nothing like the soft black of my bedroom. Or the spacious black of my rooftop. Or the rippling dark of my garden. Here the darkness moves in crashing shifts of emptiness. I feel something unravelling, something I can't articulate. I feel less centred, less sure. Frailer – more ghost than girl.

I put my hands in my pockets and grasp my glasses case, my turned-off phone, my keys. Never before have these simple items given me such reassurance, such joy. With my glasses I can see. With my keys I can escape this lonely hilltop for my warm companioned home. With my phone I can find friends and family. Every item in my pocket is a portal to people, to love, to home. Away from aloneness. Back to the light.

Above all, these familiar things remind me of who and what

I am. And on this bleak wind-flattened land I am losing bits of myself more quickly than I could ever have imagined.

Three hours later, we crest the black windswept hill, and the sky suddenly explodes into a hailstorm of light – pink, yellow, blue, violet. The beach ahead is ablaze with bonfires, fireworks, glow sticks. In one brutal step we are plunged from darkness into flashing, pulsing urban glare.

And yet I feel a deep unexpected glee. People, noise, light . . . all at once I ache for the seething genius of humanity, for the warmth and companionship, for the endless curiosity and industriousness that created fireworks and sparklers and neon glow sticks. The anthropologist Richard Wrangham believes that we became truly human only when we learned to gather round a fire.[7] And suddenly I understand. Why choose wild terrifying darkness, when you could be in the frenzied, dazzling bustle of other people?

I have an overwhelming urge to run down the hill, to lose myself in this mass of fire and flame and people. But the ground is dark and rocky, and, with a gesture of her hand, Caroline motions us to follow her, slowly and without speaking.

I'm not the first woman to have an epiphany like this. Long before me came the audacious, cross-dressing Aurore Dupin, better known as George Sand. Sand – who wrote nocturnally for forty years – nurtured her relationship with night by dressing as a man. In her youth she discovered that cross-dressing meant she could go out after dark without being accosted or inciting gossip. In 'a pair of trousers and a vest . . . in coarse grey material, with a grey hat and bulky wool necktie . . . I would fly from one end of Paris to the other'.[8] The fashions of nineteenth-century Europe made outdoor life difficult for women: 'delicate shoes' that 'split after two days', 'dainty velvet hats' that turned into 'tatters' after a spot of rain, hems that ripped and dragged. But outdoor life after dark was even more difficult. A woman couldn't roll up hems or wipe unseen dung from a sturdy boot as a man could. Stumbling along in her finery, she risked everything – clothing, reputation, safety. Sand's discovery – that clothing and darkness could liberate her from the expectations of society – opened her eyes to the *possibilities* of life.

Thanks to a period of 'ardent mysticism', during which the fifteen-year-old Sand stopped sleeping, she was comfortable being awake at night. So when, a couple of years later, she decided to educate herself, she chose the hours of 'ten until two or three in the morning' to 'read everything' from novels and poetry to 'all the philosophers, all the non-believers, all the heretics'. At night, her mind open and receptive, a teenage Sand wrangled with religion, faith and philosophy.[9]

But she also ventured out, riding her mare, Colette, round the countryside. Dressed as a man and under cover of darkness, Sand discovered what it was to feel as nocturnally and exultantly free as a man. And she liked it.

Of course, Sand was clothed and on a horse. Today's equivalent must surely be Amy Liptrot, who, in her memoir of recovery, described nights surveying corncrakes: 'These never-nights, marking off grid references and following maps in the mist, they are my own,' she wrote. One night, Liptrot did something she would surely never have done by day: 'I stop at the Ring of Brodgar . . . and I take all my clothes off and run around the Neolithic stone circle.'[10]

So here's the thing about freedom when bestowed by darkness: once unshackled from fear it's possibly the most liberating of all experiences.

Not long after my first night walk I spend a fortnight in Mallorca, inspired by Sand and her night-walking. Her memoir, *A Winter in Mallorca*, describes a pattern of being outside that brought the night startlingly alive. There, with the composer Frédéric Chopin (her tubercular lover) and her two children from an ex-marriage, Sand was thrust into the role of carer. The big question on her mind was How can I keep Chopin alive? Indeed, the trip to Mallorca had been Sand's brainwave, convinced that the island's warmth and peace would allow Chopin to rest and compose. Her plan went horribly awry. The climate of the island wasn't what they'd expected, and Chopin became weaker and weaker. They lived in a pair of dank, dark, north-facing rooms in the monastery of Valldemossa (not the charming rooms, incidentally, that are displayed as a tourist attraction today). Here, they were friendless, shunned by the local people, who were terrified of catching the 'white plague' and horrified by the unmarried couple's failure to attend mass.

Sand found solace by staying outside on the terrace until 5 a.m. admiring the scene 'lit by the moon and the perfume of the flowers . . . I was not there like a poet in search of inspiration but as an idler who watched and listened.' She became entranced by 'the sounds of the night', and began thinking of how all the places she'd inhabited had their own peculiar nocturnal soundscape: the cries of mice in pursuit of each other on 'slimy flagstones . . . the monotonous noise of the sea, or the call of . . . the watchmen in Barcelona'. In the darkness her mind floated back to 'the sounds of Lake Maggiore, different from those of Lake Geneva. The continuous crackling of fir cones in a Swiss forest [which] is nothing like the crackling that is heard on a glacier.'

Night amplified her hearing as much as it nudged free her memories of the past. 'In Mallorca,' she wrote, 'the silence is deeper than anywhere else. The donkeys and mules . . . interrupt [the night] by shaking their bells . . . the sound of a Spanish song rises out in the most deserted places and on the darkest nights.' She could also hear the sea, but so far away and so faint that 'the strangely fantastic and thrilling poetry of Djins came back to my memory'. Other sounds rose out of the dark: 'the crying of a little child . . . the mother who was singing him to sleep . . . the pigs . . .' and the farmer reciting his rosary to return the pigs to sleep.

Sand and her children (who often had rocks thrown at them during the day) began roaming the mountains after dark. Away from the judgemental eyes of distrustful villagers, they found a few hours of anonymous freedom. Until that too was taken from them. Someone else roamed at night – a drunk man. One night he spotted them, followed them home. Then he began turning up regularly, shouting and banging on their door at all hours. Sand told her children they were no longer to night walk. Once again, they had to stay in the monastery or risk being pelted with stones. A single brutish man had closed an entire world for Sand and her children. An all too familiar story.

Sand continued to roam in the safety of the monastery cloisters, where the bulky blackness gave her a feeling of 'anxiety and pleasure'. Even the bold, cross-dressing Sand wasn't immune to twinges of nocturnal fear – particularly when the rains came and the wind rocked and moaned all night. On one such stormy night, she and her son were returning from Palma. The torrential rain caused their carriage to break down, so Sand decided to walk: 'the rain fell in waves: erroneous clouds, blacker than ink, veiled the face of the moon . . . the moon, devoured by the monsters in the air, disappeared and left us in a blue black limbo where we seemed to be floating like clouds for we could not even see the ground where we dared to put our feet.' For three hours they walked through mountains 'running with waterfalls' and over uprooted trees, until they arrived home, their shoes sodden and flapping from their feet.

In the wild abandon of darkest night, Sand had an epiphany, recounted on the next page of her memoir: man is not made to live with wild nature 'but with men, his fellow men'. It isn't solitude that provides refuge, she continued, but living in peace with our own kind. 'We have a heart too loving to pass each other by; and the thing we are left to do is to support each other mutually.'[11]

I think about Sand's epiphany, bursting from her after a sleepless, lightless night. She wasn't the only one. Time and time again I come across accounts of catalysing moments springing from and crystallising in long black nights. I've experienced them myself. But if we have no darkness, if we live in a world that is permanently aglow, how do we experience Sand's dramatically catalysing moment? There are other ways, of course. But none so readily convenient as the night.

One night I go out to the balcony of our Valldemossa room. Sand's descriptions of Mallorcan darkness have left a vivid impression on my mind, and I wonder if I too might hear the distinctive night sounds of this island. As I look over the balcony, I frown. The endless flat plains disappearing eventually into the sea have become a neon blaze, a vast puddle of orange light. Where has all this illumination come from? A stadium? A motorway?

The next morning I push open the balcony doors. The vista stretches before me, flat and green-brown. Not a light in sight. Not a road in sight. Did I dream the neon blaze? Later, I ask about the night shine. Is there a football stadium out on the plains? No, no, no, I'm told, 'it is Palma airport, the lights come on at 7 p.m. and they turn off at 8 a.m. and you can see it all the way from the mountains.'

Sand's inky Mallorcan night has gone for ever.

As Matthew and I walk the hills of Valldemossa, we marvel at how sure-footed we are in the dark. I'd noticed this on my night walks with Caroline: despite covering miles and miles of ups and downs, on turfed scarps and chalk paths, through mud and over scree, no one ever fell. As our bodies became used to the darkness, and as our senses reordered themselves, so our feet placed themselves with a blend of caution, care and burgeoning confidence.

The more I night-walked the more I became aware of subtle changes in proprioception – the way our bodies move through space, a sort of sixth sense. Not only did my night vision kick in, not only did my smell and hearing become more acute, but my body began to engage differently with the landscape. Often this was in the smallest of ways: my stomach muscles contracted very slightly as if to stabilise me; my arms hung loose in readiness to balance myself; I sniffed at the air. I began to feel less human, more mammal.

And so I start to see night-walking as an act of humility. We move through darkness, wrenched from the certainty of vision and utterly reliant on senses we rarely use now. The animals our forebears once hunted are masters of this nocturnal landscape – able to see, smell or hear us although we cannot see, smell or hear them. This makes me feel – and I cannot find another word – humbled.

One night Matthew and I walk inland from the coast of Mallorca to the town of Sóller. It's midnight, the air is breathless and still, the darkness like liquid. All the shutters are closed, not a single light burns. The silent, shut-up streets, semi-circled by looming mountains, feel vaguely apocalyptic, so that idle conversation seems inappropriate, dangerous.

We're not familiar with the landscape or the route, so our nerves are sharpened, our eyes wide and darting. Our peripheral vision is working double time, with brain regions (including the amygdala) responding twice as rapidly as normal. In darkness we process images appearing peripherally before we see them – and with a greater sense of potential danger.[12]

At this empty hour and in this unknown place, we feel wary,

exposed and completely reliant on one another. But in this unspoken vulnerability, there is also closeness. We walk in silence, hand in hand, united by our sudden fragility. In unfamiliar darkness, our need for one another – so often forgotten during the light – feels stark and elemental. I want to tell Matthew this, but I have no desire to break the pin-sharp silence, so I grip his hand a little tighter and he squeezes mine in return.

My night walks have shown me that, although I like the *idea* of hopping from my bed at 2 a.m. and striding alone into the night, I prefer the *reality* of being with others. In some odd way, it's the presence of people-in-darkness that has most moved me.

I'm ashamed and disappointed that my outdoors Night Self hasn't yet managed to shed her ungovernable fear. Equally, I recognise that being with others in lonely, unknown places has allowed me to see the beauty of a star-flecked sky, to relish the yowling wind, to enjoy the sound of thudding waves. Because without the company of others I'd have heard nothing but the hammering of my own heart and the shrieking of my endless, inner fear.

Which is to say that we are all instruments of our own discovering . . . but sometimes what we discover is not what we hoped for.

As a child Caroline Whiteman was terrified of the dark. She had good reason. Every night, bundled under her duvet with her eyes screwed shut, monsters tumbled from her wardrobe, phantoms slipped out of her drawers, hideous apparitions rose from beneath her bed.

Eventually Caroline outgrew her fears, recognising that her bedroom monsters were figments of her imagination. But one night, Caroline was followed home. Hearing footsteps behind her, she recognised the quickening, heavy tread of a stalker. She felt again the terrible fear of her childhood – the vulnerability, the aloneness, the overwhelming terror. Her night fear had returned, but this time it was nothing to do with her vivid imagination.

'Being followed in the dark, realising I was prey, reinforced my sense that darkness was dangerous, and not for me' Caroline explains, from a busy, brightly lit café where we're meeting for breakfast. 'When I first intentionally night-walked, on a wilderness course, it absolutely blew me away. I completely forgot my humanity . . . all my anxieties vanished. I loved being in the dark and I felt as if I was finally reclaiming night-time for myself.'

She pauses, then describes how the anonymity of night – its *otherness* – spoke to her in another, perhaps more profound way. 'It didn't judge me, and it provided no light for others to judge me. As women we're very bound up with our physical form, but at night all that falls away. As someone who has always felt a bit different, night provided a habitat for my *otherness*.'

Caroline was so powerfully affected by her night walk that she decided to create and lead a series of guided walks, making her the UK's first female leader of night hikes. 'I wanted to share my feelings of empowerment,' she adds. 'I've been guiding night walks for six years and I've encountered the same response in hundreds of women. It's just so liberating to discover that our sources of terror can become sources of strength and joy.'

Sometimes Caroline walks all night, fifteen-mile yomps that finish with the dawn chorus. Other walks are done barefoot. 'I love feeling like an animal,' she explains. 'I love the way my peripheral vision comes to the fore, followed by my other senses. At some point my brain switches off and my feet guide me – and it's as if my brain has been relocated into the soles of my feet. It sounds odd, but I feel as if I've dropped into an ancient but still familiar version of myself.'

On the few occasions when Caroline loses her way, she sometimes senses a path that appears as a glowing thread. 'It only happens when my mind is stilled and my gaze softened . . . it's like an internal navigation system, a sort of sixth sense, enabling me to tune into a path that I wouldn't otherwise have found.' She's also learned to recognise a route through her feet 'according to whether it feels damp or hard, or sandy or whether I'm walking on crunchy bracken or twigs . . . our feet can read a terrain but we've forgotten how to listen. We don't know our landscapes any more – not with the intimacy that our ancestors knew them.'

When I ask Caroline which elements of her night walks people respond to most viscerally, she answers without a pause: 'Trees . . . and the pitch darkness you find in forests. People are really moved by being among trees at night.'

'And why d'you think women are so scared of the dark?' I ask, thinking of my own palpitating dread.

Caroline looks away briefly, then into her coffee cup, then back to me. 'No one says it, because we don't like to use the words. But we all know what it is. It goes unspoken, because they're such ugly words: We're terrified of being raped and murdered. Men have shaped the female experience of night. And every time another woman is raped and murdered, men continue to shape our experience of darkness. And then it's perpetuated by crime novels and films.'

She shakes her black curls and her jaw hardens fractionally. 'We have to carry on walking at night, whether that's in an organised group, with family and friends, or alone if we feel safe. We can't let a few men control our world like this. Women gathering at night is still a radical act – but at least no one can drown us as witches now.'

Although walking in the depths of night felt radical to me, I was following a long tradition of night-walking at times of sudden and unexpected loss. My reading had thrown up dozens of accounts of women outwalking their anguish at night, often alone. From the poet Eleanor Farjeon to the dancer Isadora Duncan to the actress Patricia Neal. Infuriatingly, we only hear about Charles Dickens, who, following the death of his father and unshackled by social expectation, could brag of his 'celebrated feat of getting up at 2 in the morning and walking . . . over 30 miles . . . through the dead of night'. Sadly, no woman could claim her night-walking to be 'celebrated'. She would neither speak of it nor publish an article about it, as Dickens did.[13] Instead, she walked by stealth and in secret.

I think about these women outstriding their suffering, fuelled by emotions too large for the confines of their bedrooms. And I wonder if we have to be at the whim of vast, unwieldy emotions before we can muster the bravura to step out into the night. Or is it merely that our bodies and brains – pulsing with excess feeling – know that there will be no rest until we've purged ourselves of cortisol and adrenalin?

Finally, I decide to put my Night Self to the test. One restless 3 a.m. I pull a coat over my pyjamas and tug on my wellington boots. I step into the darkness and feel the instant tightening of my heart, the quickening of my pulse. I long for a hand to hold, a dog at my heel, a calm sure-footed Caroline to follow. But I'm alone: me and my Night Self, escaping the trammels of my low-ceilinged bedroom, swapping its four claustrophobic walls for a glittering canopy of stars. I walk down the track, through a metal gate and into a field. As I move, my heartbeat settles, my pulse steadies. The darkness brushes against me, like a friend. The air is pungent with night perfumes – damp sheep's wool, bracken, flattened grass. I hear the wind snatching at the trees and the sudden scuffling of something in the hedge. I flash my torch. Nothing.

I turn my mind outwards, away from my ludicrous imaginings, and look ahead into the horizon. It's nothing like a day horizon. In sunlight, the horizon recedes as we approach it – always ahead of us, a tantalising, unending division between earth and sky. But at night the horizon is always within our grasp, always traversable. We can sense an end, a rim we can reach and cross.

But cross to . . . where?

My horizon is suddenly in front me. Trees and woodland. Rook-black. Branches waving into the sky like claws. And suddenly my heart is in my mouth. And I am running, stumbling. Back towards the cottage.

Then I remember what to do. I stop and look up. The moon is slender, gold, lolling on her back. Orion's sword leans to earth. The North Star is exactly where she should be. In seconds my fear has fled. I turn back to the field and walk towards the trees.

12

Wild

(

Wild Nights – Wild Nights!
Were I with thee
Wild Nights should be
Our luxury!
Emily Dickinson, 1861

Nowhere is our Night Self more altered than in a forest. When the branches of trees shut out all light, when unrecognisable noises surround us, when anything could be lurking – above, behind, below – we are transformed from an adjusted, rational person into someone we barely know. To watch ourselves trembling on the brink of hysteria, for no logical reason, reminds us of how little authority we possess, how illogical and irrational we are at heart.

I first encountered my forest Night Self when I was twenty-one. I'd been chased by a large brown bear, down the wooded flank of a Himalayan mountain. Because it was dusk, and because my boyfriend and I had run miles off course, we had to spend the night in a ruined, roofless, doorless bothy. Without food or water, without torch or blankets, we huddled and shivered as the darkness deepened, viscous and impenetrable. All night the forest heaved and hissed around us. With our imaginations in overdrive – snakes, tarantulas, panthers, the very angry bear – we begged and prayed for merciful dawn.

I knew exactly what happened to my Night Self in a forest. And it wasn't a Self I wanted to meet again.

But that was the Himalayas. And I am now in England – with a yearning for something only a wooded nocturne can provide. Because here's the thing about a forest at night: it's probably the last remaining landscape where we can cut loose from the modern world, where we can escape every glint of light and thrum of engine. Where I can find the undiluted primeval darkness that I hanker for.

I've always tamed my terrors by accumulating data. I start with forest expert Peter Wohlleben, who says 'statistically speaking, the forest [at night] is one of the safest places we could be'.[1] I tell myself that, while they once lurked in our woods, wolves and outlaws have now gone. And while my distant ancestors feared potentially fatal falls and drownings, I have a mobile phone and a torch, and I can swim.

Meanwhile, I learn about the forest at night: that trees sleep, just as we do. When darkness falls, trees stop photosynthesising. By day they take in oxygen via the undersides of their leaves (miniature 'mouths' called stomata), using sunlight to convert water and carbon dioxide into sugar. At night, however, they rely for energy on the carbohydrates banked beneath their bark. The by-product of this is carbon dioxide, exactly the same by-product of our own process of breathing.

This isn't the only way in which sleeping trees resemble sleeping people: trees curl up just as we do. When researchers surveyed a canopy of birch trees, they noticed that as the light faded, the trees' leaves and boughs started drooping. Some trees curled up so dramatically their night-height was 10 cm lower than their day-height. At night, the trunks of trees also fatten, just fractionally. Because trees sleep, water drawn up through the roots must wait until daylight to be absorbed by the sleeping leaves. So it hangs around in the trunk, which Wohlleben calls the tree's 'water belly'.

I'd often found that facts – particularly when startling and revelatory – emboldened me. They provided a sense of surety but, more importantly, they provided distraction. Instead of catastrophising about what or who might be lying *behind* a tree, my mind would now dwell on what was happening *inside* the tree. Armed with all this tree knowledge, I might be able to navigate a dark forest. Possibly.

As I swotted up on sleeping trees, I came across a woman who provided me with a much-needed dose of fortitude. She also showed me the possibilities contained within fear. I took it as an omen.

I'd been looking at the paintings of Canadian artist Emily Carr. I'd always loved Carr's work, but I'd never paid much attention to her murky forests, preferring her bold, bright landscapes. But as I was scrolling around one evening, *Stanley Park by Moonlight* popped up – in shades of jade green and charcoal – and I wondered how Carr had painted something so foreboding but also so eerily beautiful.

Carr's forest was a real place, in a rarely visited corner of Vancouver's Stanley Park. She walked here frequently, and often at night, scoffing at its reputation for 'suicides and queer things'. With her dog, Billie, she ventured into the grove of immense cedars called the Seven Sisters, hidden at the end of a grassy trail and wrapped around by thickets of sheltering undergrowth. Here she fell in love with the forest's empty wilderness, later writing: 'The appalling solemnity, majesty and silence was the Holiest thing I ever felt.' In this dark, dim place she found 'God . . . like a great breathing among the trees.'

I wondered how Carr found the courage to night-walk in a partially *urban* forest – surely the most frightening place of all? In fact, Carr had wrestled with her own night fears long before she painted Stanley Park. Her life, it turned out, was one of constantly conquering and reconquering her own fear, a process she believed gave her energy and creativity. Fear, according to Carr, was a necessary element in art. 'You have to go out and wrestle with the elements, with all your senses alert,' she wrote.

Her first epiphany struck when she travelled to the remote village of Greenville in northern British Columbia, in order to sketch. Here, she pushed open the door of the dark, deserted schoolhouse where she was supposed to be staying. Appalled by its grim desolation – 'not even a match could live in the stagnant air' – she fled. But there was nowhere else for her to sleep, so she went back to the schoolhouse and spent a wide-awake night 'in that smothering darkness . . . not knowing what was near me – what I might touch if I reached out a hand.'

Carr made peace with her fear by 're-establishing a human presence with small rituals: boiling the kettle, setting the clock, turning the calendar pages'. And later she used the same technique on her night forest walks, where she 're-established a human presence' by singing or whistling in the dark. And yet Carr never wanted to *overcome* her fear, which – at its source – she recognised as a fear of dying. According to her biographer, Carr 'could not achieve a full realisation of the vitality of the . . . forest without confronting death and the dread of death. She had [for some time] worked under the vague sense of being constantly watched from the forest by something indefinably hostile, and she had come to accept and even welcome it.'[2]

Carr's fears didn't deter her from walking the woods at night. Instead, she transformed her feelings of vulnerability and dread into creative gasoline, giving her art a tension and complexity often lacking in other nocturnal forest paintings. Residing beneath the skin of her fear, she discovered 'a quiet inexhaustible vitality'.

Carr's 'vitality' was, in part, down to the rush of biochemicals brought on by fear – an age-old response allowing us to escape impending danger as quickly as possible. When our bodies flood with adrenaline, our breathing speeds up and oxygenated blood pours into our muscles. When we realise there's no danger, we feel intense relief, even euphoria. No wonder Carr also found a God who had grown 'stuffy squeezed into a church'. Her intense nocturnal experiences bordered on the transcendent, bringing her to an understanding that 'Only out in the open was there room [for God].'

With a head full of facts and Carr's bravery as ammunition, I began building my courage by collecting firewood from a copse at the back of our garden. One night as I turned for home with my basket of kindling, I became hopelessly, dizzyingly lost. Without a path to guide me, I wandered for hours, in and out of dozens of identical trees. Everything looked the same – the tree trunks, the branches, the floor of rotting leaves. I couldn't find a route out and I didn't have my phone. No light penetrated from any direction. Blindly I walked and walked, presumably in circles although I had no sense of this. The darkness grew thicker, my toes and fingers became numb with cold. Panic rose in my throat. I knew that the cottage was no more than 100 metres away. I knew my family were there, playing board games by the fire. And yet I was utterly, stupidly lost.

I also knew about the woman who stepped off the Appalachian Trail to pee, lost her way in the forest, and became so disorientated she eventually died there. Suddenly I understood the ferocious speed with which we lose all spatial sense in a dark wood. No stars to navigate by, no distant lights to orient oneself, no guiding path or distinguishable landmarks of any sort. And a brain disintegrating beneath the weight of its own panic. In all this spiralling fear lurks the very real possibility that we might lose ourselves completely and disappear for ever.

All this raced through my head as I stumbled round and round the minuscule woodland. Forests, I was sure, were sources of terror for both lone men and women, often by day and most definitely by night. And Carr had understood it absolutely – a forest at night is a place we fear above all others because we know death is a very real possibility. Which is to say, it's not forests we fear but death. We just think – quite irrationally in the case of my tiny copse – that we are more likely to die in a dark forest than anywhere else.

Perhaps this isn't as irrational as my scoffing day brain tells me. It turns out that our night brain is more spatially frail than we might think. Buried deep are neurons known as angular head velocity (AHV) cells, which track the direction, movement and speed of our head as we move, helping us navigate through space. These neurons rely on visual cues, which – in a dark forest – are both fewer and harder to spot. When our AHV cells become metaphorically blinded, we are unable to recognise our whereabouts, and we swiftly lose our sense of place and of direction. Within minutes we can become overwhelmingly disoriented. Any longer and we struggle to accurately gage our own speed, while our 'brain compass' – which relies on properly functioning AHV cells – fails altogether, so we can no longer tell if we've turned 90 degrees clockwise or 180 degrees anticlockwise. The same effects have been found in mice, suggesting that even nocturnal animals rely heavily on visual cues to orient themselves in space.[3]

So perhaps Carr was right to fear death in a darkened forest. And yet, despite my discombobulating woodland experience, it's not the prospect of disorientation or death that bothers me. It's something else altogether.

★

I don't possess Carr's bravery, so my first late-night forest walk of any length is with a crowd. It's my birthday – the only day of the year when my family will do something I want to do.

'No presents,' I say. 'I just want one thing.'

They look at me, wide-eyed.

'You want us to weed the garden? Do the laundry? Cook you supper? Clean the house?' They begin guessing and I'm sorely tempted to take 'clean the house'. But I don't.

'I want to walk the forest late at night, with all of you,' I reply.

After much shivering, shuddering, sighing and eyeball-rolling, they agree. That evening, seven of us wrap up in coats and scarves, and drive to our nearest forest – 360 hectares of ancient woodland surrounding a lake and carved through with muddy rutted tracks.

The night is moonless, boot-polish black. Within minutes the trees close around us, like a tightly drawn cloak. Impatient for speed, we flash our torches along the paths, into the bushes, up and down the trunks of trees. Immediately, I see the source of our fear: it isn't darkness that frightens us but artificial light, hurling shadows around, throwing the distance into thick blackness, forcing our eye to see only what lies in its bright beam, blinding us to the corners and the crannies. We should have left our torches at home and let our eyes acclimatise.

It takes the human eye at least twenty minutes to adjust to darkness. Behind our eyeballs lie millions of light-sensitive cells, known as rods and cones because of their respective shapes. During daylight we rely on our cones, which give us colour. And yet we have only 6 million cones in each eye, compared to 120 million rods. Our rods distinguish light from dark. When there's not sufficient light to activate our cones, our rods – most of which are used for peripheral vision – come to the rescue, giving us our dim night vision. Nocturnal mammals typically have more rods than we do, and significantly fewer cones. The badger, for example, appears to have very few cones, and night vision that is little better than our own. I like this idea – that the shadowy landscape I see is exactly that seen by a badger.

'We should turn off our torches,' I suggest. But it's too late. Our eyes have been killed by the light. Thrown into darkness, we can see nothing, and it's too cold to hang around waiting for our eyes to adapt. So we walk on, swinging our torches, talking, laughing. When we finally get back to the car, my daughter, Imogen, turns to me and says, 'I absolutely loved that!'

That night I reach for the works of Mary Webb and reread her account of owl hunting in a moonlit Shropshire forest. Here, Webb tiptoed along 'seeding moss', through paths of black and silver, beneath a moon 'like an enormous lemon' before discovering a family of owls, which she calmly sat and watched – alone.[4] I flick through my shelf of night spinners: Anne Finch in 'A Nocturnal Reverie' feeling 'a sedate content' and 'silent musings . . . too high for syllables to speak'.[5] And on to Dorothy Wordsworth sheltering in a forest from a violent storm 'under the hollies . . . hawthorn hedges, black and pointed, glittering with millions of diamond drops'.[6] And on to Nan Shepherd, for whom 'night . . . sets the puny world in its true perspective'.[7] And on to Clara Vyvyan one stormy night 'in a lone [German] forest' where she took off her clothes and 'rolled in wet moss'.[8]

As I read and reread, I'm reminded of just how intrinsic darkness was to the lives of past women. These night descriptions – replete with elation and exaltation – evoke a darkness we have lost, a darkness we find so alienating and terrifying we have squeezed it from our very existence.

We know how this happened, of course. With artificial light – oil, paraffin, gas, electricity – we extended our days into night. Light and colour lifted our mood, imbued us with energy, drowned out our deeply entrenched fear of the dark. Capitalism lapped up the extended working hours, the promise of more, more, more.

Meanwhile, the cultural and religious connotations of darkness continue to rumble in the shadows: ignorance, the unknown, dirt, danger, deviancy, devilry. Today in our secular society, darkness has yet to be uncoupled from depression, anxiety, grief, mental illness. However you look at it, darkness is unwanted. And the lighter and brighter our world becomes, the less we want it. Is it any wonder so few of us can stroll willingly in a darkened forest?

And yet I've come to love outdoor darkness. I love the way perfumes unfold in the night air. I love how urgent-eared I become, picking out the tiniest and most forgotten of sounds. I love the sense of living so fully in my skin. I love the magical way in which the night sky calms me. I love the crunch and thud of my boots. I love the strange indecipherable sounds that float through the air. I love how darkness renders the familiar unfamiliar, the known unknown. I love the way time shifts and stops – the past slipping away, the future ceasing its endless whine – every second equally weighted with urgency. Here. Now. Utterly alive.

But a forest *alone* in the dark? No gifts there, screeches my Night Self. The mere thought causes every fibre of my body, every inch of bone and sinew, to resist. I will never walk a forest alone at night. Never.

It takes a gentle nudge from my editor, and an intervention from my Day Self, to finally propel me into a pitch-black forest. Doing things that terrify us are easier when we tell ourselves they are for another person (my editor), and when we know that others have gone before (my night spinners). They are also easier when we have less time to dwell on them, less time for our galloping fear to drown out all counter-arguments. And so one night, after I've dropped my daughter at an airport for a ludicrously early flight, I seize the moment. My route home passes the forest and, because I've been night driving for an hour, my eyes hurt, my back is aching and my alert, sensible Day Self is in the ascendancy. She suggests I pull over, take a walk, shake out my limbs, get this chapter finished. My body stiffens immediately, my heart tightens. I find excuses: I'm not in the right footwear. I don't have my night-walking stick. There's no moon, no stars. I have no dog. No – it's impossible.

But here's the thing about our Day Selves – they temper the heightened emotions, the fear, the sweeping irrational and illogical thoughts that render us *not quite ourselves* at night. They curb our imagination, talking down its ballooning terrors. I hear her steady, practical voice now: Take the umbrella from the back seat in lieu of a stick. Stop using your footwear as an excuse. Hold your door keys in your hand. Just ninety minutes of pure darkness before dawn breaks.

I park outside a pub. The car activates the pub security light, so I step out into its searing white beam, feeling suddenly exposed. I clutch my umbrella to my chest, cross the road and take the path into the woods. Something clangs in the wind, metallic and shrill. Instantly, I feel the sprinting heat of fear. My heart rattles against my ribs, my arms are pressed rigidly to my body, my Night Self shrieks in my ear: Turn back, turn back – or risk rape, murder, death!

Then I hear the long low lilt of an owl and I am so entranced my fear falls away. For reasons I cannot fathom, the owl call placates me, distracts me, calms me. She seems to be inviting me into her forest.

I follow the track, mud slopping beneath my trainers. The trees shimmy wildly above me, branches scrape against boughs, trunks creak and wheeze, the darkness whispers. The forest closes in – a cave of black roses – and my heart jumps into my throat. But then the owl call floats through the canopy again, beckoning me on. I look back – I am completely alone except for my companions: a solitary owl, the wind, thousands of trees, and the darkness. I press on, encouraged by the calm, constant reminders of my Day Self (murderers do not stalk forests at night) and the gently swelling wonder of my Night Self.

I've walked this track before but never without light of any sort. Inevitably, I miss turnings, walking too far or not far enough. But eventually I find the lake, asleep and blackly glinting. I walk its shore, intoxicated by my own puny courage. But feeling, too, the relief of open space.

With my fear curtailed, I start enjoying my walk. The dread I felt earlier seems absurd, and eventually my mind wanders a little. A phrase I found in my father's notebook comes to me over the soughing of the wind: *Darkness is but the privation of Light.* I want to tell him that I disagree, that he has misunderstood the nature of darkness. It isn't the absence, lack or *privation* of light. Darkness has its own qualities, its own soul, its own wisdom and beauty. Here in the forest, swathed in its folds, I see this with a particular clarity. And I want to tell my father that it is because of his death that I have seen this, that the many gifts of darkness have their genesis in him.

I return to my car in the half-dark of dawn, euphoric. Drunk on my own wild bravado. It's not darkness I've mastered, but fear. Ancient, obsolete fear.

I know the fear will return. It's written too deeply in my bones to be defeated with such ease. But I also know that it was defeated tonight because I no longer see darkness as an enemy. Because darkness has become my friend.

13

Enchanted

The night was vast with all the other things. No need to sleep.
Dorothy Richardson, *Pilgrimage 1*

Buoyed by my wild forest walk, my Night Self relinquishes some of her fear. I have learned that fear is greatest in the *anticipation* of danger, either real or imagined. Once I move, it shifts, shrinks. And yet it never fully leaves me. Instead, I remain in a state of heightened emotion, my senses like scissors, the blood running giddily beneath my skin. I know my fearful Night Self can return within a nanosecond: an unfamiliar sound, a moving light, any sign of another human. I have also learned that my fear rises and falls with the phases of the moon. Which is to say, light continues to appease her.

But over the next few weeks, as I diligently habituate myself to outdoor darkness, I discover something that does more to curtail my Night Self's fears than anything else. I call it enchantment. Others call it awe or wonder or the sublime. In the moment it feels more like magic than anything else. Psychologists attempt to explain it as 'the science of awe'. But here's the thing: when gilded by our night brain (imaginative, inventive, receptive, curious) and with our senses in full blossom, enchantment becomes amplified, sharper, more memorable. And in our utter absorption, fear slips silently into the undergrowth.

My night spinners show me that it doesn't take the drama of a meteor shower or the rarely heard song of a nightingale to spark night wonder. The smallest, humblest and most overlooked of insects can out-awe the more predictable events.

My revelation started with the writer Gene Stratton-Porter. Between 1908 and 1925, Stratton-Porter's novels sold at a mind-boggling rate of 1,700 every day. They were read by over 50 million Americans and translated into twenty languages. As well as being a literary phenomenon, Stratton-Porter was a conservationist, pioneering wildlife photographer, movie producer, columnist and poet. But it was her unconventional love of moths, documented in her 1915 book, *Moths of the Limberlost*, that transformed her into an adventuress of the dark.

When a friend pointed me to Stratton-Porter's book on moths, I winced. Decades back, when I was a teenager waiting tables at night, the restaurant boss – a large, muscle-bound Yorkshireman – had confessed to a skin-crawling aversion to moths. We'd had to move away from a wall light because he couldn't stand being so close to the endless swarming moths whose wings sizzled on the blue fluorescent bulb.

'They give me the creeps,' he'd said with a shudder. 'Ugly blind little beasts . . .'

His sense of repulsion stayed with me, reinforced by repeated attacks of house moths that gnawed their way through carpets, curtains, clothes. For years our house was festooned with moth traps. And yet the moths continued chomping and chawing through our socks, scarves, skirts and sweaters. Like mosquitoes and cockroaches, they were undesirable insects that appeared sneakily at night, deserving no mercy.

'What's wrong with butterflies?' I asked my daughter, Bryony, when she admitted to a burgeoning fascination for the drab, blundering moth.

Her eyes widened. 'Moths are amazing. They're like flying tongues, tasting everything they land on, and they have ears under their wings! They're way more interesting than butterflies.' Gene Stratton-Porter would have agreed wholeheartedly.

Like our Night Selves, moths are a gift of darkness, with an alchemy all of their own. In the last decade lepidopterists have made a series of startling discoveries about the overlooked moth. Not only do moths taste via their feet (many also have taste receptors at the end of each hair and scale, so that every millimetre of them can seek out food), but some of them also hear through their stomachs. Many can jam the ultrasonic echolocation capacities used by bats, who are very partial to a moth meal. Meanwhile, other moths have no mouthparts and never eat, living for weeks on the nutrients they stored as caterpillars.

Weirdly, moth caterpillars can see through their skin. And new studies suggest that caterpillars can retain memories even as they transition into moths – a mind-bending process that takes place in the darkness of their self-spun silk cocoon. Here, the caterpillar's wormy body is dissolved, then resurrected as an intricately patterned, winged beauty that can recall lessons it learned as a caterpillar.[1] No other metamorphosis is as bafflingly beguiling as that of caterpillar into moth.

Equally beguiling are their names: the hummingbird hawk-moth, the scarlet tiger moth, the cinnabar moth, the Merveille du Jour, the green-brindled crescent, the crimson-speckled footman. How to resist such an evocative litany of names?

I can't. And neither could Stratton-Porter, who never intended to investigate moths. Her passion was for birds. But one evening, while observing and photographing birds in the swamps of the Limberlost (in Indiana, America) where she lived, she noticed that these delicately downy insects were investigating *her*. 'These fragile night wanderers, these moon flowers of June's darkness literally thrust themselves upon me,' she recalled.[2] The more she peered at them, the more entranced she became. Moths, she realised, were 'one of the most amazingly complicated and delicately beautiful creatures in existence'. And night was viewing time: 'The most important class of big, exquisitely lovely [moths fly] only at night,' she explained in her guide-cum-memoir. Which was why so few people were aware of them, she lamented. 'It is a great pity for the nocturnal non-feeding moths are birdlike in size, flower-like in rare and complicated colouring, and of downy, silent wing.'

Stratton-Porter began collecting moths and attempting to breed them in boxes from where she could also observe, draw and photograph them. Although July and August nights are best for moth-watching in my English garden, in the Limberlost 'the most beautiful form of life' appeared during May and June nights – some of which became the happiest times of Stratton-Porter's life.

The clock had just struck midnight on a 'perfect night during the middle of May, all the world white with tree bloom, touched to radiance with brilliant moonlight, intoxicating with countless blending perfumes' when Stratton-Porter found the night sky of her orchard 'alive with Cecropia [silk moths] . . . From every direction they came floating like birds down the moonbeams . . . the exquisite big creatures came swarming around me. I could feel them on my hair, on my shoulders, and see them settling on my gown and outstretched hands. Far as I could penetrate the night sky more were coming . . . I revelled with the moths until dawn drove them to shelter.' This particular night was to rank in Stratton-Porter's memories as 'the most delightful experience of my life'.

While reading Stratton-Porter's moth-hunting memoir, I became convinced that darkness played a bigger part in these 'most delightful experiences' than she was letting on. It seemed to me that her revelations were inspired as much by being out at night as they were by moths. Later, when Stratton-Porter ventured into woodland at night, her prose reached a crescendo of excitement. 'Of all the beauties of a June night in the forest, these moths are most truly [the man in the moon's],' she wrote feverishly. So enchanted was Stratton-Porter that she thought nothing of lifting her skirts and wading into a dangerous swamp, alone, when night was at its thickest. The capture of a luna moth, she explained, was worth it: 'Nowhere in nature can you find such delicate and daintily shaded markings or colours so brilliant and fresh as on the wings of these creatures of night.'

Enchantment shunts fear aside, creating a hiatus in which we are enlarged, bolder versions of ourself. During times of loss and grief, with fret and fear in freefall, moments of wonder remind us of who we once were and who we can become. They remind us that – in spite of everything – we remain an intrinsic, connected part of the world. They show us that we need not be defined by absence. And when we slip back into sadness or fear (as we will), these memories sustain us. Stratton-Porter teaches me that, in such moments, we can find not only meaning but an unexpected bravery. Even in the darkest of swamps.

Once she'd caught her 'creatures of night', Stratton-Porter took them to her bedroom, where (for a good two months) every surface was covered with moths, cocoons and pupa cases. Unsurprisingly, there was little opportunity to rest: 'I did not average two hours of sleep in a night and had less in the daytime,' she wrote. All night long pupating caterpillars burst from their cocoons, many resembling small birds that grew, as if by magic: at midnight 'they measured two-thirds of an inch', she wrote breathlessly. By 1 a.m. they were three inches, and by 3 a.m. they 'measured six and a half inches strong'. In her bedroom, the moths swooped and plunged so exuberantly that next-door sleepers often woke up in alarm.

Her family protested, of course. They thought she should spend more time sleeping and less time roaming the woods and breeding caterpillars in her bedroom. But Stratton-Porter took no notice. As far as she was concerned, she was witnessing a nightly marvel: 'To see those brilliantly coloured wings droop, widen, and develop their markings, seemed little short of a miracle.' Besides, why sleep if you could 'go to [work] with delight'?

Bryony and I capture moths on sheets and in a special trap. We find tiny silver-washed moths in shades of bitter chocolate and milky coffee, with markings so intricate we can barely see them. But we also find huge moths, exquisitely patterned, mind-boggling in their hues. Some have wings so palely, fraily delicate I wonder how they survive on a breezy night. Others are large and so softly velvety I yearn to stroke them. One moth has dramatically scalloped wings and looks as if it's been carved from the trunk of a tree. Another is so silkily translucent I can almost see through its folded wings. Some have red squares on their heads, like sirens. Their symmetry enchants me – no matter how complex their markings or the whittled edges of their wings, moths are symmetrically perfect. In the disorder of darkness, my Night Self finds their perfect fractal harmony deeply reassuring.

My moth book tells me that there are many more varieties of moth than butterfly, and that they occupy every part of the world, from high mountains to bees' nests to water. That light usually only attracts them after midnight. That some moths cannot fly, while others live for only a few hours. I learn that certain moths migrate for hundreds of miles, reaching an astonishing speed of 30 miles an hour, while others have a nectar-sucking proboscis measuring more than 10 cm.

Where I live, on the southern rim of the British Isles, moths have been decimated. In fifty years we have lost 40 per cent of the moths we once had. A few years ago, our car headlamps were routinely swarmed by moths, and our darkened windows regularly battered by their softly fluttering wings. Now a moth is a rarity.

Eighteen years before he died, my father edited an anthology of poetry called *Earth Songs*. In among the poems celebrating peacocks, kingfishers, dragonflies and butterflies are poems celebrating the less loved and the loathed: wasps, aphids, spiders. Insects that creep, crawl or fly *by night* are among the most loathed and feared of all. But poems about these particular insects are the ones I read and reread. Because words lavished upon such un-feted creepy crawlies help me see them anew.

My favourite poem is 'Moths' by the Irish poet Eavan Boland. Boland has an affinity for darkness and for all those that make their home there. She understood its strange allure, both tantalising and terrifying. She recognised its curious capacity for nurturing change, reminding us (in her poem 'This Moment') that 'Apples sweeten in the dark'.

Above all, Boland shows us how to 'measure the sanctuary of darkness by a small danger'.[3] Like moths, says Boland, we are drawn to the light. And yet it's darkness, both mystical and perilous, that reveals us to ourselves. Like moths, we can perish at 'the kitchen bulb'.[4] Or, like apples, we can sweeten in the dark.

We move the moth trap round the garden, collecting different species in different locations. By the poplar trees we find the poplar hawkmoth – the size of my palm, with ruffled wings and amber veins. We watch lime-speck pugs, lunar thorns, little greys, dark arches, buff arches, dingy dowds, buttoned snouts, oak eggars and apple moths. We identify common white waves, dot moths, flame shoulder moths and a species known as 'the uncertain'. I repeat the names over and over: each contains a history that we shall never know. Who first spotted and named the 'dingy dowd'? Why? When? Moths are rarely studied and many have become extinct without ever being identified.

In 2020 researchers at University College London discovered that night moths transport pollen from dozens of plants not commonly visited by bees and butterflies. 'Nocturnal moths have an important but overlooked ecological role,' they wrote. Moths complement the work of daytime pollinators, helping to keep plant populations diverse and abundant. 'Without them many more plant species and animals, such as birds and bats . . . would be at risk,' they added before concluding that moths 'have been strongly neglected, like most nocturnal insects'.[5]

Which reminds me of how blinkered by light we humans are, of how we have consistently refused to accept what we cannot easily see, of how our dogged preoccupation with vision has snuffed out the full richness and wonder of our world.

As for the moths I thought were 'blind' and 'blundering' . . . how wrong I was! In 2021, scientists put tiny radio transmitters on fourteen nocturnally migrating hawkmoths. Like me, they assumed the moths to be 'blundering', blindly blown by the wind to wherever the wind deposited them. The tracking experiment was intended to see how the hawkmoth coped with changing wind conditions. Instead the astonished researchers noticed that the moth flew in a perfectly straight line direct to its chosen destination, regardless of wind.[6]

It's very rare for a migratory animal to follow a straight path, and yet the hawkmoth had mastered several sophisticated methods for exploiting or circumnavigating wind conditions. When the wind blew in the direction they wanted to go, the moths allowed themselves to be propelled, blown. When the wind blew in the wrong direction, the moths dropped height and picked up speed, flying fast and low to the ground. Whatever the wind, the moths frequently adjusted their trajectories so that they never drifted off course.

How do they do this? By following earth's magnetic field? By recognising landmarks? By following scents? No one knows. But I've learned that the little things we overlook are sometimes the most miraculous and misunderstood of all. A bit like the Night Self really.

There are some words of Stratton-Porter's that stay with me for longer than they should, like a riff lodged in my head: 'The most delightful experience of my life.' When she wrote this line, Stratton-Porter had only two years left to live. She had married (happily), written bestselling novels, given birth to an adored daughter, restored a much-loved house, had numerous encounters with wildlife and set up her own movie business. And yet this rich profusion of life-altering experiences was trumped by a night out in her mothy orchard.

As I raked through my notebooks, rereading three years' worth of scrawled notes on the antics of my night spinners, I realised that powerfully memorable nocturnal experiences weren't unusual. There was something about events at night that rendered them particularly intense and poignant. They often carried a significance that marked them out from similar daytime experiences.

Australian writer Charmian Clift was constantly struck by experiences gleaned during her nocturnal wakings – which she too called her 'night watches' – finding in them 'a sort of elation . . . a sense of quickened heartbeats, of heightened perceptions, of self-surprise, of complicity even'.[7]

Clift is right: things felt, seen, experienced by night come with our own 'heightened perceptions'. The darkness adds layer upon layer of additional emotion, from surprise to disorientation to an alert wariness to feelings of aloneness or undiluted fear. Our senses are transformed into beacons of vigilance – ears, nostrils, the tips of our fingers as we feel our way along a lightless hall, the soles of our feet as they attempt to divine our location, our anxiously straining eyes. Our brain, wired to sleep at night, must venture into its own elusive byways.

Again, Clift is right – there *is* a sort of elation in this. And perhaps this is why experiences at night often acquire a profundity and magic of their own, and why the memory of them endures and endures.

My fascination with moths was soon joined by a growing interest in other nocturnal creatures. I spent long, sleepless hours hunting glow-worms (to whom I lost my heart completely) and bats, seeking out nightingales and owls, watching foxes and badgers. During these encounters I often sensed something almost divine. The writer Helen Macdonald once described such moments as those 'in which the world stutters, turns and fills with unexpected meaning'.[8] These moments of wonder, meaning, awe – call it what you will – were amplified and exaggerated by the secret alchemy of nocturne, and by the traits of my Night Self. With fear tamped down, she displayed a boundless propensity for enchantment.

As summer drew to a close, a final thought struck me: that the cavity left by the death of my father was, in fact, a valuable space, a gap for replanting. I felt the aching void of grief slowly shrinking, its edges filling out with the soft peachy wings of moths, the lucent green of glow-worms, the startling trill of nightingales, the dim plunging and tumbling of bats. And so, like the darkness they inhabited, these night creatures also became healers of sorts.

Reckless

At night I fret about the day and no longer trust myself:
A bad swimmer, far out, and more than startled by the deep.
Peter Abbs, 'On Not Being Able to Sleep'

For months I walk the empty stretch of Sussex coast my father walked on the last day of his life. I'm convinced he's still here – in the salt-sharp, sea-damp air, in the flash of light on the ocean. I come by day and by night. A sort of pilgrimage. Already I know that my day walks will disappear into the shrinking folds of memory. But my night walks will endure, stamped hard and bright through a combination of fear, sensory novelty and something I will call 'mystery'.

At a time when everything in my life seems inexplicable and unpredictable, the beach at night provides both certainty, with its regular ebb and flow, and a sense of the unknown as the ocean disappears darkly into nothing. Known and unknown in a single space. I walk between the two, finding solace in the strange balance of this borderland.

'The true spirit of the sea does not reside in the gentle surf that laps a sun-drenched bathing beach on a summer day,' wrote the marine biologist and writer Rachel Carson. 'It is on a lonely shore at dawn or twilight, or in . . . midnight darkness that we sense a mysterious something we recognise as the reality of the sea.'

In a 1958 article written for *Holiday* magazine, Carson urged her readers to leave their 'trappings of human existence' at home in order to hear 'the accents of sublimity in which [the sea] speaks'. She described full-moon nights 'when the sea and the swelling tide and creatures of the ancient shore conspire to work primeval magic from Maine to Florida . . . and . . . the shore speaks of life in a mysterious and magical way'.

The mystery of the sea, said Carson, could never be fully grasped in dull daylight. Nor could it be adequately described in plain old words. She guided her readers instead to Beethoven's Ninth Symphony.

But Carson knew more than most people about the mysterious life of the ocean at night. She was fascinated by a recent discovery of 'living creatures [that] spread like a cloud over much of the ocean . . . no one is sure what these creatures are,' she explained in a 1951 speech.[1] They had never been seen by the human eye. And yet their existence had been noted by the echo-sounding instruments used to record the depth of water under a moving vessel. This 'phantom bottom' of the sea had been mistaken for a sunken island, but a new consensus was emerging – 'that the layer is composed of living creatures'. At night – in darkness – the 'layer' moved up to the surface. At daybreak, it returned to the deepest water 'where light cannot follow'.

Like her contemporaries, Carson didn't know what these mysterious nocturnal creatures were. Some people thought they might be shrimp – billions and billions of them – others thought they were vast shoals of fish or squid. 'The answer to this enigma may come very soon,' concluded Carson. And she was right.

In 1995 Deborah Steinberg, an ocean researcher, took her first night dive, tipping from the edge of a boat and plunging through 13,000 feet of darkest water. To her surprise she found herself in 'a totally different community . . . with animals of every single kind'.[2] The experience was so startlingly illuminating that Steinberg changed the direction of her career. Twenty-five years later, she still speaks of it as a defining moment in her life.

Like the night world on land, the night world at sea thrums with extraordinary unseen activity. Every night trillions of miniature creatures, known collectively as zooplankton, rise 1,000 feet from the ocean floor to the sea's surface. Millions more join them in their upward propulsion: krill, fish larvae, copepods, salps. It's an unstoppable nightly migration of gargantuan proportions (an estimated 10 billion tonnes, to be precise).

Known as diel vertical migration (DVM), this exhausting journey is driven by the need to eat in safety. At night zooplankton can feast on the tiny aquatic plants growing at the ocean's surface without being gobbled up by roaming fish. Until very recently scientists knew almost nothing about this mass nocturnal movement or its ramifications. We now know that these creatures organise themselves into clusters, travelling together according to type and size, in a series of immaculately timed ascents and descents. As they shift up and down, they take in carbon dioxide from their phytoplankton supper and deposit it – via their faeces – on the ocean floor, where it can remain for thousands of years. Oceanographers think this remarkable night migration prevents the planet from being as hot as it might otherwise be. They also fear that we humans are on the verge of utterly disrupting this delicate dance – overfishing, excessive light at night, climate change, who knows what else – with implications we cannot possibly foresee.

I'm thinking about Steinberg's night dive when my sister – an accomplished diver – casually mentions that she has night-dived.

'It's amazing,' she says. 'Completely different. People think that, because the ocean is dark, diving by night is the same as diving by day. But it's not. Everything about it is different.'

'In what way?' I ask.

'You have a torch, and everything is smaller. So you go very close to tiny things ... plants ... sea life ... It's colder, lonelier, eerie. But very calming, almost meditative. Once you concentrate on looking at all the minuscule life, you don't think about the scary things – drowning, running out of air, getting lost.'

She tells me I should do a night swim, but then says that night swimming is more unsettling than night diving: 'It's just empty ocean nothingness that goes on and on. With a night dive there's lots to distract you. A night swim is ... well, exciting. You should try it.'

When I was fifteen and getting into my pyjamas one night, a friend knocked on our door and demanded I join her on 'an adventure'.

'It has to be you,' she said. 'Everyone else is too scared of getting into trouble, but you ... well, you like trouble.'

'What do I need?' I asked, piqued.

'Nothing,' she said with a laugh. 'Just follow me.'

I followed her to a neighbouring street where large houses stood in rock gardens with Audis on the drives.

She put her finger to her lips, then motioned at the biggest, grandest house of all. Then she pointed at the house next door, where our friend Jane lived. Jane and her family were on holiday and their house was dark and curtained. We crept down the side of the house, through a gate and into Jane's garden.

I felt momentarily perplexed: surely we weren't going to break into Jane's house? I could no longer see my friend in the dark – where was she?

But then I heard her scrabbling over the fence, followed by a thud as she landed in the next-door garden. I pulled myself over the fence in time to glimpse her naked body disappearing into a vast swimming pool.

We swam for hours in water as warm and black as coffee. Floating on our backs, we stared at the million heedless stars above. We felt invincible. For the next week we returned nightly. Swimming naked in pitch darkness was liberating, calming and exhilarating all at the same time. When Jane's family returned from their holiday, our midnight swims came to an end.

Decades later, that remains my only experience of being immersed in dark water. But the ocean? Already I feel the tremulous twitch of my Night Self. Can I?

A week later, my friend Kate messages me with a tantalising description of being in the sea at night. She describes the experience as 'somatosensory', saying it heightens her awareness of every aspect of her body's physical capabilities, that it generates 'an absolute trust' in 'knowing through sensing'. She explains how she swims out to sea for a count of sixty strokes, then judges whether to swim on, or to turn back. 'It's not a time trial,' she writes. 'It's about testing and paying heed to what my body's feeling. Instead of looking at the colours and patterns of water and sky, night swimming focuses attention on buoyancy and movement through eddies, currents and waves. I can feel if the tide is ebbing or flowing, and the speed. I can feel from the movement of the water and I experience Leonardo da Vinci's drawings of water turbulence through my skin.'

Most people think she's crazy, she says. But it's the encounter with an 'unknown' that she most treasures, and the sense of tuning into a different sort of body, one that's both supremely powerful and supremely sensitive. 'And I like the rush,' she adds. 'Knowing that I've done something challenging and reckless but not stupid gives me a long-lasting dopamine high.'

A few days later, I meet an elderly woman from Brighton who tells me she too swims at night on full moons. And then a Scottish friend mentions that she also swims on full-moon nights. All year round. Suddenly it seems as if night swimming is perfectly normal. And I wonder why I feel so fearful. What's wrong with me?

For a long time I've dreamed of walking the coast while everyone sleeps. I've been inspired by Rachel Carson's description of the shore at night as 'a different world, in which the very darkness that hides the distractions of daylight brings into sharper focus the elemental realities'. Carson described coastal night as 'the darkness of an older world, before Man . . . no sound but the all-enveloping, primeval sounds of wind blowing over water and sand, and of waves crashing on the beach'. It was a catalysing moment for Carson, who was suddenly overcome by an 'odd sensation' of understanding the ocean 'as never before', of suddenly grasping 'the essence of its being'.

Yet again, darkness had precipitated illumination. Carson's words remind me, once more, of all the life I've failed to experience because I've been welded to light, sleep, safety indoors.

And so one night I drive ten miles to my nearest beach and sit on the pebbles until darkness falls. When the last dog walker has left and the sky is a bruised black, I get up and walk. My boots crunch over the pebbles for no more than five minutes when I realise that I'm not alone. People are with me. I hear them slipping down the banks of shale. I hear the chip of their boots on the stones. They have appeared, wordlessly, from nowhere. I can see their outlines against the sky, moving, stooping, bobbing and bending. Things are being dragged and dropped. I hear chinkings and rattlings and the odd curse. Why are they here at 10 p.m.? What are they doing? Suddenly I feel frightened. I don't want to be alone by the sea with strangers. With men.

I turn on my torch and angle its beam into the darkness – men are everywhere, putting up tents and setting up fishing rods and lines. I lose my nerve. What am I doing here anyway? This isn't Carson's wild empty beach – it's a grey stony English beach, backlit by the skyglow of Eastbourne, and bereft of any 'darkness of an older world'. I scuttle back to my car, feeling small and silly.

But Carson continues to urge me out. I read her enthralled investigations along the shores of the Atlantic, which she described in a letter to a friend: 'Lots of swell and surf and noise . . . it was most exciting down there towards midnight . . . to get the full wildness we turned off our flashlights and then the real excitement began . . . the surf was full of diamonds and emeralds and was throwing them on the wet sand by the dozen . . .'

So I forget about the beach of fishermen. Instead I find a coastal stretch renowned for its rockpools, and one moonless October night Bryony and I take our UV torches and go in search of Carson's 'diamonds and emeralds'.

To reach the beach we must climb down several flights of steps in complete darkness. We descend slowly, gingerly, by the dim red light of our head torches. We feel as though we are trespassing, that any minute now a coastguard will leap from the shadows and ask us what we're doing or accuse us of illicit activities. Apparently smuggling still happens at night here, along with illegal fishing.

The beach is deserted and utterly black but for a distantly winking lighthouse. We hear nothing but the slap of the sea and the tumble of pebbles beneath our boots. We cross the shingle to the rock pools – acres of them, draped in slippery bladderwrack – then turn off our head torches. We wobble and stumble over the seaweed, the scooped rocks and crevices, the braided rivulets of seawater. Then we crouch down and point the blue beam of our UV torches into the pools. In the eerie lilac light, we see hundreds of crabs, their shells a muted green. Sea anemones – fluorescently green, violet, sapphire, scarlet – wave their tentacles at us. Every pool contains chips of neon, translucent shrimps, weed of brilliant crimson. Suddenly we are looking into jewelled crevices, aquariums of rainbow light, prismatic troves of phosphorescence, a fantastical otherworld that thrills, enchants and captivates us. We stagger around, exclaiming at every shade and hue, every splendid sidling crab, every strange, pulsating sea creature. All of it transformed by darkness in combination with the blue beam of our UV torches.

And then Bryony tells me to bend low and put my ear to the rocks. 'Listen . . . Can you hear it?'

With my head millimetres from a barnacled rift, I catch the sound of crackling and popping.

'It's all the limpets, sucking and un-sucking as they detach themselves from the rock and then reattach themselves.'

I listen, mesmerised. One ear roars with surf and the other is full of the snap, crackle and pop of a million moving limpets.

Carson was right. The true spirit of the sea can be found only in midnight-dark.

One night, towards the end of October, I finally muster the courage to swim in the English Channel in darkness. Matthew and I drive to our nearest beach, where I've swum before in midwinter. The cold doesn't worry me, but dark, turbulent water terrifies me. Matthew refuses to come in, but promises to rescue me if I get blown out to sea.

The beach is wind-whipped, deserted. There's neither moon nor stars. It is utterly dark. The waves are ominously large, and sound like huge trees being felled, one after another. I can see the roiling water spilling on and on and on. A vast expanse of moving darkness, flinging its frothing edge repeatedly against the shingle, then noisily slurping sand and stones back out to sea. I imagine the waves bludgeoning me, dragging me out, losing me for ever.

I shine my torch on the surface of the water. Its beam barely covers anything. If I'm pulled under, how will Matthew find me?

'You can't go out.' He shakes his head. 'The waves will knock you over and I can't see a thing.'

'Oh,' I say, trying to sound disappointed. Because surely I should be disappointed? But I've never felt so relieved in all my life. I leave the wild loneliness of the beach with a lightness in my step, floating like a bubble through the black air.

In the cold light of morning, my too-swift capitulation disgusts me. So on the next full moon I return to the beach with Imogen. She refuses to swim with me (too cold) but agrees to sit on the shingle and call for help if I disappear. This time the tide is out, the air is still and silvery light ripples over the surface of the ocean. It's a different place altogether.

I step into the water, which gently foams and swirls like Guinness. The cold is shocking, but it's the unending darkness wrapped around my body, rolling into the horizon, that worries me. Except that, with the bright elegant eye of the full moon above me, the darkness is utterly unintimidating. Instead of having to corral my fearful imaginings – of being sucked under by invisible tentacles, or clamped in the jaws of an unseen shark – I am entranced by the moon, by her blue hollows and craters, by her dappled light on the water.

I move further and further out until I am bathing in a surf of liquid silver. The water eddies deliciously against my skin. The sand undulates beneath my feet. The air smells of seaweed. The long pebbled beach lies like a bolt of sequinned silk. The fear and aloneness I'd expected never materialise. Instead I feel oddly companioned. By Imogen, of course, cheering from the shingle. But also – a little peculiarly – by the moon. She seems to watch me, to witness me.

I know my Night Self is appeased and mollified by the bounteous light, but I also sense that the moon is offering more than mere illumination. I can't find words for something that makes so little sense. But I have learned that not everything should be named and explained. My accumulated night journeys have shown me that our world will always contain elements that lie beyond our understanding. As I float in an inarticulate embrace of moonshine, my whirring mind stops its endless efforts to understand, to measure, to *know*. Explaining a thing can strip it of its fearfulness, of course. But too much explaining can strip away its power and mystery.

'What's it like being in the sea alone at night, then?' asks Imogen as I wrap myself in a towel.

'Magical,' I say, suddenly tingling with cold, with *not-knowing* – and with the sheer magnificence of my own becoming.

15

Fearful

> It is the same woman, I know, for she is always creeping,
> and most women do not creep by daylight.
> Charlotte Perkins Gilman, *The Yellow Wallpaper*

When I was a child, the dark was a place of excitement – we turned out the lights to play sardines, we donned blindfolds to play blind man's buff, we roamed the darkened streets on Halloween, we rushed around with sparklers on Bonfire Night.

But one evening, something happened that made me question how to behave, dress, move after dark. It was 7 p.m. and I (aged fourteen) was going to a friend's house, which meant walking through town after nightfall – as I'd often done without any sense of trepidation. On this particular evening I decided to put on some lipstick and wear a new skirt that sat several inches above my knees. When I stopped at the kitchen to say goodbye to my parents, my father stared at me.

'You can't go out like that,' he said.

I stared back, confused. 'Why not?'

'You look . . .' He paused as if groping for the right word.

'Yes?' I felt bewildered and hurt. I liked my new skirt. It was red corduroy, picked up from a jumble sale. The lipstick matched and I'd felt glamorous and sophisticated as I ran it over my lips.

'Tarty,' he said after a long pause. 'People will think you're a . . .'

'You should rub some of the lipstick off,' suggested my mother.

'And the skirt . . .' mumbled my father. 'It's too short.'

'But I'm not a tart,' I said, angry tears pushing at the backs of my eyes.

'No,' agreed my father, 'but it's night . . . you have to be careful.'

From that moment, my safe, friendly little town became unsafe, unfriendly. I understood then that clothes I wore by day could not be worn by night. Alone in the dark I was exposed, vulnerable to the judgements and actions of others. To avoid danger and censure I must never draw attention to myself. I must be inconsequential, of no importance, a perfectly behaved ghost.

Despite the generous illumination and the proximity of fellow humans, few women enjoy an urban ramble at night. Not for us the nonchalant nocturnal saunters of Charles Dickens or the 'gently recalcitrant' night stroll proposed by a male writer in a recent edition of the *Guardian*.[1] Instead, we walk with sharply swivelling necks, ears twisted into the silence, eyes straining at the edges, fists gripping keys, hearts hammering against ribcages. It can hardly be called a 'walk' . . . more of a half-run, in which we sweat and fizz with fear.

And yet the idea of walking the city at night endures as a powerful fantasy of liberation. As the artist Helen Frankenthaler wrote in a letter dated 1957: 'New York . . . quiet strolls, 9 p.m. on Madison Avenue. Somehow that's my dream of freedom.'

We dream of it, we fantasise about it. A few women do it. But rarely alone. When I want to experience the city on foot, at night (and who wouldn't?), I take female friends.

Eleven months after my father dies, I have a yearning for churches at night. I invite three friends to walk with me along a bygone funeral route linking eight historic churches on a straight line. On this smudgy November night we walk from a fifteenth-century church in the City of London via St Paul's Cathedral to a church in Trafalgar Square, admiring the palely lit stone, the moonlight catching on gold, the hushed feel of a city asleep.

I wonder where this urge has sprung from – this urge to walk church-to-church at an hour when all their doors are shut fast. My friends busily make plans to return by day, to explore *in the light*. But I like the churches looming, bone-white, out of the shadows. I like the emptiness and quietness of the city, the way each church has space to breathe. St Paul's Cathedral is illuminated by artfully angled spotlights so that it floats out of the darkness, in an exaggeration of shadows. The smaller churches – St Bride's, St Clement Danes, St Martin within Ludgate, St Dunstan-in-the-West – sit modestly in gloom, as if asleep. We rattle at the handles, but to no avail – all are locked and bolted.

At the end of our line of churches, the lights brighten and the party crowd swells. We're approaching London's West End – a frenzy of 24-hour, neon-lit bustle. Julie, a photographer, begins reminiscing about darkrooms, telling me that she only uses digital now despite loving the grain, atmosphere and depth of film.

'Digital is easier, more convenient and much cheaper,' she says. 'But I miss my darkroom days. I miss that sense of mystery. The whole process was rooted in chemicals of course, but it had a magic that nothing else compares with.'

I've come across photographic darkrooms only in films and books, where they frequently precipitate romance or lust. But Julie says this barely scratches the surface of what constitutes a darkroom, or what a darkroom offers.

'The darkness is fundamental,' she explains. 'Without it, there's no picture. When you go in, you have no idea what you'll come out with. So expectations are intensified – potential disappointment, potential glory. For years, photography was dependent on darkness, and the darkroom was really a place of transformation, of magic.'

For female photographers of the past, a darkroom of their own was rather like Virginia Woolf's much-lauded 'room of one's own'. It was a place where the door could be legitimately locked (a single slice of light ruined any developing photograph), and where a woman too might find herself transformed. For many, it 'became a sort of safe haven'.[2]

For pioneering photojournalist Margaret Bourke-White, borrowing a man's darkroom for her school project inspired her to become a photographer. For Annie Leibovitz, it provided an almost spiritual place of solitude: 'I fell in love with the darkroom, and that was part of being a photographer . . . The darkroom was unbelievably sexy. I would spend all night in the darkroom.'[3]

All too often darkrooms were only truly lightless at night, so photographers often spent long sleepless hours locked up there – away from distraction, safe from predation, and a human part of the eerie, alchemical process of development.

'Most of us can't afford darkrooms now,' adds Julie. 'We've lost that sort of mucky, embodied process. You can always tell, though – a picture developed from film in a darkroom has texture and depth and a softness. Digital is really very different.'

I think about this as we walk towards Piccadilly Circus, in a crush of light, people, traffic. We've left the sanctuary of darkness – the churches in their soft shawls of shadow – and reached London's equivalent of 'digital'. Like walking out of a darkroom print into the sanitised technicolour of a screen shot.

★

Despite the dangers, real or imagined, illuminated cities have always attracted women. Virginia Woolf found London nights 'enchanting . . . amazing'. She loved the lit windows and lamps: the 'oblong frames of reddish yellow light . . . points of brilliance burning steadily like low stars . . . the floating islands of pale light'.[4]

Anaïs Nin wrote of Paris with a similar sense of rapture and excitement: 'I step out . . . into darkness. It is a sensual experience. I recognise no one. I stumble. I hear the voice of a man I am sure I could have loved, but he vanishes. Mysterious blue and green lights, here and there.'[5] To feel the full sensual effect, Nin often walked without underwear. She called it 'walking dispossessed' or 'walking poor' and claimed it made her feel 'less enveloped, protected . . . purified'.[6]

Like Woolf, Nin was attracted to light: 'My eyes seek the lights, crude artificial lights, illuminating drugstores . . . endlessly circling Michelin tyres; burning in red darts down the dark stairs of the Metro . . . All in black I follow the lights.'

Clara Vyvyan was also drawn to light when walking alone: 'I would walk at night along the Thames Embankment, round its great semicircle from Westminster to Blackfriars Bridge and watch the reflected lights quivering in the water . . . until I was dizzy with beauty.'[7] And then there's Sylvia Plath night-walking the streets of Wellesley, Massachusetts, a 'unique and strange delight' that she described as akin to walking across 'a bare stage' in which the street lamps were stage lighting. 'I am part man,' she wrote exultantly, 'I would walk . . . all night.'[8]

The lure of artificial light – I know it well. In thirty years of city night-walking, light tugged me as a moth to a flame: shop windows, street lamps, illuminated billboards. I routinely took long circuitous routes to stay close to light. And when it wasn't available I sought it out on my phone, watch, torch. But something has changed. The lights of the West End are brighter than ever, eye-achingly, piercingly brilliant. Apparently many shops and petrol stations are ten times brighter than a decade ago. And I wonder what Woolf, Nin and my other night spinners would make of a city centre so glaringly, blindingly bright.

Clara Vyvyan would have embraced it. For Vyvyan, even distressing experiences became sources of excitement. One night she and her friends were mistaken for 'suffragettes'. Six of them were chased and attacked by a mob in a 'midnight brawl'. Afterwards, Vyvyan wrote, 'despite the dirt and humiliation and fear, I felt a curious exhilaration both during and afterwards . . . even the rough side of life is better than stale monotony'.

Vyvyan's account reminded me of Caitlin Myer, a city night-walker, who – after her first night walk in Paris as a teenager – realised that 'I am scared but the fear wakes me, moves me. I grow larger and stranger out here in the dark.'

Caitlin Myer began walking cities at night after a series of tragedies – the death of her mother, an emergency hysterectomy and then a marriage break-up. 'My warrior years,' she called this period, in her memoir *Wiving*.[9]

Myer night-walks wherever she is and whatever the hour. 'People tell me it's dangerous to walk alone . . . [but] the silence at night calms me . . . It feels like being in on a secret. In the dark I am in communion with the breathing whole of the universe. My solitude shifts back to a sense of rightness.'

Myer has night-walked in more than thirty cities across the world, from San Francisco to Istanbul, from Barcelona to Oslo, with a penchant for the 'deep silent hour long after the bars have closed and before the early risers are off to work'. In this pocket of sleeping stillness, she finds room for herself: 'I take in a breath and feel it roar between buildings, in and out of the spaces between my ribs.' In the space and secrecy of city nights, she stumbles across secrets that she's kept from herself. And so her night walks act much like one of Julie's darkrooms – a space in which she is slowly revealed to herself.

And yet throughout Myer's night journeys, men appear. They touch her. They proposition her. They 'jack off' in front of her. They threaten her. But for Myer 'bed' is more dangerous – a place where she watched her bipolar mother disappear into mental illness. When we're trapped inside, escape from ourselves is infinitely more difficult. Besides, Myer refuses to submit: 'I walk down the street alone and men's eyes stick to me. Their eyes full of want and resentment . . . I will not escape punishment. And, so? That's no reason to stop.'

Myer takes photographs as she walks. Focusing on the small things (the slant of a shadow, the light reflecting from foil in a shop window) turned her night walks into a form of meditation. 'Taking photos helped me focus on the astonishing beauty out there,' she says.[10] 'It takes about 20 minutes of walking' before Myer's attention shifts from herself, outwards, at which point she recognises the city's absolute indifference to her. 'I realise how unimportant I am,' she explains. Being out on the street 'restores my place in the world'.

In 2015 Myer began posting her photographs on Instagram. To her surprise, women responded in droves. They loved her mysterious images. They loved seeing a place that (for most of us) is on our doorstep but rarely seen. And they loved her fearlessness. For Myer, who was raped at sixteen, the worst had happened and it had happened during daylight: 'Night doesn't feel dangerous for me,' she says with complete serenity. 'It wakes me up in the best way.'

I share Myer's 'gargantuan hunger to be free' but I want to share her bravado too. So one very early morning I get up, pull on some clothes and sling my bag round my neck. It's almost 4 a.m.

– the sweet spot for a city walk, says Myer, 'the quietest point of the night'.

Normally when I wake at this hour in need of urban space and air, I sit on my balcony wrapped in a blanket and watch the foxes slinking in and out of my neighbours' bins. So tonight I feel nervous. I dredge up the (very few) women of the past who roamed cities at night for pleasure, getting stuck at Gwen John walking the streets and parks of 1920s Paris. I turn to the fictional Miriam Henderson in 1930s London 'strolling home towards midnight'.[11] And then I remember Peace Pilgrim, who, alongside Myer, must surely be the bravest city stroller of all.

Peace Pilgrim walked the roughest and most dangerous neighbourhoods after dark, often sleeping on roadsides, in bus stations and abandoned houses. But her favourite place to sleep (other than a haystack) was an urban cemetery, which she described as a 'wonderful place to sleep . . . quiet . . . nobody ever bothers you'. Whether she was walking, sleeping rough or sitting up all night talking to the homeless, Peace Pilgrim was never harmed. 'I always think of the dark as being friendly . . . restful,' she said.

And so I leave my house with her words turning over and over in my head. Friendly. Restful. Friendly. Restful.

In the harshly lit stillness of a London night, I feel as if I'm the only person alive. I turn on to an arterial road with a steady stream of traffic. A bicycle clanks towards me. To my surprise and relief, the cyclist is female. But for the next hour I see only men. A man in a hoodie sits on a step smoking and scrolling. Other solitary men appear and disappear. Who are they? Where are they going? People out in the depths of night rouse our curiosity. Robert Louis Stevenson once wrote, 'There is a romance about all who are abroad in the black hours.' I feel less romantic, more wary. In these shadowy roads, my mind is a hovering broth of curiosity, sleepiness and vigilance.

Some men look like personal trainers – they carry backpacks and wear sports shoes. Others are in suits, headed early to their City jobs. A few are drunk, swaying and singing. There's not a single woman on the streets. I walk past a bakery, fully lit, and see two women inside taking trays of muffins out of industrial ovens. A quick search on my phone tells me that the Underground opens soon, so I decide to take a train into the centre of London. At the station I wait half an hour on a deserted platform. A train arrives on the opposite side – empty but for a single man. For the five minutes that it sits in the station I feel lighter, less heart-thumpingly alert. But when the train pulls out I'm alone again, pacing a garishly lit empty station like someone in an Edward Hopper painting. One by one, men arrive – one pulling a wheelie case, two with briefcases, another with a backpack. I am still the only woman.

Where are all the women who work night shifts, I wonder? The cleaners, nurses, carers . . . Later I find them. They don't take the train. They take the night bus. Cheaper. Better lit. Safer.

It's not only our choice of routes and modes of transport that make women different at night. It appears that the biological sexes often *behave* differently in darkness. When researchers observed male participants in dimly lit streets, they noticed a tendency to disinhibition; the men were more likely to behave in ways deemed antisocial on a dimly lit street than on a well-lit street where they might be seen or admonished. But when researchers observed the female participants, they were surprised to find the reverse: women behaved even more 'correctly' on dimly lit streets than they did on well-lit streets.

The researchers then ran a second experiment in which participants were observed while playing a trust game, firstly in a brightly illuminated room and then in a semi-dark room.

Female participants played the game in the same way, regardless of how well lit the room was. But male participants played differently, according to the level of illumination. They were significantly more likely to bend the rules under low lighting than in bright lighting. The authors concluded that, in darkness, men are 'more likely to exhibit ethically problematic behaviors than women'.[12]

How to read this? An indicator of genuine biological difference or merely a reflection of social conditioning? A piece of research that reflects the cultural roots of the respondents? Or the result of evolutionary adaptation?

Either way, the authors' summary ('Darkness decreases men's trustworthiness but increases women's. Darkness decreases men's prosocial behaviors but increases women's.') suggests that most women don't see night as somewhere they naturally belong. Desperate not to attract critical attention – for which we might be punished – we go out of our way to appear 'well behaved', to conform, to be as unseen and invisible as possible.

A 2021 survey bears this out: one in two women feels unsafe walking alone after dark on a quiet local street, compared to one in seven men. One in two women feels unsafe walking alone after dark in a busy public place, compared to one in five men. Four out of five women feel unsafe walking alone after dark in open space, compared to two out of five men.[13]

How did this come to be? How did so many of us allow so few of us to control so much of our time, our space, our lives?

If women are to freely walk cities at night, good lighting is essential. As I walk London's streets I notice that the lighting isn't always designed to protect. Shop lighting exists to attract customers. Roads are lit for cars. Excessively lit areas render unlit areas as black as liquorice. This is the perversity of night lighting: the more you have, the more you need. Light one half of a street, and the other half suddenly looks viscerally dark. Besides, the well-lit half of the street destroys our night vision, making the unlit section terrifyingly shadowy.

In 2018 the engineering company Arup investigated the relationship between lighting and female safety, concluding that most lighting designs 'overlook the . . . vulnerable after dark'. City planners, said Arup, had mistaken quantity for safety, flooding cities with unnecessary lighting or the wrong sort of lighting, and focusing on traffic and business rather than pedestrians. Importantly, artificial night light should fall as sunlight does (engineers call this 'rendering'), allowing women to distinguish between a bush and a person, for example.

'Our current standards prioritise lux levels – which are easy to measure. Yet we don't see the amount of light coming out of a street light. We see what bounces off the surfaces around us,' explained lighting designer Hoa Yang.[14]

Arup's study also found that the wrong sort of lighting often forced women and the more vulnerable to change their habits altogether (taking taxis rather than walking, for example), while others simply decided not to leave their homes at all.

Walking round London – dark streets, well-lit streets, empty streets, peopled streets – I come to understand what makes me feel safe. It's neither lighting nor police on the beat. It's the presence of other women.

My urban night walks leave me in a quandary. I love the idea of cities where women casually saunter through darkness, experiencing the strange joys of a sleeping metropolis. I love the thought of a million female Night Selves freely floating home – no fist of keys, no urgent phone calls or hastily messaged ETAs, no pulsing, pounding heart. But how can we reclaim the urban night – let alone rethink darkness– when unlit streets are sources of irrepressible fear?

'We need more lighting,' says an outraged friend. 'Our safety is more important than darkness. Or moths. Look at Singapore . . .'

She has a point. I once visited Singapore – the brightest place on the planet. So bright that it regularly ranks as the world's most light-polluted country.[15] So bright that 99.5 per cent of stars are no longer visible. The Singapore government recently replaced most of its street lamps with LED (light-emitting diode) bulbs, making the island more radiantly illuminated than ever.

Perhaps unsurprisingly, Singapore – steeped in sticky, seductive light – is renowned for its safety. According to the Women's Danger Index, Singapore is the world's second safest country.[16] Indeed, 92 per cent of women feel safe night-walking in Singapore, making it the safest city on the planet for a lone woman out after dark.[17]

I too had roamed Singapore at night, astounded by the plentiful lighting. Every restaurant sign was backlit. Every tree had lights in it, on it and beneath it. Pavements and handrails were illuminated. Walls were studded with lamps. Neon screens, light installations and signs beamed down from every skyscraper. All of this was cleverly reflected in water and mirrors. It was all so garishly, gaudily brilliant my jet-lagged eyes had ached for hours. But no stars. And no hint of the Milky Way.

As I walked, Singaporeans streamed past me – on bicycles strung with neon lights, on illuminated rollerblades, or wielding light sabres. The city was high on light, its inhabitants exuding the frayed, near-manic energy of the perpetually sleep-deprived or the chemically intoxicated.

Amid this feast of light were dozens of solo women. They sat beneath trees fiddling with their phones. They strolled the illuminated paths. They jogged, and pulled at small fluffy dogs, and heaved bags of shopping, and flashed their phones in an endless succession of selfie poses. All safely visible, all contentedly on their own.

But behind all this safety-in-light lies another narrative: Singaporeans are among the most sleep-deprived people in the world. In a survey of the forty-three most sleep-starved cities, Singapore came third after Tokyo and Seoul (also renowned for their brightly lit nights), with an average 6.8 hours of sleep a night.[18] Another survey found that Singaporeans sleep less than the residents of any of the twenty other countries polled. Could it be the surfeit of artificial light?

In 2022 researchers published a study revealing the startling truth about light-as-you-slumber. Even when we are asleep, light penetrates our eyelids and steals into our brain, unsettling our heart and playing havoc with our metabolism. Night light leaves its toxic traces, no matter how long we sleep, or how many melatonin pills we've swallowed. A single night sleeping in a puddle of dim light (100 lumens is the equivalent of a bulb used to light a European walkway) had multiple consequences: more time trying to get to sleep; less time in deep and REM sleep; a faster heart rate; less heart rate variability; more insulin resistance.[19]

Previous studies found elderly people who slept with a light on were more likely to get Type 2 diabetes, while women who slept in the presence of a flickering TV were more likely to become obese. A 2022 study discovered that female mice repeatedly exposed to very dim night light died at a younger age than mice who slept in darkness. Worryingly, the researchers suggested that 'females are more susceptible to the detrimental consequences' of light disruption. Singapore's breast cancer rates have also been linked to this excess of light. According to one study, 'Singapore has among the highest breast cancer incidence in Asia'.[20]

So is darkness more biologically necessary for women than for men? We don't know. We only know that artificial light-at-night affects us in mysterious, deleterious ways, whether that's a sputtering TV or street lighting seeping through the cracks in our curtains.

Incidentally, a 2019 poll found that a staggering 78 per cent of Singaporeans are afraid of the dark. In fact, darkness was more frightening to them than loneliness, enclosed spaces or going to the dentist.[21] To put this in perspective, the equivalent US figure is around 50 per cent. A substantial difference, suggesting that the more light we have, the more we fear darkness.[22]

On my last evening in Singapore I'd visited the world's only night safari, flabbergasted at the thought of nocturnal wildlife existing in this perpetual aquarium of light. The night safari turned out to be a zoo that stayed open until midnight. When I arrived, there was a squirming mass of overexcited children wearing illuminated wheelies and waving iPhones. Throughout the 'safari' there were coloured lights on tall pedestals, but every now and then I encountered a few seconds of authentic darkness – and I realised how much I'd missed it. I inhaled the smell of night, of damp soil, sap, foliage. I listened to the rattling and scraping of insects. A mosquito whined in my ear. It had taken darkness for my smell cells to awaken, and for my ears to reopen. The glut of Singaporean light had so dazzled my eyes that my other senses had become paralysed, forgotten.

This too is why we need darkness – so that we can live a fully embodied life, so that all our senses can work together in synergy. So that our eyes can rest. So that our lost senses of smell, touch and sound can spring back to renewed life.

In Singapore there was very little distinction between night and day. The one rolled seamlessly into the other. For five days I occupied an everlasting diurnal universe that ended, not with the infinite enigma of a distant star, but with the biggest, brightest screen imaginable. The sizzling, illuminated nights left me fractious and exhausted. After the initial exhilaration of so much brash beauty and night-walking freedom, I longed for the grace and purity of a dark sky, for its seductive chips of starlight and its ungraspable mysteries. I longed for a moon with dignity – in Singapore, even the full moon looked desultory and defeated, lounging in a sweep of electric skyglow. And I longed for the companionable intimacy of friends-in-darkness. Because this too is lost without night.

Thinking back to Singapore makes me want to retreat into cave-ish blackness, particularly as the first anniversary of my father's death is looming. Quite suddenly, I long to be in the darkest place on earth. Me and my memories, wrapped up in the downy darkness of for ever.

16

Revelatory

It is a pity that in Europe they can imagine only the terrors
of the polar night . . . They have no idea that under this
radiant heaven a man's spirit is also calm, clear and radiant.
Christiane Ritter, *A Woman in the Polar Night*

December is the darkest month. And so, five days before the
anniversary of my father's death, I board a boat bound for the
Arctic Circle. I shall be spending *my* darkest day – a day I'm
dreading – in near 24-hour darkness.

In the wintry Arctic Circle, the sun neither rises nor sets. It
crosses the sky beneath the horizon, so that the further north
you go, the less light there is. At its most northerly point,
darkness endures for twenty-four hours. I'm not going quite
that far, so my darkness will prevail for a mere twenty-one hours
each day.

In my bag are my father's collected poems and a copy of *A
Woman in the Polar Night*, Christiane Ritter's hypnotic memoir
of a year lived on one of the world's most northerly islands,
much of it spent alone in total darkness. In 1933 Ritter left her
young daughter in Vienna to live in a rudimentary, isolated hut
on Svalbard, as 'housewife' to her hunter-trapper husband,
Hermann. Her memoir – the only book she ever wrote –
became a bestseller and has never been out of print. The

unending darkness left a powerful impression on Ritter. Later, when her Viennese family home burned to the ground, she watched without any distress, explaining that the polar night had taught her what mattered and what didn't.

For three days we cross the North Sea, chopped green and white. The boat rises and falls, tipping and tilting so that everything in my little cabin flaps, bangs, rattles. Disposable vomit bags are handed out and many of my fellow 'explorers' (which is what this particular ship likes to call us) retire, white-faced and groaning. On we roll, plunging through the half-cracked light. From the empty windblown deck, I watch for whales but see only an impossible immensity of ocean. Every now and then an oil rig looms from the mist, and I wonder about life on board, the weeks spent stranded in windy darkness, far from friends and family.

A fellow passenger – who once worked on a rig – tells me how dangerous it is, that workers must be flown in by helicopter in drysuits that weigh a ton. He reminds me that, although we think of oil rigs as places of men, the support staff are frequently women.

'Oh, don't pity them,' he snorts. 'They make a lot of money and the life on a flotel isn't so bad. You can't drink alcohol but they have cinemas and gyms. And you build a camaraderie that's like no other.'

Thoughts of camaraderie in adversity (the powerful bond forged when human beings are thrown together in unsettling situations) reminded me of the instinct for companionship I'd noticed in my Night Self. With our age-old sense of nocturnal vulnerability, we're more inclined to befriend others after dark. Besides, there are practical reasons. In a group, the surveillance can be shared. We can relax our tendency to vigilance. We feel safer.

Every night I walk around the ship, looking at the stars, feeling the sea wind on my face. Most of the gangways are lit.

But there are no lights on the bow. This is the darkest corner, kept lamp-free so that the Northern Lights can be clearly seen. No matter how many times I circle the ship, this corner fills me with terror. The same old terror: of someone creeping up behind me and hurling me overboard, into the waves, where I'll drown, abandoned and unnoticed.

On the night before the anniversary of my father's death, my sleep is riven with nightmares – of bone-numbing cold, of the boat sinking in a *Titanic*-style disaster, of the North Sea's oil-black waters closing over my head. I pull back the little curtains and peer out of my porthole. The night is clear, stars shining like bright expectant eyes. A battered moon drifts past, and I stare at the distant edge of things, hoping I might glimpse the green and violet of the Northern Lights. Bucked by the wind, the boat rocks and sways, and eventually I return to sleep.

When I wake up night has rotated into day. The sky is a deep indigo blue, with a faint line of pinky-gold smudged along the horizon. Spume crackles beneath my window. Ahead, the hills rise like pale glittering teeth.

Later, I step off the boat and walk towards a hill. My booted feet, in their steel crampons, crunch through the ice, and the thin frozen air seems to loosen the tightness in my chest – the pinch that hovers at the rim of my ribcage. I glance up and see something that surprises me. I've seen nothing but seagulls for the last four days, but above me a pair of eagles circle lazily. Confounded by this sudden appearance, I ask a passer-by if the birds are really eagles.

'Oh yes, they are golden eagles,' the man says. 'We have many eagles in this part of Norway.'

I smile and thank him. I don't tell him the truth: that these are not regular Norwegian eagles, these are the spirit of my father come to fortify me.

That evening a voice blares into the cabin: *Northern Lights! Northern Lights!*

I grab my coat and gloves, pull on my boots and dash up to the bow. The ship's lights have been turned off so that, as I stagger down the walkway, familiar things are now unfamiliar, bulked with strangeness. Blackness humped upon blackness. Shadows pounce from cracks and corners. The wind roars in my ears. I turn onto the bow and the wind shunts me backwards so brutally I have to cling to the iced handrail and press forward half choked. My feet slip and slide on the frozen deck, and the metal rail unloads its glassy chill through my gloves, into my fingers.

Eventually I drag myself through the violent squalls, and turn out of the wind. A small cluster of passengers huddle, pressed against the body of the ship and pointing at the sky. I'm expecting the neon brilliance – emerald green, electric purple – of the photographs in *National Geographic* magazine. But this isn't the aurora borealis I see. Instead, an arc wavers faintly in the sky, a spectral ribbon of faintest light. It shifts in a pale slow-motion dance.

'It's just a cloud,' says one woman, crossly. 'It's not like the pictures is it?' She stomps off, teeth chattering with cold and fury.

I lean on the deck and watch this strange ethereal light that only reveals itself in the depths of night. As my vision adapts to the dark, I notice that the light in the sky is tinged a pale bleached green. It shifts and sways: a scarf of diaphanous silk rippling from the heavens.

The days get shorter, darker. Each night I return to the abandoned deck, my hand gripping the railing as my feet slide round on the ice. The wind tears at my throat as I stare into the sky. The stars seem lower here, closer. Indeed, they seem to hang directly over my head. At night Cassiopeia is my crown. When I come out at dawn, she has been replaced by the Big Dipper.

The stars are not only larger and closer but also brighter and more abundant. I want to lie down and gaze upwards, but the deck is like glass. So I strain and crane.

Later, Matthew messages me: *Of course the stars aren't closer! You are still at sea level obviously. But the darkness will make them seem brighter. That's all . . .*

Quite.

The further north we go, the colder it gets, and the brighter and more dramatic are the Northern Lights. It seems to me that the aurora borealis is yet another gift of darkness. Its soft green hues are endlessly mesmerising. Like the broad beam of some celestial spotlight, the lights sweep through the sky, pale lofty arcs, hovering behind hills, shimmying starwards or simply pausing, floating, before disappearing into nothing.

The drama of their nocturnal appearance adds to the excitement. Most of us are in bed when the announcements come. We leap up, throw clothes on back to front and inside out, and scurry to the deck, missing a glove or a sock, pyjama legs hanging from beneath our coats, hats skewed and scarves dangling, clutching cameras and tripods. Some passengers flash their camera at the sky, mutter about the arctic winds, and shuffle back in as quickly as they came. A few of us lurk for hours, watching silently as our fingers grow numb and our tilted necks stiffen into lines of pain. And beyond the aurora, through the thick clots of darkness, a billion points of chilling light flash out – specks of hope in the amorphous blue of night.

Why sleep when the sky is so wondrously alive?

Dawn limps in later and later each morning. When we reach Tromsø – the gateway to the Arctic – the sun neither rises nor sets. And although the morning is illuminated with gauzy slices of pink and blue light, most of the day is pitch black. Finally we reach the North Cape, the most northerly point in Europe. A sunless place where the polar night persists for two months, and where I plan to hike in snowshoes for the three scant hours of light we've been promised.

Shortly before leaving London I'd had supper with a writer who once spent a season on Svalbard. I confessed my concern about being in constant darkness, and admitted that I'd bought a SAD lamp and extra-high-dose vitamin D pills. Would I feel depressed? How would I sleep if I couldn't set my circadian clock with a decent dose of bright dawn light?

'I was there in summer,' she explained. 'It was light for twenty-four hours a day. There was no night.'

I frowned, unsure which most horrified me – unceasing light or perpetual dark? I'd once spent a summer week in Norway, awake until midnight and then waking at 4 a.m. as the sharp light filtered into my bedroom, like blades on my eyes.

'Oh, the body gets used to anything,' she said breezily. 'I loved the 24-hour light. I just wrote for hours. I didn't sleep much, I didn't seem to need it.'

'Yes, but that's the summer,' I muttered. I didn't say that, although I was learning to love the darkness at night, I didn't think I would love it during the day.

'Oh, you're worried about going *rar*,' she laughed. *Rar* was Christiane Ritter's term for the Svalbard hunters, who 'lost all standard of reality in the loneliness and darkness'. Many threw themselves into the floe-cold sea and died. Ritter herself travelled to the edge of sanity in her early days of perpetual darkness, writing: 'They [her husband and his friend, Karl] maintain that I am moonstruck . . . [they] are very strict with me. They do not let me out of their sight and often keep me under house arrest.'

I nodded and thought of the physiological symptoms experienced by Ritter, who, after seventy-eight days of darkness, wrote, 'we look pale yellow, like plants kept in a cellar, and our skin is flaccid and shrivelled'. Karl turned 'very pale' and his eyes grew 'more and more colourless. But that is what happens in the winter night,' Ritter explained.[1]

At the most northerly corner of Europe, the wind yowls, lifting and blowing the snow so that it rolls across the bleak barren land in great sugary gusts. We arrive in a thin misty light of palest blue and plod, in our cumbersome snowshoes, through deep-sifted snow, up and up towards . . . nothing. The land has no beginning and no end, it simply rolls into the sky. The wind freezes my face and my fingers become so bloodlessly numb I must wriggle them constantly.

At midday, the sky's rim turns a pale apocalyptic yellow. The light then drains from the sky and by 1 p.m. it's twilight – a deep cobalt blue. The Norwegians call this the 'blue hour', when the residual light reflects from the snow and the sea, dousing the landscape in a glass-blue radiance. It's a time (and hue) beloved of Norwegian landscape painters, who must snatch it before it disappears. As winter passes, the blue hour shifts, becoming a few minutes later each day. In the depths of December, though, it arrives at around 1 p.m., sidling into darkness an hour later.

But I'm in the most northerly corner and by 1.30 p.m. the 'blue hour' has passed. It's pitch black, which makes me feel curiously disorientated. We return to the boat, but the darkness has induced in me such a sense of sleepiness I can do nothing but crawl into bed. Later, a Norwegian crew member tells me this is quite normal, and that inhabitants of the Arctic Circle often feel sleepier in winter.

And yet repeated studies show that, contrary to expectation, the long polar nights often result in more insomnia and a greater prevalence of sleep disruption than during the endlessly light summer. In 2011 researchers examined the sleep habits of a community in northern Norway, comparing them to a community in Ghana where both light and temperature are constant and unchanging. The Ghanaians' sleep patterns were consistent throughout the year, but the Norwegians recorded shifting sleep patterns that reflected the seasons. Their mental and physical energy waned during the colder darker months, while their tendency to insomnia increased. They went to bed later, found it harder to fall asleep, and slept less well than during the light-filled summer months – despite *feeling* significantly more fatigued.

How so? Because we need morning light to set our circadian rhythms. Or, as the authors of this study say, if we don't get enough morning light we find it harder to sleep. We're inclined to feel lethargic, less mentally alert and – if we're female – fractionally more depressed. In other words, it's not the surfeit of darkness our body and brain dislike, but the paucity of morning light.

Morning light – with its high proportion of blue waves – hits the back of our retina, prompting our body to blast us with cortisol, the hormone that makes us feel alert and energetic. Morning light also reminds our brain to turn off the melatonin that makes us feel sleepy.

But since that study was published the picture has become a little murkier. Contradictory studies have appeared. Researchers have criticised earlier reports for having too-small sample sizes. The swamping artificial light we live with has made it harder to untangle study findings. Other overlooked factors play a role – altitude, temperature, social isolation, activity patterns, the age and sex of participants, and so on. Despite this, the general consensus remains: we feel sleepier but we actually sleep less well during 24-hour darkness.[2] As Ritter put it in her memoir, 'at night we lie down, neither tired nor wakeful'.[3]

Given that we produce more melatonin in extended darkness, it seems right that we should *feel* listless and sleepier. But what actually happens is more complex. In a 2017 study two participants spent ten days in constant darkness, during which time they began producing melatonin in the morning while their night-time supplies dwindled. By the end of the experiment, they produced as much melatonin during the day as during the night.[4]

Studies of laboratory rodents subjected to long periods of darkness found other effects, including reduced thyroid activity (lethargy, low mood, poor concentration) and plunging sperm count.[5] Certain hormones simply dried up (like hypothalamic thyrotropin-releasing hormone or TRH, which acts rather like an antidepressant), and the rodents quickly exhibited signs of low mood and fatigue, with a marked disinclination to move. Female rats became more depressed than male rats, suggesting a biological sex effect that needs unpicking further.

Meanwhile constant darkness also affected the rodents' hippocampi (the brain region associated with memory and learning), so the animals began to display impaired cognition and failing memory. All of this happened within seven days of total darkness, to the surprise of researchers, who concluded that 'light deprivation shapes the brain in developing pups and in adults, which end up with damaged neural systems, maladaptive behaviors, dysfunctional physiology, and impaired cognition'.

Incidentally, most research into the effects of extended light or dark is now carried out on animals and the same effects may not be replicated in humans. Either way, it's generally accepted that both animals and humans need a predictable balance of light and dark.

So how will I feel in this ever-expanding darkness?

I keep returning to the study that compared Ghanaian and north Norwegian students, because what really strikes me is this: despite the Norwegians' seasonal sleep disruptions, their long polar nights, their dramatically altered sense of mental tiredness, the Ghanaians reported the highest levels of anxiety and depression. Despite all that consistently predictable light and warmth.[6]

It goes to show that there's always another story lurking beneath the data.

That evening I'm lured out to the deck by another display of the Northern Lights.

As the North Sea pounds against the ship, arching veils of light rise to a green turbulence, razor-sharp winds squall and blow, and the deck pops with passengers and their phones and tripods, stumbling around in the briny darkness, cursing and exclaiming and click-click-clicking.

Most of my fellow passengers seem more interested in capturing a vivid image (which they then edit to make yet more vivid) than in watching the aurora borealis. This ethereal otherworld has become a photo opportunity, a moment to be captured, consumed and shared on social media. I hadn't bothered to master the necessary settings on my camera, so it rebelled, refusing to capture anything. Instead, I spent the next few hours huddled on the stern, shivering with cold, watching the aurora gently wavering across a sky of blinking stars, unimpeded by the need to angle, frame, focus, share. As I crouched there, I thought back to my earlier night walks, when the deck was deserted and the black sea thrashed all around me and the raging wind filled my ears. I had felt frighteningly alone then, subjected to the illiterate imaginings of my Night Self. Now I feel an immediate and companionable calm. I even relish the endless flashing of iPhones.

Ritter learned a similar lesson: alone in the dark for days on end, she felt herself 'disintegrating . . . [in] the intense loneliness'. She had no phone, radio or pet. She had no idea if her husband and Karl would ever return. 'There is nothing like me, no one I can meet face to face who can confirm my existence. I feel as if I am losing the limits of my being . . . for the first time I realise what a heavenly gift a human being is.'

When the men finally returned, Ritter felt as joyous as 'a canary', writing, 'Now I know who I am again.'

The shorter the days, the more I appreciate the glow of light as it creeps, tantalisingly, over the horizon. At 10 a.m., swaddled in layers, I go on deck to watch the sky brighten. I've noticed that the longer and darker the night, the more pleasurable is the mid-morning dawn. Temperature works in the same way: the colder I become, the more gratifying is the return to my cabin. Company also works in this way: the longer I'm alone, the more I appreciate other people. And so it goes on. This sudden flash of understanding was one of Ritter's polar epiphanies, striking her after a 'titanic storm' that prompted an unprecedented appreciation of the ensuing 'peacefulness'. In her memoir, she asked, 'Do we really need the force of contrast to live intensely?' Yes, we do, she concluded, adding that 'Perhaps in centuries to come men will go to the Arctic as in biblical times they withdrew to the desert, to find the truth again.'

Alone, in the cold and dark, I experience Ritter's 'force of contrast'. And it reminds me that the death of someone we love works in a similar way: their absence magnifies their earlier presence. And in the vacuum created by their departure, our own feelings are amplified, be they feelings of regret, guilt, sadness or gratitude.

Which is really to say that we must have absence to appreciate presence, loss to appreciate life, darkness to appreciate light. Or, as Ritter put it on the final page of her memoir, 'You must live through the long night . . . You must have gazed on the deadness of all things to grasp their livingness.'

I wake up regularly during the long nights. Sometimes the swell of the sea awakens me; sometimes it's the sudden rattling of a cupboard door. I draw back the curtains and peer out. In urban areas, the coastline is strung with blazing artificial lights. The black, empty stretches of coastline are marked by the faintest of lines and angles where mountains rise and fall. At sea, the darkness has a texture and quality all of its own. At home I can guess the time from the sound of traffic or the quality of light seeping through the shutters. But here there's only the rocking of the ocean, the soft throb of the ship's engine and the smouldering night sky. I dream of staying up late on deck, sitting under the chilly stars for hours, but all this darkness is so soporific I can barely keep my eyes open. I return to sleep with a speed I've never previously experienced. A speed I slightly resent. My customary night watch is being swallowed by sleep, with barely a moment to enjoy the soothing sensations of the deep polar night.

We're fast approaching the shortest day of the darkest month. Daylight has dwindled to a paltry two hours of dusky blue. Despite my plentiful sleep, I start to feel a little sad at the edges. I felt better when I slept less but spent my days doused in light. My bed beckons to me constantly. So I go back to Ritter, back to her advice for avoiding the 'long paralysis' – which is to keep constantly, mindlessly busy. Ritter nurtures a mania for 'sewing, mending and polishing'. I write, and fiddle around on social media, and turn my desk away from the black porthole and the soft allure of my single bed. Do not sleep. Do not lie down. Do not even remove your shoes . . .

When news reached the Ritters of Europe's imminent war, Hermann told his wife they'd be catching the next ship home.

She agreed. Until one insomniac, revelatory night when she knew she couldn't leave the isolated, bleakly beautiful island of Svalbard. The next morning she told Hermann she couldn't go. Not yet. She was so smitten with the polar night that even the prospect of seeing her daughter couldn't entice her away.

Sometimes it takes a wide-awake night to hear the murmurs of our deepest yearnings. Our most secret *rars*.

My sleep starts fragmenting, until I'm waking up three or four times a night. Sometimes I'm too hot, sometimes I'm too cold, sometimes my wardrobe doors wake me with their ceaseless rattle. Sometimes I wake from a nightmare in which the ship is sinking. One night I dream of the 6,000 men drowned in a single battle during the Second World War, their bodies lying at the bottom of the ocean at the North Cape.

The ship turns round and we start the journey home. Darkness sets in at 2.30 rather than 1.30 and, one day, as I watch the illuminated coast rush by, I realise that it's not the early darkness I dislike but the gaudy glut of electric light. It looks pretty enough from a distance, reflecting on the water, illuminating the cheerful interiors of family homes. But who wants to live constantly in the uniform blandness of artificial light?

In Svalbard, where darkness fell for 132 days, of which around 75 were pitch black, Ritter had no electric light. She slept when she needed to, unconstrained by any obligations to socialise, to work, to deliver a child to school. Light came from the stars and the moon, from the fire in her wood stove, from candles or an oil lamp – a light that was soft, supple, many-hued.

As the darkness settled in, Ritter felt her 'living senses begin to go their own way'. Her soul sprang to life: 'a strange light spreads before the inner eye ... it is as though here ... we develop a particularly sharp awareness of the mighty laws of the spirit'. In the light of this revelation, Ritter recalled the Europeans she had left behind, noting that 'the people who live under the sun seem distant and small . . . With bent heads they are running round in circles, the circles of their anxieties and troubles.'

Daylight, Ritter suggested, is not all it's cracked up to be. For our inner eye to open, we need darkness.

'I like all this dark,' says a woman over supper. 'It's comforting, like having a blanket wrapped round you. I feel it gives me permission to relax, to stop being so busy. To just *be* . . .'

'I've been to bed twice today,' says another woman. 'I just feel so tired. I have a morning nap and then an afternoon nap. So indulgent!'

'I hate it,' says a man at our table. 'It makes me on edge. I could never live here.' He shivers, then shakes his head. 'Not in a million years.'

After two weeks of darkness, I've read 173 of my father's poems. I feel as if I've lifted the bonnet of his mind, peered into its dusty corners. I've seen the fruits of his compulsive night spinning and watched him navigate his own darkness.

Five years before he died, my father stopped writing. For the previous two decades he'd been working on a project of epic proportion – a tome he called *The Story of the Self*. For years it gripped his imagination, becoming almost an obsession. This, he said, was to be the world's first and fullest history of autobiography, an audacious quest to examine the ways in which *Homo sapiens* constructs an identity and a sense of self. Every now and then the postman would deliver a large brown envelope containing a draft of his latest chapter. Sometimes I read them; other times I hurriedly put them in a pile for later.

And then the envelopes stopped coming. When I asked about the progress of his life's work (for that's how he spoke of it), he mumbled, avoided my question. After three years of silence, he confessed that he was taking a break from it. In truth he had lost his way.

One evening he phoned and told me there was something I needed to know. Not only had his book stalled, he said, but he hadn't written any poetry for three years either. He was about to start therapy, he explained. He'd been suffering from depression, 'a sort of darkness', he called it, but he hadn't wanted anyone to know. He still wasn't sleeping, he added, although he had some pills now. Anyway, he was getting help and he just wanted to keep me informed.

I was startled at this late confession. Why hadn't he told me earlier? Why hadn't I noticed anything? What should I do? When I relayed our conversation to Matthew, he looked at me, baffled. 'How could you not have seen?'

But no daughter, whatever her age, wants to see her father bludgeoned by his own inner darkness. Physical illness is different. We can care for him, coax him to eat the delicacies we've cooked, adjust the pillows at his back. We can *do* something. Which is not to say it's any easier, only that we can find a sort of purpose, a role for ourselves.

I conferred with my brother and sister. We agreed to send him regular messages. Just checking in, we called it. And then the busyness of our lives consumed us once again.

Slowly, my ship returns to the light. On our first day outside the Arctic Circle, the sun is so low and so glaringly bright I'm half blinded. Its rays flash and leap from windows, creating shimmering pools of gold that ripple over the sea. *Look at me*, it shrieks. *Look at me! Aren't I beautiful?*

The ship stops and we disembark in a small town. I take shadowy streets in a bid to avoid the sun's garish dazzle, which makes my eyes hurt. Besides, all this light makes me feel suddenly visible and exposed. Any of the other strolling passengers might spot me and decide I need a companion. So I find a dark sunless street and start walking out of town.

I've become one of those shadowy nocturnal animals, terrified of the light that makes it instantly visible and immediately vulnerable to predation. Darkness has become my new protector.

'The winters are long,' says Hilde, who works on the ship and used to live in Svalbard. 'But mostly people die by suicide when the sun comes. Not when it's twenty-four hours of dark.'

She's right. Studies have consistently found that death from suicide peaks in spring and summer and is at its lowest in December, the darkest month of all.[7]

I keep waking in the dead hours, restive, pulled remorselessly from sleep to which I cannot return. I shake out the duvet, remove a pillow, rearrange my limbs. I lie very still for a bit, then get up and look out of the porthole. I contemplate visiting the captain and his navigator up on the bridge. The navigation crew work in shifts of four hours, twenty-four hours a day. Four hours on, then four hours off. The Norwegian coastline is one of the most challenging in the world. There are strong currents, shallow waters, rocky outcrops, fast-changing weather conditions, and some stretches are so complex that a specialist navigator must come aboard. 'You have to sail the Norwegian coast for five years before you can captain a ship like this,' the navigation officer had explained earlier.

Needless to say, this doesn't help me sleep. Haunted by dreams of hitting an iceberg, I eventually plug in my earbuds and listen to an audiobook. I wake an hour later, toss and turn, doze, wake, fantasise (again) about visiting the night captain, then wonder if he's fallen asleep in his navigating chair . . . in which case surely we are all dead?

All these thoughts set the darkness echoing.

I can barely imagine a full night of sleep. How dull it would be – bereft of strange imaginings and discourses, of delusions and fantasies, shorn of all night thoughts and night smells and night sounds . . . My Night Self shunted into oblivion . . .

Nor can I imagine a life without darkness. And yet our lust for light is changing the world irrevocably. Artificial light drains the shadows, edges, corners from life. It blots out stars, comets, the Milky Way. It threatens moths, glow-worms, bats and birds. It feeds and fattens our primal fear of darkness. It weakens our night vision. It dulls our ability to smell, to hear, to register temperature and texture. It deprives us of the healing capabilities of nocturne.

I'm beginning to realise that it's no longer darkness or death or a few evil men that frightens me. It's the prospect of a future deprived of darkness. As Sigri Sandberg wrote in *An Ode to Darkness*, 'Scarcity of darkness is more frightening than darkness itself.'

On our last evening on land we hike up a mountain on the edge of Bergen, starting in the city centre, which is awash in Christmas glow, every street hung with festive lights, every window illuminated. As we climb higher and higher, we leave the city and begin zigzagging through dark pine woods. We can no longer see the detail of things, but as our eyes adjust we make out darkened outlines and shapes – the tips of branches, the massed foliage, the twisting path ahead. The cloud cover is too thick for stars, but a veiled waxing moon floats above us, her vague light reflected in the acres of snow and ice. The landscape feels still and peaceful, so that when our guide hands out head torches we take them but do not use them.

After three miles of winding through fir trees and darkness, we reach the summit and look down on the gleaming flickering city, its edges marked by the floodlights of stadiums and running tracks and the dazzle of ships in the port. We sigh, exclaim, pull out our phones. With its thousands of gold and silver lights, reflecting from the black waters of the harbour, stretching into the dark mountains, the extravagantly lit city is indisputably, ravishingly beautiful.

And yet a mere century ago it would have looked nothing like this. Although oil and fat have been burned for hundreds of years in order to create light, this was done only when necessary. Burning fat made houses smelly, smoky and dirty. It carried the ever-present risk of fire, and the light it produced was indistinct and cloudy. In the 1840s we discovered how to distil lamp oil. Suddenly oil could dazzle with its clean, clear light. By the 1860s, oil was a vital part of our lives. But by then we had electricity. And now we have LEDs, and our world is saturated in cheap, homogeneous and addictive light.

Much later, when I looked back on my time in the Arctic Circle, it was the polar light I remembered: the misty aurora borealis streaming through the thick unending darkness; the stars so silver-bright they seemed to hang immediately above my head; the moon a crescent of thinnest ice; the few hours of scraped light – opaquely blue and fraily pink turning to amber, tangerine, gold.

In the failing heart of winter, free from the sun's grip, the light was the cleanest, softest, most serene light I'd ever encountered.

An ice wind blows as I take my last turn round the deck. For the last two weeks I've been scouring the ocean for whales, dolphins and unusual birds. But the middle of the North Sea is a lonely place, and I've seen nothing except the odd gull. As I'm hovering at the stern, watching the wind's calligraphy on the sea and the grey slanting light, a bird comes into view. Is it a gull? It seems larger than a gull . . . and it's not white but brown. It follows the ship for a bit, the only bird in this impossibly vast and hollow sky. I squint at it. Yes, it's definitely brown, speckledy brown. And such a large wingspan . . .

Then it changes direction, its wings beating against the cold air. The ship ploughs on, churning its trail of white and green foam. I crane over the railing, and the bird becomes smaller and smaller until it's a mere dot on the horizon.

'Dad?' I say.

But the bird has gone.

17

Healing

I am what I apprehend.
What I have struggled with is who I am.
Peter Abbs, 'Epilogue Poem: The Apple'

I return from the Arctic Circle to repeat an experiment carried out
by psychiatrist and researcher Thomas Wehr in the 1990s. Wehr
wanted to know if a primeval sleep pattern was encoded in our
genes. Had cave people slept differently? And if so, could modern
humans return to those primitive sleep rhythms somehow? Wehr
hypothesised that our brightly lit post-industrial world had caused
us to cram our once-natural sleep into a single (less natural) block.
He also speculated that – in the right conditions – we moderns
might be able to revert to ancient sleep patterns.

For a month, eight men lived without artificial light, spending
fourteen hours (dusk to dawn) in darkness and ten hours in light,
a light–dark ratio typical of a British winter. The men were
allowed out during the day, but after dusk they were confined to
rooms without music, screens, entertainment or light.

For the first three weeks, the men slept in a single segment.
But in the last week they began sleeping in two blocks (of
between three and five hours) with a wakeful one to three hours
in between. During these sleepless hours the men appeared to
be neither fully awake nor fully asleep, but in a state of mystical,

Zen-like calm they had never previously experienced. Wehr's tests revealed that, during this partially conscious time, the men had raised levels of prolactin – a semi-sedative hormone produced at night and typically higher in breastfeeding mothers and nesting birds.[1] I wanted to know if a woman might respond differently.

I tell my family that the cottage is returning to 'cave' conditions and that electric light is banned. Unsurprisingly, they show no interest in the deep mystical sleep allegedly enjoyed by our ancestors. Instead they flee – clutching their many screens – to London.

This December has been the greyest and darkest month since 1956, with a mere twenty-six hours of sunlight. It has rained almost every day and the sky is a perpetual sagging blanket of cloud. The thought of being without light fills me with foreboding, more so since our remote and gloomy cottage has recently been burgled. I decide to modify Wehr's 'cave' experiment: I'll use candles and firelight after dark.

On my first night of darkness I light a candle and go straight to bed, a cricket bat on either side of me. The flame is too wavering and dim to read by, so I blow the candle out. To my astonishment I sleep all night, the first night in weeks that I've slept through. When I wake it's 6 a.m. I light the candle and watch my shadow moving: I am two people now, one flesh and blood and one vast and trembling, stretched across the ceiling. The room springs to life as the flame reflects in every surface, sending shapes and shadows across the walls. But it's too dark to do much, so I pull up the blind. The sky is as black as tar and boiling with stars. I wonder how it is that I can barely see by candlelight and yet the light from a star millions of miles away is so clearly visible.

★

In 2018 Dr Diane Barret began collecting cow's eyeballs from a local abattoir. For two years her days were spent in the most arduous and painstaking of work, as she extracted a tiny protein from the membrane wrapped round the rod cells in each eyeball. By examining this protein beneath a very powerful microscope, Barret worked out how cows' eyes – and the eyes of crocodiles, eagles and humans – evolved to see distant shreds of light.[2]

The rod cells we use for night vision are so light-sensitive that, although they can't see colour, they can detect a single photon of illumination even when it's from the outer reaches of the galaxy. These light beams, however small or far away, are then turned into a visual impression (a light burst) by our brain – thanks in part to this microscopic protein that opens up the rod cells in darkness but closes them during the day. Our night-eyes, it appears, were designed to recognise the tiniest fragments of light – the far-off flicker of fire, the gleaming eye of a predator, a distant star.

Miraculous really, how the tiniest of things (a hidden thread of protein on an invisible cell's membrane) can reveal to us the most colossal of all things – the universe.

I get back into bed, feeling sleepy after my eyeball thoughts. An hour later I take a shower by candlelight – an oddly enjoyable experience that my ancestors wouldn't have bothered with, but I need to wash my hair. I take my candle to the kitchen, make coffee, then stare out of the window as the sun slowly rises, a thin tissue of blue light, then a band of pale gold lifting from the frosty fields. It's the first morning in weeks that I've drunk coffee in the promise of sunlight, and that too feels miraculous.

Did I sleep all night because I went to bed early with a candle? When Sean Cain surveyed the homes of Melbourne, he found half were so brightly lit that melatonin production was suppressed by 50 per cent. We've known about light-at-night for decades:

Professor Richard Stevens, a cancer epidemiologist, had his catalysing moment in the early 1980s when he linked electric light to a rise in breast cancer. Subsequent studies showed that melatonin could shrink breast tumours in rats. Stevens is unequivocal: 'Our use of electric light in the modern world is disrupting our circadian sleep and our biology. There is no question about that.' Artificial light, he says, is the major factor in spiralling rates of obesity, depression and cancer.[3] Oh – and insomnia.

In the wild, our bodies start producing melatonin around dusk. So when the light falls at 4 p.m. I let the cottage darken. To avoid chopping vegetables – or my fingers – in candlelight, I cook supper now. As the light dwindles I feel myself becoming more anxious. It's not the incoming darkness that worries me any more. It's the prospect of my own irrepressible fear. A fear born of knowing that thieves have been inside my (largely security-less) cottage, that I am alone and out of all earshot, that I am vulnerable – and that this will be amplified by my biochemically altered night brain.

By 4.30 p.m. the cottage is completely dark. I blindly prod spaghetti in a pan of boiling water, then I light the fire, fumbling and cursing. The fire goes out. So I light my candles and wonder how I'm to survive six hours with nothing but a pair of puny flames. I briefly turn my laptop on (yes, cheating) and am shocked at the flaring light of the screen, which is a hundred times brighter and whiter than any candle.

By 5 p.m. I have no light other than a fire roaring away in a gush of orange flames. But how beautiful it is, like warm liquid gold. The whole room seems to dance in this moving, living light; even the shadowy corners possess tones and contours. Without the blank, bland light of the filament bulb, the room has become a place of liminal spaces and imaginative possibilities.

But as time slowly ticks by, the initial romance of sitting in flame-lit darkness wears off. It's only 6 p.m., but the dark is beginning to feel oppressive. I keep thinking of all the things I should be doing but can't because my laptop is experimentally banned and it's too dark and I'm by myself in the middle of nowhere. The cottage night music begins – inexplicable thumps and thuds, raspings and rattlings. At every sound I stiffen instantly, feel my heart become a fist.

Funny how a home can turn so swiftly from a place of joy and gaiety to a place of unsettling emptiness. No wonder we humans are so fond of music, TV, social media, company. I love our little cottage: my favourite pictures hang here, my favourite books line the shelves. Which is all very well, but I'm coming to see that it's people who make a place, not things. Especially after dark. Suddenly I long for the press and sweat of London.

Anthropologist Richard Wrangham believes that the discovery of fire turned us from primate to *Homo sapiens* because fire gave us digestible cooked food, enabling us to spend less time chewing and giving us the biological resources to reshape our bodies and brains. But he also argues that cooking over fire marked the beginning of patriarchy. Cooked food was so valuable that women became 'cooking chattels' in need of 'protectors' to ensure their food wasn't stolen by other men (and yes, Wrangham says, it was always men). Two hundred thousand years ago the campfire provided light, warmth and quick-to-eat cooked food. But it also made women vulnerable, its smoke and cooking smells alerting men to the possibility and location of food-to-be-pilfered. Only by surrounding herself with others or by having a strong male 'protector' could a woman stay safe.[4]

And this is why my experiment is destined to fail. To be alone beside an open fire is not a happy molecular memory. I need companions to help quash the out-of-control feeling that accompanies all this firelit darkness. Besides, flames require perpetual work and surveillance – the fire must be kept alive with logs, sparks must be swiftly stamped out, excess smoke must be cleared. To be alone with a fire is unproductive, dangerous, lonely.

History confirms this: women invariably shared the precious heat and light of a fire as well as the work needed to maintain it. Spinning bees were a popular after-dark activity that took place communally, around a fire. Friends, family and neighbours rotated round each other's houses, bringing their own spinning wheels and often walking three or four miles to and from their local spinning bee. Sharing the light and heat made fiscal sense. And it was safer. More importantly, the physical intimacy of a fire-after-dark lent itself to the exchanging of confidences and the cementing of neighbourly bonds. This was often the only time women had to socialise, to share problems, to escape abusive husbands, to nourish a vital sense of community. The truth is, women were very rarely alone by firelight. Little wonder I feel oddly vulnerable.

Earlier in the day a friend had told me about an Israeli experiment in which volunteers gave up artificial evening light and then slept much better, with dramatic improvements in mood and attention the following day.[5] 'Stick with it,' she urged me.

So, again, I go to bed by candlelight. But on this night my sleep is as fragmented as ever. When I wake up it's only 1 a.m. I hear distant traffic and, for the first time, I find it deeply comforting. I can't get back to sleep because I ate supper nine hours earlier and my stomach is growling incessantly. I don't want to light my candle, carry it to the kitchen and grope about in the brightly lit fridge. So I pull the duvet over my head. But tonight my mind whirls with fragments of ghost stories, clips of horror films, the plots of ghoulish tales told at spinning bees.

Then I hear a loud thud. I freeze. Are the burglars back? Is the cottage haunted?

I summon my Day Self with her voice of reason. But it's too late – she hasn't got a chance.

And then I remember what to do. I get up, lift the blind and stare out at the prickling stars above. My pulse slows, my breath lengthens, my mind opens like a clam. The immediacy of my recovery – for what else is it? – feels like wizardry.

And in my sudden calmness I remind myself that a dearth of light fuels fear, much as being alone beside a fire does – but only if I let it. It's our biology, put in place to protect us. But it's also evolutionary. Over millennia, we have learned to fear anything that makes us vulnerable. Whether that's predators, adverse weather conditions or merely the chance of falling over in the dark. For centuries this fear was exploited by anyone who wanted women confined to the home. And so we must accept our neurobiological fear, and accommodate it as best we can. But we must never be contained, controlled or diminished by it. Instead, we must look it in the eye, speak to it.

And this is why I grope my way to the wardrobe, blindly drag on clothes and step out into the blackness.

If we're not lying awake ruminating or frightened of our own fear, we're lying awake frightened of our sleeplessness. 'The anticipation of sleep,' declared David Robson in *New Scientist* magazine, can 'put someone in a state of high arousal at the very time they need to be relaxing. There is evidence that people with insomnia show heightened activity in the amygdala . . . if anything reminds them of sleep.' Robson calls this 'a type of self-fulfilling prophecy' where our fears of not sleeping strangle all chance of actually sleeping. 'The more that people worry about their sleep loss,' he adds, 'the worse their symptoms – independent of how well they are actually sleeping.'[6]

I make a pledge to myself: I will never ever worry about my sleep – the quantity, quality or shape of it – again.

With all this mingling in my head I walk over the darkened fields, my boots squelching in the sodden grass, my ears full of the low shivering calls of unknown birds. The stars have gone, replaced by heavy cloud and leaving the sky so thickly dark I can almost touch it. Far into the distance I see the scattered lights of farms and houses – my neighbours to the north, south, east and west. A few months ago their lights infuriated me. I wanted every light extinguished. I wanted our night skies returned in all their inky purity. But now I thrill at each glimmer of buttery yellow. They speak to me of human life, of safety, of company and community, softening the edge of my amygdala-kindled fear.

The fear I felt inside, in bed, vanishes as quickly as it came, reappearing only briefly when the sudden fluster of a pigeon startles me. The aloneness and vulnerability disappear too. Not just because I can see the faraway lights of neighbouring houses but because I have company now. The truth is, our Night Selves are never alone. They exist in a giddy, unfamiliar cauldron of activity, in a whirl of ravishing unseen beauty. Seventy per cent of mammals and 50 per cent of insects are nocturnal. Venture into the ocean and we find an entire world on the move. Even now, as I pick my way over the fields, I am companioned by a myriad of unseen creatures.

I walk on, slowly, quietly, because this is their time and their place. I am merely passing through. A guest, of sorts.

A day later a friend tells me her local pack of wolves has been hunted almost to extinction. 'All I want to do is sit round a campfire with close friends, drink beer and cry,' she says, adding that her fire pit has become her unconscious place of catharsis. 'Fire feels important . . . the space it makes for silence, for the grief we rarely allow ourselves.'

A fire encourages us to pause, to note its bright flicker, to hear its cracklings and mutterings. Fireside silence is an utterly sociable silence. But, alone, my experience of it had shifted.

'Would your fire pit have been as cathartic if you'd been alone?' I ask.

She pauses. Then says, with complete certainty, 'Oh I could never be truly alone with fire. I don't like the sound of that at all . . . No, I like being alone by a fire for a few minutes of decompression, but only with family and friends close by. *Very* close by.'

And so I also learn that, although I'm not ready to sit alone with fire, I'm not the only one. And that's quite all right. For now, and perhaps for ever, fire is for sharing.

That afternoon I manoeuvre my desk into the broad beam of the sun. I raise my face to its white-gold light and for a second I'm lulled by its warmth. We need sunlight by day, I think. And dark by night. When we have both in balanced abundance, life seems more spacious but also more precious. We find our equilibrium. We feel day and night as a continuum of contrasts, the one slipping smoothly into the other.

And when we spend time with both our Day Self and our more elusive Night Self, we encounter the chequered fullness of ourselves. We meet the Self that draws together disparate, tenuous thoughts, that sometimes feels unfiltered fury and a quiet recklessness, that reflects with broad-minded curiosity, that peers into the spangled firmaments, that steps tingling and terrified through cloistered woodland, that learns to recognise an object by its heft rather than its colour. The self that is more mammal than human. More spirit than bone.

When we live alongside both selves, with each attentive to the other, life becomes both richer and sweeter. We are whole. We can heal.

★

And eventually we sleep. Thirteen months after my father's death, my sleep slowly returns to its more usual pattern: I still wake regularly, but broken–awake nights are interspersed with luxurious sleep-filled nights. If I have a run of unbroken nights, I miss my 'sweet vigil'. It has become a constant in my life, allowing me to check in on my Night Self. The reverse is also true: too many restless nights, and I long for the energetic cheer and steady mood of my well-rested Day Self. The dominion of darkness was never intended for lengthy stays. Even I know that.

I've learned something else too: there's a violence to sudden, inexplicable loss – a wrenching so seismic that we must live for months, years, in a blur of bewildered disbelief. Plenty has been written on the pain and despair of bereavement. But disbelief is different. When something we thought was for ever – parent, child, partner, pet, home, job – is unexpectedly severed from us, we find ourselves in a state of anguished ambiguity. In one fell swoop, our past and future are snatched from us, for reasons we cannot comprehend. We long, more than ever, for certainty, pattern, assurance. For something that will restore our belief in the order and stability of life. At the same time, we crave mystery and the unknown – these are the uncertain spaces in which our frail hopes breathe. The waterholes at which our souls must drink in times of disbelief. Both needs – for knowing and not-knowing – are important. But they don't always make easy bedfellows.

By allowing one to roam by day and one by night, I found a kind of balance. A sense of certitude returned. An ease with enigma and the unknown quietly blossomed. While my Day Self calmed me, my Night Self inspired me, the two existing in a delicate dance of symbiosis. I came to accept both. Not because of any wisdom of my own but thanks to the forensic diligence of researchers, who enlightened me on the shape-shifting night brain, and courtesy of my night spinners, who wrote so eloquently of their own sleepless nocturnes.

Every now and then we are nudged into a complicated and intimate form of kinship with a place. We don't always understand why this place takes on such significance. We feel only its powerful allure – an allure that can be utterly predictable or an astonishing *coup de foudre*. For me, night became my place. And it took me utterly by surprise.

But looking back, as I am now, it seems to me that my preoccupation with darkness was a search for the souls of those I had lost. Particularly for the spirit of my father. After he died I searched for him, unable to comprehend his absence. I didn't know it at the time but my night journeys were an attempt to locate him. For in darkness lie innumerable imaginative possibilities that dull quotidian day rarely offers.

And so my wide-eyed nights were never 'insomnia'. They were cravings for a darkness we've lost, for a mystery we've mislaid, for the deep time and infinite space that we've cast aside in deference to clock time, screen time, ceilings and certainty. Over decades, my cravings had twisted into anxieties and fears – of the dark, of being asleep for too little or too long, of being awake, of being tired, of dying from sleep deprivation or dementia, of having a disease called 'insomnia', of rape and murder, of the contents of my own meandering mind, of the unknown.

It isn't medication and sleep trackers we need, or endless bright light, so much as a radical new approach to sleep, to nocturne, to the firmaments, to all that has been swept away with the darkness. To our missing Night Selves.

I didn't find my father in the dark, of course. We cannot dredge up the dead. But I found other things of comfort – the stories of my stealthily subversive night spinners, an unexpected love of glow-worms, a newfound appreciation of moths and green-backed crabs, a fledgling fondness for the moon and stars, a billowing celestial world of beyond.

Above all, I found my Night Self – a whimsical creature previously crushed into a chest of sleep aids. And I liked her. It has taken time to comprehend her, to tease apart her ineluctable fears, to recognise her frailties, to accept that she is not always as ordered or as predictable as I might like. And it has taken time to understand that her wistfulness is neither grumpiness nor depression. It is merely thinking in the absence of light.

I've accepted her predilection for mothy fluttering thoughts that dip and skim. It is not that she is utterly disordered. It is merely that new territories of the brain reveal themselves at night – and she wishes to explore. And yes, sometimes these are strange and baffling places.

I'm slowly buffing the sharp edges of her (my) fear. But I do this in the knowledge that they too are a biological imperative – a necessary ingredient of the night watch, enabling our senses to bloom, bestowing on us an animal vigilance, helping us exist in the very moment of life. Not fear at all, perhaps. Merely an acutely physical attention prompted by darkness.

And yet my Night Self can be maddening. She no longer ruminates as she once did, but there are brief moments of the supine, limb-locked night when her anger leaps on a whim. I now know this sudden sprinting fury is nothing more than the frustrations of life boiling over at night, thanks to a brain freighted with nocturnal churning chemicals. And so I have learned to resist her snarling demands by getting up and moving. Away from the bed, the bedroom. She follows, of course, but subdued.

Here's the other thing I've learned: my Night Self comes in many guises. She is fractionally altered according to the soup of circumstance. Many things muffle her: alcohol; excessive fatigue; a glut of light; caffeine; pain. She can change hour by hour, and according to her situation and her geography: midnight in a sweating crowd is quite unlike 3 a.m. alone in an icy sleeping bag. I am still learning to decipher the many notes of her song – for they too will change as time passes.

We all have Night Selves. And yours is not mine. Each is conjured from our own idiosyncratic brew of circumstance, history, genes, hormones, memories, physiology and much more besides. Those of you who sleep through the darkness like logs may never encounter your Night Self until – perhaps – you too find yourself mired in grief or loss. As Katherine Mansfield said, she often comes as a 'consolation prize'.

My Night Self, and my subsequent discovery of a world after dark, were infinitely more than a 'consolation prize'. They were an unexpected gift. Part of my father's legacy to me. And a poignant reminder that the legacies of the dead can never be predicted.

And yet we can all experience our Night Selves. And we can all encounter starry skies, sleeping trees, night perfumes, darkness. Switch off your lights and screens. Turn down the volume of your Day Self. Open a window. Venture out on fox feet. Listen to that nocturnal inner voice. She is there. She is with you. Always.

Author's Note

My night journeys were the result of regular night awakenings (sometimes called sleep maintenance insomnia). But we can all take night journeys in the way that best suits our personal circumstances. Or we can live vicariously by reading about the night journeys of others. The latest research suggests that some night awakenings may indeed be beneficial for the brain, rather than detrimental,[1] and that there are many ways to rest.[2] Take your rest when you can. Embrace light during the day and darkness at night. Make peace with your restive brain. Embrace your Night Self. Chances are, you too will sleep again.

This book is not intended to provide medical guidance. Anyone with chronic insomnia should consult a doctor.

Acknowledgements

Dozens of people helped me write this book, sharing their knowledge, expertise and experiences, and willingly answering endless questions. Without them, this book would not exist. I apologise to those who were edited out – nothing personal; I simply had far too much material and far too many night spinners! In no particular order, I wish to thank the following: Juliet Nicolson, Vanessa Nicolson, Rosemary Selmes, Caroline Whiteman, Kate McLean, Julie Derbyshire, Geraldine van Heemstra, Kate Lowe, Maggie Humm, Alice Vincent, Clare Pooley, Sean Cain, Antonia Malchik, Mason Currey, Elizabeth Klerman, Duncan Minshull, Javier Hidalgo Jimenez, Kathryn Aalto, Martin Siefkes, Inga Simpson, Robin Scagell, Linda Worrall, Linda Clark, Andrew Tubbs, Caitlin Myer, Valerie Shrimplin, Annie Harris, Sarah Thomson, Antoinette Koutsomihalis, Charly Peacock, Amy Robson, Susan Saunders, Caroline Williams, Allison Brown, Meredith McKinney, Keith Grant, Michael Perlis, Chris McDermott, Chris Beetles, Roger Wong, Sepiedeh Keshavarzi, Isabelle Chopin (thank you for Barbara, *la grande insomniaque*), Tim Hearn, Nancy Golin, Lyndsy Spence, Kieran Moore and Coltan Scrivner. Special thanks to the many scientists and researchers who explained complicated studies to me. Any mistakes are mine, and mine alone.

Thank you to my wonderful agents for helping me wrangle

with early versions of this book and for encouraging me to continue when I had (completely) lost my way: Rachel Mills, Stuart Krichevsky, Laura Usselman. And to Alexandra Cliff for getting early versions to all my brilliant overseas publishers.

An enormous thank you to Abigail Scruby and Michelle Howdry, whose impressive editorial talents helped me cut tens of thousands of words. Your skill and insight are extraordinary, and you have made this an infinitely better book. Thank you to Lisa Highton whose early enthusiasm was the genesis of this book. Thank you also to Judy Spours, Hilary Hammond, Jasmine Marsh, Diana Talyanina, Sofia Hericson and the team at John Murray for their work towards this book and its publication.

Thank you to all the writers, biographers, historians, podcasters, researchers, neuroscientists and nightologists whose work helped inform this book and who frequently kept me company on long, sleepless nights, with a special mention to podcasters Vanessa Lowe at Nocturne, Katherine May at How We Live Now, Matt Walker at the Matt Walker Podcast and Vicky Derksen at Night Sky Tourist.

Thank you to the Authors League Fund and St Bride's Church, joint literary executors of the estate of Djuna Barnes, for permission to quote from *Nightwood* by Djuna Barnes; to Faber & Faber for permission to quote from 'Zoo-Keeper's Wife' by Sylvia Plath; to Erlend Clouston and the Nan Shepherd Literary Estate for permission to quote from *The Living Mountain* by Nan Shepherd; to Pushkin Press and Ullstein Buchverlage GmbH for permission to quote from *A Woman in the Polar Night* by Christiane Ritter (© 2010 Ullstein Buchverlage GmbH, Berlin. English translation © Jane Degras 1954. First published by Pushkin Press in 2019); and to the *Paris Review* for permission to quote from its interview with Toni Morrison, Issue 128, Fall 1993 ('The Art of Fiction 128: Toni Morrison' by the *Paris*

Review. Copyright © 1993, The Paris Review, used by permission of the Wylie Agency (UK) Limited).

Thank you to my father, whose poetry veins this book. If you spot a line you like, chances are I plundered it from his work.

As always I am grateful to several libraries and librarians for their service and sanctuary, particularly the British Library, the Wellcome Library, Gladstone's Library, the City of Sydney Library and the London Library.

And finally, to my long-suffering family – Matthew, Imogen, Bryony, Saskia and Hugo – who have never complained about my night roamings or odd hours: thank you, thank you, thank you!

Notes

Prologue

1 'The evening hour, too, gives us the irresponsibility which darkness and lamplight bestow. We are no longer quite ourselves.' Virginia Woolf, 'Street Haunting', in *The Death of the Moth and Other Essays* (Mariner Books, 1974).

2 Zhang Bin and Wing Yun-Kwok, 'Sex Differences in Insomnia: A Meta -Analysis', *Sleep*, vol. 29, issue 1 (January 2006), 85–93, https://doi.org/ 10.1093/sleep/29.1.85

3 Mats Fredrikson, Peter Annas, Håkan Fischer, et al., 'Gender and Age Differences in the Prevalence of Specific Fears and Phobias', *Behaviour Research and Therapy*, vol. 34, issue 1 (January 1996), 33–9, https://doi.org /10.1016/0005-7967(95)00048-3

4 Seán T. Anderson, Hu Meng, Thomas G. Brooks, et al., 'Sexual Dimorphism in the Response to Chronic Circadian Misalignment', *Science Translational Medicine*, vol. 15, issue 696 (17 May 2023). Expanded in email correspondence with Dr Tim Hearn of Newnham College, Cambridge, who is investigating the (seemingly) more robust circadian clock of women and speculates that this arose, over time, to provide 'evolutionary advantage', enabling women to better 'handle the physical demands of raising children'. Genetically, females may be more resilient to disrupted nights, and less likely to suffer from metabolic disease associated with shift work. Research continues.

Chapter 1: The Night Self

1 Marike Lancel, Margaret Stroebe and Maarten Eisma, 'Sleep Disturbances in Bereavement: A Systematic Review', *Sleep Medicine Reviews*, vol. 53 (October 2020), https://doi.org/10.1016/j.smrv.2020.101331

2 Ibid.; see also C. F. Reynolds, C. C. Hoch, D. J. Buysse, et al., 'Electroencephalographic Sleep in Spousal Bereavement and Bereavement -Related Depression of Late Life', *Biological Psychiatry*, vol. 31, issue 1 (1 January 1992), 69–82, https://www.sciencedirect.com/science/article/abs/pii/000632239290007M

Chapter 2: Disobedient

1 Andrew S. Tubbs, Fabian-Xosé Fernandez, Michael A. Grandner, et al., 'The Mind after Midnight: Nocturnal Wakefulness, Behavioral Dysregulation, and Psychopathology', *Frontiers in Network Physiology* (3 March 2022), https://www.frontiersin.org/articles/10.3389/fnetp.2021.830338/full. Most of the 'dysregulated' behaviour studied here involved things like drug-taking, homicide, rape, suicide, self-harm and eating. I am hypothetically extrapolating and extending to ways of thinking.

2 Ibid.

3 All quotes taken from Laura Cereta, *Collected Letters of a Renaissance Feminist*, ed. Diana Robin (University of Chicago Press, 1997).

4 Daniel G. Amen, Manuel Trujillo, David Keator, et al., 'Gender-Based Cerebral Perfusion Differences in 46,034 Functional Neuroimaging Scans', *Journal of Alzheimer's Disease*, vol. 60, issue 2 (18 September 2017), 605–14, https://content.iospress.com/articles/journal-of-alzheimers-disease/jad170432. The researchers who discovered this also found that the female prefrontal cortex was subject to more intense blood flow, speculating that this may have a bearing on women's higher risks for depression, anxiety, eating disorders and Alzheimer's.

5 Cereta, *Collected Letters*.

6 Michael L. Perlis, Michael A. Grandner, Gregory K. Brown, et al., 'Nocturnal Wakefulness as a Previously Unrecognized Risk Factor for Suicide', *Journal of Clinical Psychiatry* (June 2016), 726–33, doi:10.4088/JCP.15m10131

7 Andrew S. Tubbs, Fabian-Xosé Fernandez, Michael Perlis, et al., 'Suicidal Ideation is Associated with Nighttime Wakefulness in a Community Sample', *Sleep*, vol. 44, issue 1 (January 2021), doi:10.1093/sleep/zsaa128

8 Or, as they put it, 'changes in cognitive and emotional regulation'. Ibid.

9 Some of the hormones that rise and fall according to light and dark also function as neurotransmitters, helping neurons communicate with one another. For the sake of simplicity, I refer to them throughout as hormones.

10 Anneke Graf, '24 Hours in the Life of a Hormone: What Time Is the Right Time for a Pituitary Function Test?', *Endocrinologist*, vol. 134 (Winter 2019), https://www.endocrinology.org/endocrinologist/134-winter19/features/24-hours-in-the-life-of-a-hormone-what-time-is-the-right-time-for-a-pituitary-function-test/ Other night/dark peaking hormones include the growth hormone prolactin and, in women, estradiol. This is a hugely complicated subject and considerably more research is required.

11 Andrew Huberman, 'The Science of Vision, Eye Health & Seeing Better', *Huberman Lab Podcast* #24 (June 2021).

12 Yonghua Wu, Haifeng Wang and Elizabeth A. Hadley, 'Invasion of Ancestral Mammals into Dim-light Environments Inferred from Adaptive Evolution of the Phototransduction Genes', *Scientific Reports*, vol. 72 (2017), https://doi.org/10.1038/srep46542

13 Report on the sleep aids market, Precedence Research, July 2022, https://www.precedenceresearch.com/sleep-aids-market The sleep industry is forecast to be worth $125 billion by 2030.

14 All quotes taken from Cereta, *Collected Letters*.

Chapter 3: Imaginative

1 Alex Dueben, 'The Looming Dark: An Interview with Linda Pastan', *Paris Review*, 6 January 2016.

2 Anna Steidle and Lioba Werth, 'Freedom from Constraints: Darkness and Dim Illumination Promote Creativity', *Journal of Environmental Psychology*, vol. 35 (2013), 67–80, https://doi.org/10.1016/j.jenvp.2013.05.003

3 Greg Johnson, 'On the Edge of an Abyss: The Writer as Insomniac', *Virginia Quarterly Review*, vol. 66, issue 4 (Autumn 1990), 643–55, http://www.jstor.org/stable/26437923

4 Stephan A. Schwartz, 'Consciousness, Creativity, Innovation, and

Survival', *Explore*, vol. 18, issue 2 (March–April 2022), 136–9, https://doi.org/10.1016/j.explore.2021.12.011

5 K. M. Heilman, 'Possible Brain Mechanisms of Creativity', *Archives of Clinical Neuropsychology*, vol. 31, issue 4 (June 2016), 285–96, doi:10.1093/arclin/acw009

6 For example J. A. Easterbrook, 'The Effect of Emotion on Cue Utilization and the Organization of Behavior', *Psychological Review*, vol. 66 (1959), 180–201, https://pubmed.ncbi.nlm.nih.gov/13658305

7 For more on dopamine and creativity, see Daniel Z. Lieberman and Michael E. Long, *The Molecule of More* (BenBella Books, 2018), or Darya L. Zabelina, Lorenza Colazto, Mark Beeman, et al., 'Dopamine and the Creative Mind: Individual Differences in Creativity Are Predicted by Interactions between Dopamine Genes DAT and COMT', *PLoS One* (19 January 2016), https://journals.plos.org/plosone/article?id=10.1371/journal.pone.0146768 In the latter article the neuroscientists concluded 'that creativity relies on dopamine'.

8 Quoted in Matthew Parris, *Fracture: Stories of How Great Lives Take Root in Trauma* (Profile, 2020), p. 259.

9 Interview with author, 14 September 2022.

10 All quotes taken from Katherine Mansfield, *Journal of Katherine Mansfield*, ed. John Middleton Murray (Persephone, 2006).

11 Polly W. Wiessner, 'Embers of Society: Firelight Talk among the Ju/'hoansi Bushmen', *Proceedings of the National Academy of Sciences*, vol. 111 (22 September 2014), doi:10.1073/pnas.1404212111

12 'What I found was a big difference between day and night conversation, the kinds of information transmitted and the use of imaginary thought,' Wiessner says in her 'Firelight Talk of the Kalahari Bushmen', Unews Archive, 22 September 2014, https://archive.unews.utah.edu/news_releases/firelight-talk-of-the-kalahari-bushmen

13 Janet Flanner, *Paris Was Yesterday* (Virago, 2011), p. xxxii.

14 Judith Thurman, *Secrets of the Flesh: A Life of Colette* (Bloomsbury, 1999), p. 308.

15 For more on Rita Dove's night-writing, see William Walsh, 'The World Has to Fall Away: An Interview with Rita Dove', *Georgia Review* (Spring 2016), https://thegeorgiareview.com/posts/the-world-has-to-fall-away-an-interview-with-rita-dove/

16 L. Pizzichini, *The Blue Hour: A Portrait of Jean Rhys* (Bloomsbury, 2009), p. 287.

17 Interview with author, 19 October 2022.

Chapter 4: Receptive

1 Selina Hastings, *Rosamond Lehmann: A Life* (Vintage, 2002), pp. 344-345.

2 A. Roche, *Lives of the Saints* (Bruce Publishing Company, 1934).

3 The canonical hours are matins 12 a.m. (or night watch), lauds 3 a.m., prime 6 a.m., terce 9 a.m., sext 12 p.m., none 3 p.m., vespers 6 p.m. and compline 9 p.m.

4 S. Handley, *Sleep in Early Modern England* (Yale University Press, 2016), p. 147.

5 A. Roger Ekirch, 'The Modernization of Western Sleep: Or, Does Insomnia Have a History?', *Past & Present*, vol. 226, issue 1 (February 2015), 149–92, https://www.jstor.org/stable/24545188 Ekirch cites the Tiv of Nigeria, the Woolwa of South America and the Sinhalese, but a 2017 report claims the Malagasy people of Madagascar still sleep in two phases. See David R. Samson, Melissa B. Manus, Andrew D. Krystal, et al., 'Segmented Sleep in a Nonelectric, Small-Scale Agricultural Society in Madagascar', *American Journal of Human Biology*, vol. 29 (8 July 2017), doi:10.1002/ajhb.22979

6 Isabelle Arnulf, Agnès Brion, Michel Pottier, et al., 'Ring the Bell for Matins: Circadian Adaptation to Split Sleep by Cloistered Monks and Nuns', *Chronobiology International*, vol. 28, issue 10 (December 2011), 930–41, doi:10.3109/07420528.2011.624436

7 Christopher Timmermann, Leor Roseman, Michael Schartner, et al., 'Neural Correlates of the DMT Experience Assessed with Multivariate EEG', *Science Reports*, vol. 9 (2019), https://doi.org/10.1038/s41598-019-51974-4

8 Javier-Hidalgo Jiménez and José Carlos Bouso, 'Significance of Mammalian N, N-Dimethyltryptamine (DMT): A 60-Year-Old Debate', *Journal of Psychopharmacology*, vol. 36, issue 8 (2022), 905–19, doi:10.1177/02698811221104054

9 Bryony Sheaves, Paul E. Bebbington, Guy M. Goodwin, et al., 'Insomnia and Hallucinations in the General Population: Findings from the 2000 and 2007 British Psychiatric Morbidity Surveys', *Psychiatry Research*, vol. 241 (30 July 2016), 141–6, doi:10.1016/j.psychres.2016.03.055

Chapter 5: Raging

1 Louise Bourgeois archive, Easton Foundation, New York: LB-0188, loose sheet, *c.* 1965.

2 According to her biographer Robert Storr, Bourgeois's 'roller coaster up all night crash at dawn bipolar patterns' of sleeplessness continued to the end of her life. R. Storr, *Intimate Geometries: The Life and Work of Louise Bourgeois* (Monacelli Press, 2014).

3 Fabon Dzogang, Stafford Lightman and Nello Cristianini, 'Circadian Mood Variations in Twitter Content', *Brain and Neuroscience Advances* (January 2017), doi:10.1177/2398212817744501. See also Scott A. Golder and Michael W. Macy, 'Diurnal and Seasonal Mood Vary with Work, Sleep, and Daylength across Diverse Cultures, *Science*, vol. 333, issue 6051 (30 September 2011), 1878–81, and Vasileios Lampos, Thomas Lansdall-Welfare, Ricardo Araya, et al., 'Analysing Mood Patterns in the United Kingdom through Twitter Content' (2013), Cornell University, https://arxiv.org/abs/1304.5507

4 William D. Todd, Henning Fenselau, Joshua L. Wang, et al., 'A Hypothalamic Circuit for the Circadian Control of Aggression', *Nature Neuroscience*, vol. 21 (2018), 717–24, https://doi.org/10.1038/s41593-018-0126-0

5 See for example University of California, San Francisco, 'Comparison of Anger Expression In Men And Women Reveals Surprising Differences', *ScienceDaily*, 31 January 2000, https://www.sciencedaily.com/releases/2000/01/000131075609.htm and Kateri McRae, Kevin N. Ochsner, Iris B. Mauss, et al., 'Gender Differences in Emotion Regulation: An fMRI Study of Cognitive Reappraisal', *Group Processes and Intergroup Relations*, vol. 11, issue 2 (April 2008), 143–62, doi:10.1177/1368430207088035 Incidentally, violent crime – from homicide to rape – peaks at night, although whether this is because of the opportunity afforded by not being at work or from alcohol and drug abuse is unclear.

6 Storr, *Intimate Geometries*, p. 31.

7 Ulf Küster, *Louise Bourgeois* (Hatje Cantz, 2012).

8 Jonathan Jones, 'The Night Stuff', *Guardian*, 9 January 2001, https://www.theguardian.com/culture/2001/jan/09/artsfeatures1

9 Tubbs, Fernandez, Grandner, et al., 'Mind after Midnight', based on evidence from T. A. Bedrosian and R. J. Nelson, 'Timing of Light Exposure Affects Mood and Brain Circuits', *Translational Psychiatry*, vol. 7 (31 January 2017), doi:10.1038/tp.2016.262

10 Jing Xu Alison and Aparna A. Labroo, 'Incandescent Affect: Turning on the Hot Emotional System with Bright Light', *Journal of Consumer Psychology*, vol. 24, issue 2 (April 2014), 207–16, https://doi.org/10.1016/j.jcps.2013.12.007

11 See, for example, Jessica Salerno and Liana Peter-Hagene, 'One Angry Woman: Anger Expression Increases Influence for Men, but Decreases Influence for Women, during Group Deliberation', *Law and Human Behavior*, vol. 39, issue 6 (August 2015), 581–92, doi:10.1037/lhb0000147

12 Zahid Saghir, Javeria N. Syeda, Adnan S. Muhammad, et al., 'The Amygdala, Sleep Debt, Sleep Deprivation, and the Emotion of Anger: A Possible Connection?', *Cureus*, vol. 10, issue 7 (July 2018), doi:10.7759/cureus.2912

Chapter 6: Ruminative

1 Francine du Plessix Gray, *Simone Weil* (Weidenfeld & Nicolson, 2001), p. 198.

2 Quoted in Heather Clark, *Red Comet: The Short Life and Blazing Art of Sylvia Plath* (Jonathan Cape, 2020), p. 686.

3 Sylvia Plath, *The Journals of Sylvia Plath 1950–1962*, ed. Karen V. Kukil (Faber & Faber, 2014), p. 646.

4 Michele L. Okun, Roberta A. Mancuso, Calvin J. Hobel, et al., 'Poor Sleep Quality Increases Symptoms of Depression and Anxiety in Postpartum Women', *Journal of Behavioral Medicine*, vol. 41 (20 July 2018), 703–10, doi:10.1007/s10865-018-9950-7

5 Clark, *Red Comet*, p. 752.

6 All references to sleep, insomnia and fatigue are taken from Plath, *Journals*, ed. Kukil.

7 Juliet Nicolson, *Frostquake: The Frozen Winter of 1962 and How Britain Emerged a Different Country* (Chatto & Windus, 2021), p. 144.

8 SP to Olive Prouty, quoted in Clark, *Red Comet*, p. 859.

9 SP to Michael Carey, 4 February 1963, in Sylvia Plath, *The Letters of Sylvia Plath, Volume II: 1956–1963*, ed. Peter R. Steinberg and Karen V. Kukil (Faber & Faber, 2018), p. 966.

10 All Sylvia Plath quotes taken from the following: *Journals of Sylvia Plath*, ed. Kukil; *Letters of Sylvia Plath, Volume II*, ed. Steinberg and Kukil; *Letters Home*, ed. Aurelia Plath (Faber & Faber, 1975); and *The Collected Poems of Sylvia Plath*, ed. Ted Hughes (Faber & Faber, 1981).

11 Michael L. Perlis, Michael A. Grandner, Gregory K. Brown, et al., 'Nocturnal Wakefulness as a Previously Unrecognized Risk Factor for Suicide', *Journal of Clinical Psychiatry* (June 2016), 726–33, doi:10.4088/JCP.15m10131

12 The brains of depressed people show more frontal cortex theta and delta activity and less beta and gamma activity; Michael L. Perlis, Michael A. Grandner, Subhajit Chakravorty, et al. 'Suicide and Sleep: Is It a Bad Thing to Be Awake When Reason Sleeps?', *Sleep Medicine Reviews*, vol. 29 (October 2016), 101–7, doi:10.1016/j.smrv.2015.10.003

13 Sylvia Frey, Angelina Birchler-Pedross, Marcel Hofstetter, et al., 'Young Women with Major Depression Live on Higher Homeostatic Sleep Pressure Than Healthy Controls', *Chronobiology International*, vol. 29, issue 3 (April 2012), 278–94, doi:10.3109/07420528.2012.656163

14 Nicolson, *Frostquake*, p. 246.

Chapter 7: Anonymous

1 All Webb quotes are taken from her essays and poems, in Mary Webb, *The Collected Works of Mary Webb* (Jonathan Cape, 1928).

2 All quotes taken from *Joan Mitchell*, ed. Sarah Roberts and Katy Siegel (San Francisco Museum of Modern Art and Yale University Press, 2020).

3 P. Albers, *Joan Mitchell: Lady Painter* (Knopf, 2011), p. 14.

4 Krisztina Kopcsó and András Láng, 'Korai maladaptív sémák és kötődési minőség összefüggései a sötéttől való félelemmel' ['Relationship between Early Maladaptive Schemas, Attachment Quality and Fear of Darkness'], *Orvosi Hetilap*, vol. 155, issue 49 (7 December 2014), 1967–72, doi:10.1556/OH.2014.30045 'From the age of 8, research [into night fear] showed remarkable gender differences, with higher levels of fear of the dark in females.' Another study came to the same conclusion: 'women experienced more frequent and intensive fear of darkness than men'.

5 M. F. K. Fisher, *Stay Me, Oh Comfort Me: Journals and Stories 1933–1941* (Pantheon, 1993), p. 322.

6 Joan Didion, *The Year of Magical Thinking* (Harper Collins, 2006).

7 Quoted in Kashmira Gander, 'Why Are We Afraid of the Dark?', *Independent*, 22 February 2016, https://www.independent.co.uk/life-style/health-and-families/features/why-are-we-afraid-of-the-dark-a6889086.html

8 Email correspondence with researcher Sean Cain, 29 September 2022.

9 Yadan Li, Wenjuan Ma, Lei Qiao, et al., 'Night or Darkness, Which Intensifies the Feeling of Fear?', *International Journal of Psychophysiology*, vol. 97, issue 1 (July 2015), 46–57, doi:10.1016/j.ijpsycho.2015.04.021

Chapter 8: Curious

1 Manuel Fernández-Alcántara, Juan Verdejo-Román, Francisco Cruz-Quintana, et al., 'Increased Amygdala Activations during the Emotional Experience of Death-Related Pictures in Complicated Grief: An fMRI Study', *Journal of Clinical Medicine*, vol. 9, issue 3 (20 March 2020), doi:10.3390/jcm9030851

2 Gerardo Aldana, *Calculating Brilliance: An Intellectual History of Mayan Astronomy at Chich'en Itza* (University of Arizona Press, 2022). Aldana makes the case for a prominent female Mayan astronomer.

3 Cunitz's book, *Urania Propitia*, was a sophisticated revision of an earlier book of planetary tables by Johannes Kepler, which she self-published in 1650.

4 Quoted in Renee Bergland, *Maria Mitchell and the Sexing of Science* (Beacon Press, 2008), p. 53.

5 After ten years of sleeping on a fold-out bed in the dome, a tiny bedroom was made for Mitchell in the observatory coal hole.

6 *Cecilia Payne-Gaposchkin: An Autobiography and Other Recollections*, ed. Katherine Haramundanis (Cambridge University Press, 1996).

7 Jacqueline and Simon Mitten, *Vera Rubin: A Life* (Harvard University Press, 2021), p. 16.

8 Interview with Alan Lightman, 1989, https://www.space.com/vera-rubin.html

9 Mitten and Mitten, *Vera Rubin*, p. 148.

10 Ibid., p. 147.

11 Bergland, *Maria Mitchell*, pp. 38–9.

12 Emily Dickinson to Thomas Wentworth Higginson, 26 April 1862, https://www.theatlantic.com/magazine/archive/1891/10/emily-dickinsons-letters/306524/

13 All Emily Dickinson lines are from either *Emily Dickinson: The Complete Poems* (Faber & Faber, 2016) or Emily Dickinson, *The Single Hound: Poems of a Lifetime* (Little, Brown, 1914).

Chapter 9: Restless

1 R. L. Stevenson, *Travels with a Donkey in the Cevennes* (Chatto & Windus, 1908). All quotes from the chapter 'A Night Among the Pines'.

2 More on male 'vagabonding' in Morris Marples, *Shanks's Pony: A Study of Walking* (Country Book Club, 1960), and Miles Jebb, *Walkers* (Constable, 1986).

3 Stephen Graham, *The Gentle Art of Tramping* (Holden & Co, 1927).

4 Patrick Leigh Fermor, *A Time of Gifts: On Foot to Constantinople: From the Hook of Holland to the Middle Danube* (John Murray, 1977).

5 Michael Holroyd, *Augustus John: The New Biography* (Vintage, 1997), p. 185.

6 *Peace Pilgrim: Her Life and Works in Her Own Words* (Ocean Tree, 1994), p. 46.

7 Vicki Goldberg, *Margaret Bourke-White: A Biography* (William Heinemann, 1987).

8 Etel Adnan, *Journey to Mount Tamalpais* (Litmus Press, 2021). See also Adnan's *Night* (Nightboat Books, 2016).

9 Katharine Trevelyan, *Fool in Love* (Victor Gollancz, 1962).

10 All quotes taken from Clara Vyvyan, *Roots and Stars* (Country Book Club, 1963), pp. 56–65.

11 M. Edith Durham, *High Albania* (Edward Arnold, 1909), pp. 234–35.

12 Tatiana de Rosnay, *Manderley Forever: The Life of Daphne du Maurier* (St Martin's Press, 2017), p. 231.

13 Ibid., p. 236.

14 Margaret Forster, *Daphne du Maurier* (Chatto & Windus, 1993), p. 301.

15 De Rosnay, *Manderley Forever*, p. 238.

16 Krisztina Kopcsó and András Láng, 'Uncontrolled Thoughts in the Dark? Effects of Lighting Conditions and Fear of the Dark on Thinking Processes', *Imagination, Cognition and Personality*, vol. 39, issue 1 (2019), 97–108, doi:10.1177/0276236618816035

17 Anna Steidle and Lioba Werth, 'In the Spotlight: Brightness Increases Self -Awareness and Reflective Self-Regulation, *Journal of Environmental Psychology*, vol. 39 (September 2014), 40–50, https://www.sciencedirect.com/science/article/pii/S0272494413000972

18 De Rosnay, *Manderley Forever*, p. 237.

19 Nan Shepherd, *The Living Mountain* (Canongate, 2019), p. 90.

20 Chenjing Wu, Fuqun Liang, Xiaoling Liang, et al., 'Spacious Environments

Make Us Tolerant – The Role of Emotion and Metaphor', *International Journal of Environmental Research and Public Health*, vol. 18 (7 October 2021), doi:10.3390/ijerph181910530

21 Joan Meyers-Levy and Juliet Zhu, 'The Influence of Ceiling Height', *Journal of Consumer Research*, vol. 34 (August 2007), https://assets.csom.umn.edu/assets/71190.pdf

22 Gaston Bachelard, *The Poetics of Space* (Penguin, 2014), p. 222.

23 Michael Craig, Michaela Dewar, Matthew A. Harris, et al., 'Wakeful Rest Promotes the Integration of Spatial Memories Into Accurate Cognitive Maps, *Hippocampus*, vol. 26 (February 2016), https://pubmed.ncbi.nlm.nih.gov/26235141

24 S. Y. Wang, et al., '"Sleep-Dependent" Memory Consolidation? Brief Periods of Post-Training Rest and Sleep Provide an Equivalent Benefit for Both Declarative and Procedural Memory', *Learning & Memory*, vol. 28, issue 6 (19 May 2021), 195–203, doi:10.1101/lm.053330.120

Chapter 10: Changeable

1 See, for example, Meredith Mendelsohn, 'The Emotionally Charged Paintings Lee Krasner Created after Pollock's Death', Artsy, 13 November 2017, https://www.artsy.net/article/artsy-editorial-emotionally-charged-paintings-lee-krasner-created-pollocks-death

2 D. Anfam, *Lee Krasner: The Umber Paintings 1959–1962* (Paul Kasmin Gallery, 2018), catalogue for the Pace Gallery's 2017 exhibition.

3 Krasner in conversation with Richard Howard in ibid.

4 Ibid.

5 Ibid.

6 Krasner in interview with Barbara Novak, October 1979, reprinted in ibid.

7 Anfam, *Lee Krasner*.

8 Alanna Dorsey, Luis de Lecea and Kimberly J. Jennings, 'Neurobiological and Hormonal Mechanisms Regulating Women's Sleep', *Frontiers in Neuroscience*, vol. 14 (2021), doi:10.3389/fnins.2020.625397

9 Cindy Nemser, 'A Conversation with Lee Krasner', *Arts Magazine*, April 1973, p. 47.

Chapter 11: Courageous

1 Mirande Candito, Dominique Pringuey, Yves Jacomet, et al., 'Circadian Rhythm in Plasma Noradrenaline of Healthy Sleep-Deprived Subjects', *Chronobiology International*, vol. 9, issue 6 (1992), 444–7, doi:10.3109/07420529209064557.

2 Matthew Nayor, Ravi V. Shah, Patricia E. Miller, et al., 'Metabolic Architecture of Acute Exercise Response in Middle-Aged Adults in the Community', *Circulation*, vol. 142, issue 20 (17 November 2020), doi:10.1161/CIRCULATIONAHA.120.050281

3 Caroline Williams, *Move: The New Science of Body over Mind* (Profile, 2021), p. 27.

4 Author interview, 25 April 2022.

5 See S. Greenough, *My Faraway One: Selected Letters of Georgia O'Keeffe and Alfred Steiglitz*, Vol. 1 (Yale Uni Press, 2011).

6 Annabel Abbs, *Windswept: Why Women Walk* (Two Roads, 2021), pp. 213–62.

7 Richard Wrangham, *Catching Fire: How Cooking Made Us Human* (Profile, 2010).

8 Quoted in Martine Reid, *George Sand* (Pennsylvania State University Press, 2018), p. 10.

9 All quotes from ibid., pp. 41–7.

10 Amy Liptrot, *The Outrun* (Canongate, 2016).

11 George Sand, *A Winter in Mallorca* (Classic Collection Carolina, 1942), pp. 270–4.

12 Dmitri J. Bayle, Marie-Ann Henaff and Pierre Krolak-Salmon, 'Unconsciously Perceived Fear in Peripheral Vision Alerts the Limbic System: A MEG Study', *PLoS One* (9 December 2009), doi:10.1371/journal.pone.0008207

13 Charles Dickens, 'Shy Neighbourhoods', published in *The Uncommercial Traveller* (London, 1860).

Chapter 12: Wild

1 Peter Wohlleben, *Walks in the Wild* (Rider, 2019), p. 205.

2 All quotes taken from Paula Blanchard, *The Life of Emily Carr* (University of Washington Press, 1987).

3 Sepiedeh Keshavarzi, Edward F. Bracey, Richard A. Faville, et al.,

'Multisensory Coding of Angular Head Velocity in the Retrosplenial Cortex', *Neuron*, vol. 110, issue 3 (2 February 2022), 532–49, https://doi.org/10.1016/j.neuron.2021.10.031

4 Mary Webb, 'Laughter' and 'The Spring of Joy', in Mary Webb, *The Collected Works of Mary Webb* (Jonathan Cape, 1928).

5 Anne Finch, 'A Nocturnal Reverie', *c.* 1690.

6 Dorothy Wordsworth, *The Journals of Dorothy Wordsworth: The Alfoxden Journal, 1798, the Grasmere Journals, 1800–03*, ed. Mary Moorman (Oxford University Press, 1971).

7 Nan Shepherd, 'On Noises in the Night', in *Wild Geese: A Collection of Nan Shepherd's Writing*, ed. Charlotte Peacock (Galileo, 2018).

8 Vyvyan, *Roots and Stars*, p. 113. Vyvyan called this a 'moss bath' and one of 'life's best moments'.

Chapter 13: Enchanted

1 A 2008 study found that caterpillars taught to dislike the smell of nail polish remover retained the dislike after they had pupated and become moths; Douglas J. Blakiston, Elena Silva Casey and Martha R. Weiss, 'Retention of Memory through Metamorphosis: Can a Moth Remember What It Learned as a Caterpillar?', *PLOS One* (5 March 2008), https://doi.org/10.1371/journal.pone.0001736

2 All the quotes in this section are taken from Gene Stratton-Porter's guide-memoir, *Moths of the Limberlost* (Hodder & Stoughton, 1912), pp. 96–7, 194–5, 248.

3 Eavan Boland, 'A Sparrow-Hawk in the Suburbs', from *Earth Songs*, ed. Peter Abbs (Green Books & Resurgence, 2002).

4 Eavan Boland, 'Moths' and 'This Moment', both from *Earth Songs*, ed. Abbs.

5 Richard E. Walton, Carl D. Sayer, Helen Bennion, et al., 'Nocturnal Pollinators Strongly Contribute to Pollen Transport of Wild Flowers in an Agricultural Landscape', *Biology Letters*, vol. 16, issue 5 (May 2020), http://doi.org/10.1098/rsbl.2019.0877

6 Myles H. M. Menz, Martina Scacco, Hans-Martin Bürki-Spycher, et al., 'Individual Tracking Reveals Long-Distance Flight-Path Control in a Nocturnally Migrating Moth', *Science*, vol. 377, issue 6607 (11 August 2022), 764–8, https://www.science.org/doi/abs/10.1126/science.abn1663

7 Charmian Clift, *Sneaky Little Revolutions: Selected Essays of Charmian Clift* (NewSouth Books, 2022).

8 Helen Macdonald, 'The Numinous Ordinary', in *Vesper Flights* (Jonathan Cape, 2020), p. 248.

Chapter 14: Reckless

1 *New York Herald Tribune* Book and Author Luncheon Speech, 1951, in Rachel Carson, *Lost Woods: The Discovered Writing of Rachel Carson* (Beacon Press, 1998), pp. 80–1.

2 Katherine Harmon Courage, 'Greatest Migration on Earth Happens Under Darkness Every Day', *Scientific American*, 1 August 2022, https://www.scientificamerican.com/article/greatest-migration-on-earth-happens-under-darkness-every-day

Chapter 15: Fearful

1 Nick Dunn, ' "When Streets Become Supernatural": The Joy of Walking in Cities at Night', *Guardian*, 18 November 2016, https://www.theguardian.com/cities/2016/nov/18/nocturnal-night-city-nick-dunn-streets-supernatural-joy-walking-cities This article that quotes nine men and not a single woman.

2 The words of Diana Silvers, photographer and actress, from Emily Sundberg, 'Diana Silvers Started Photography Because of a Crush', *The Cut*, 14 May 2018, https://www.thecut.com/2018/05/california-native-diana-silvers-shares-photos-of-ojai.html

3 Hans-Ulrich Obrist, 'Life Through Annie's Lens', *GQ*, 29 March 2012, https://www.gq-magazine.co.uk/article/annie-leibovitz-pilgrimage-interview#:~:text=I%20fell%20in%20love%20with,all%20night%20in%20the%20darkroom

4 Woolf, 'Street Haunting', *Death of the Moth*.

5 Nin, diary entry, September 1939, *The Diary of Anaïs Nin 1934–1939*, ed. Gunther Stuhlmann (Harcourt Brace, 1970), p. 339.

6 Nin, diary entry, 23 July 1936, *Fire: From a Journal of Love: The Unexpurgated Diary of Anaïs Nin 1934–1937* (Harcourt Brace, 1995), p. 266.

7 Vyvyan, *Roots and Stars*.

8 Plath, *Journals*, pp. 54–6.

9 Caitlin Myer, *Wiving: A Memoir of Loving Then Leaving the Patriarchy* (Arcade, 2020).

10 Myer in interview with Vanessa Lowe, 'Forward Momentum', 11 Nocturne podcast, August 2015, and interview with author 16 October 2022.

11 Dorothy Richardson, *The Tunnel* (1919), volume 4 of her Pilgrimage series of novels, Project Gutenburg, https://www.gutenberg.org/ebooks /56447

12 Guofang Liu, Xiaoxiao Niu and Lin Lin, 'Gender Moderates the Effect of Darkness on Ethical Behaviors: An Explanation of Disinhibition', *Personality and Individual Differences*, vol. 130 (August 2018), 96–101, https://doi.org/10.1016/j.paid.2018.03.036

13 Office of National Statistics, 'Perceptions of Personal Safety and Experiences of Harassment, Great Britain: 2 to 27 June 2021', 24 August 2021, https://www.ons.gov.uk/peoplepopulationandcommunity/ crimeandjustice/bulletins/perceptionsofpersonalsafetyandexperiences ofharassmentgreatbritain/2to27june2021

14 Arup, Perceptions of Night-Time Safety Women and Girls Project, 'Lighting the Way for Women and Girls: A New Narrative for Lighting Design in Cities', https://www.arup.com/projects/perceptions-of-night -time-safety-women-and-girls

15 Fabio Falchi, Pierantonio Cinzano, Dan Duriscoe, et al., 'The New World Atlas of Artificial Night Sky Brightness', *Science Advances*, vol. 2, issue 6 (10 June 2016), https://www.science.org/doi/10.1126/ sciadv.1600377

16 Asher Fergusson and Lyric Fergusson, 'A Study of the World's Most Dangerous Countries for Women Traveling Alone Reveals the Good, the Bad and the Ugly', Asher & Lyric, 15 July 2019, https://www. asherfergusson.com/solo-female-travel-safety The UK equivalent is 51 per cent of women feeling safe while walking at night, according to a recent survey.

17 Kate Ng, 'Half of Women Feel Unsafe Walking Alone After Dark, Says ONS', *Independent*, 24 August 2021, https://www.independent.co.uk/ life-style/women/office-national-statistics-women-safety-b1907807. html

18 Philips News Center Singapore, 'Philips Global Sleep Study Finds Singaporeans' Sleep Woes Compounded by Pandemic, Yet More Turning to Telehealth for Help', 17 March 2021, https://www.philips.com.sg/a-w

/about/news/archive/standard/news/press/2021/20211703-philips-global-sleep-study-finds-singaporeans-sleep-woes-compounded-by-pandemic-yet-more-turning-to-telehealth-for-help.html
19 Ivy C. Mason, Daniela Grimaldi, Kathryn J. Reid, et al., 'Light Exposure During Sleep Impairs Cardiometabolic Function, *Proceedings of the National Academy of Sciences of the United States of America*, vol. 119, issue 12 (14 March 2022), https://www.pnas.org/doi/10.1073/pnas.2113290119
20 Ana Richelia Jara-Lazaro, Shyamala Thilagaratnam and Puay Hoon Tan, 'Breast Cancer in Singapore: Some Perspectives', *Breast Cancer*, vol. 17, issue 1 (2010), 23–8. doi:10.1007/s12282-009-0155-3
21 Kim Ho, 'Singaporeans' Greatest Fears Revealed', YouGov, 31 October 2019, https://sg.yougov.com/en-sg/news/2019/10/31/singaporeans-greatest-fears-revealed
22 Joshua Levos and Tammy Lowery Zacchilli, 'Nyctophobia: From Imagined to Realistic Fears of the Dark', *Psi Chi Journal of Psychological Research*, vol. 20, issue 2 (Summer 2015), https://www.psichi.org/page/202JNSum2015

Chapter 16: Revelatory

1 All quotes from C. Ritter, *A Woman in the Polar Night* (Pushkin Press, 2010).
2 See for instance Pierpaolo Zivi, Luigi De Gennaro and Fabio Ferlazzo, 'Sleep in Isolated, Confined and Extreme (ICE): A Review on the Different Factors Affecting Human Sleep in ICE', *Frontiers in Neuroscience*, vol. 14 (11 August 2020), https://pubmed.ncbi.nlm.nih.gov/32848590, or Børge Sovertsen, Oddgeir Friborg, Ståle Pallesen, et al., 'Sleep in the Land of the Midnight Sun and Polar Night: The Tromsø Study', *Chronobiology International*, vol. 38, issue 3 (2021), https://www.tandfonline.com/doi/abs/10.1080/07420528.2020.1845191?journalCode=icbi20
3 Ritter, *Woman in the Polar Night*, p. 139.
4 Ashutosh Jnawali, Be'njamin T. Backus, Elizabeth M. Quinlan, et al., 'Physiological Effects of Ten Days of Total Darkness in Humans', *Investigative Ophthalmology & Visual Science*, vol. 58, issue 8 (June 2017).
5 Mónica M. C. González, 'Dim Light at Night and Constant Darkness: Two Frequently Used Lighting Conditions That Jeopardize the Health and Well-being of Laboratory Rodents', *Frontiers in Neurology*, vol. 9 (2 August 2018), https://doi.org/10.3389/fneur.2018.00609

6 Depending on the data used, Norway is typically ranked 6 in the league of wealthiest countries, while Ghana is around 50 in the table of poorest countries.

7 Martin Plöderl, 'Suicide Risk over the Course of the Day, Week, and Life', *Psychiatria Danubina*, vol. 33, issue 3 (Fall 2021), doi:10.24869/psyd.2021.438 Recently scientists have discovered that when the light–dark balance changes (autumn and spring) we are more vulnerable to feelings of despair. According to Andrew Tubbs, 'it is speculated that serotonin levels and/or receptor availability changes in proportion to sunlight. One proposal is that serotonin sensitivity increases during the winter because decreasing sunlight leads to reduced serotonin. Then, during spring, increasing sunlight drives up serotonin before sensitivity can decrease, leading to excess serotonergic activity.' (Email exchange with author, 27 October 2022.)

Chapter 17: Healing

1 Thomas A. Wehr, 'In Short Photoperiods, Human Sleep is Biphasic', *Journal of Sleep Research*, vol. 1, issue 2 (June 1992), 103–7, https://doi.org/10.1111/j.1365-2869.1992.tb00019.x

2 Diane C. A. Barret, Gebhard F. X. Schertler, U. Benjamin Kaupp, et al., 'The Structure of the Native CNGA1/CNGB1 CNG Channel from Bovine Retinal Rods', *Nature Structural and Molecular Biology*, vol. 29 (2022), 32–9, doi:10.1038/s41594-021-00700-8

3 Rebecca Boyle, 'The End of Night', Aeon, 1 April 2014, https://aeon.co/essays/we-can-t-thrive-in-a-world-without-darkness

4 For more on this see Richard Wrangham's seminal book, *Catching Fire: How Cooking Made Us Human* (Profile, 2010).

5 Jiexiu Zhao, Ye Tian, Jinlei Nie, et al., 'Red Light and the Sleep Quality and Endurance Performance of Chinese Female Basketball Players', *Journal of Athletic Training*, vol. 47, issue 6 (November–December 2012), 673–8, doi:10.4085/1062–6050-47.6.08

6 David Robson, 'Rest Easier', *New Scientist*, vol. 256, issue 3406 (1 October 2022), 38–42, https://doi.org/10.1016/S0262-4079(22)01780-8

Author's Note

1 Roger Wong and Margaret Anne Lovier, 'Sleep Disturbances and Dementia Risk in Older Adults', *American Journal of Preventive Medicine*, vol. 64, issue 6 (June 2023), 781–7, https://doi.org/10.1016/j.amepre.2023.01.008 In correspondence with Wong, he confirmed that in his study those who awoke at night were 40 per cent less likely to get dementia than those who slept all night long, speculating that they used this time to think, read and engage in other brain-building activities that might contribute to cognitive reserve. Note: these were people over sixty -five who, presumably, could nap or catch up during the day.

2 See the following articles which show the powerful effects of yoga nidra and breathing exercises on the body's ability to rest and repair: Seithikurippu R. Pandi-Perumal, David Warren Spence, Neena Srivastava, et al., 'The Origin and Clinical Relevance of Yoga Nidra', *Sleep and Vigilance*, vol. 6 (2022), 61–84, https://pubmed.ncbi.nlm.nih.gov/35496325/; and Melis Yilmaz Balban, Eric Neri, Manuela M. Kogon, et al., 'Brief Structured Respiration Practices Enhance Mood and Reduce Physiological Arousal', *Cell Reports* Medicine, vol. 4, issue 1 (17 January 2023), https://pubmed.ncbi.nlm.nih.gov/36630953